Baptist Hymn V
By H

ANABAPTIST HYMN WRITERS AND THEIR HYMNS

Wackerxagel, in his celebrated work on German Hynmology, has a section entitled "Hymns of the Martyrs," These hymns, for the most part, were written by certain Anabaptists of Switzerland and southern Germany, who chose rather to die than to deny the truth which they had accepted as the truth of God. These hymns, twelve in number, are taken from a collection published in 1583, entitled "Some Beautiful Christian Hymns, Composed by the Swiss Brethren" in the Prison in the Castle at Passau, and by other evangelical Christians here and there.

Luther, as early as 1523, composed a martyr hymn, commencing:

Ein newes Lied wir Iieben an,

and referring to two former Augustinian monks, who were burned at Brussels, July 1, that year, for having accepted the views which Luther held. This hymn, with music also by Luther, was soon carried to every part of Germany, and on the lips of the common people did much to advance the reform movement. Luther's hymn, together with two other martyr hymns composed by followers of Luther, one in 1524, and one in 1525, are the only Lutheran martyr hymns that have come down to us. The Anabaptists furnished the martyrs from this time on, and it is their hymns that we have in the collection to which I have referred.

FELIX MANTZ

The first of these martyrs was Felix Mantz, a Swiss Anabaptist. He was a native of Zurich, a man of scholarly attainments, and from the beginning of the reform movement in Switzerland he entered into it heartily, standing at Zwingli's side. But differences at length arose in reference to infant baptism. At first Zwingli, like Luther, thought that faith before baptism was indispensable. In conversation with the Anabaptist leaders, he frequently took this position. As he himself afterward confessed, there was a time when he believed it would be better not to baptize children until they were somewhat advanced in years. But he at length changed his mind. "He saw that the setting aside of infant baptism was the same as the setting aside of the national church, exchanging a hitherto national reformation of the church for one more or less Donatist. For if infant baptism were given up because faith was not yet there, then there only remained as the right time for it the moment when living faith and regeneration were certain. And then baptism would become the sign of fellowship of the regenerate, the saints, who bind themselves together as aliens out of the world." And so Zwingli and the Anabaptists drew apart, and the latter very soon became the objects of relentless persecution. Mantz was at length arrested and thrown into prison Jan. 5, 1527, he was sentenced to death. Since he had embraced Anabaptism, he was told, and had become one of the leaders in the Anabaptist movement; since he would not be induced to retract his errors, but, in spite of the edict and of his oath, clung to his errors, separating himself from the Christian church, and laboring to organize a sect; since, further, he rejected the magistracy [which Mantz, however, stoutly denied], opposed the death penalty, to the destruction of the common Christian peace,—he should be delivered to the executioner, who should bind his hands, place him in a boat, and throw him, bound, into the water, there to die.

Mantz received his sentence in a true martyr spirit. In an exhortation which he left to his brethren, for their comfort and admonition, he said: "My heart rejoice in God, who giveth me such understanding, and guide me, that I may escape eternal death. Therefore I praise thee, Christ, Lord of heaven, that thou succorest me in my affliction and sorrow, which the Savior God hath sent me for an example and a light, who hath called me to his heavenly kingdom before my end is come, that I may have eternal joy with him, and love him in all his judgments, which shall endure both here and hereafter in eternity, without which nothing avails or subsists."

In this spirit Mantz went to execution. Bullinger says that as he was led to the boat he praised God that he was about to die for the truth. When bound upon the hurdle, and about to be thrown into the stream, he sang with a loud voice, "Into thy hands, Lord, I commend my spirit." The waters then closed over him, and he obtained the martyr's crown. His heroic death was reported far and wide. Capito, a friend of Zwingli, wrote to the latter from Strasburg, Jan. 22, 1527: "It is reported here, that poor Felix Mantz has suffered punishment, and died gloriously, on which account the cause of truth and piety which you sustain is greatly depressed."

Mantz's martyr hymn contains eighteen stanzas of seven lines each. It expresses his joy in God, and praises him for salvation through Christ, who compels no man to accept his righteousness, but welcomes all who repent of their sins and obey his commandments. The hymn opens with these lines:

> With rapture I will sing,
> Grateful to God for breath,
> The strong, almighty King
> Who saves ray soul from death,
> The death that has no end.
> Thee, too, O Christ, I praise,
> Who dost thine own defend.

MICHAEL SATTLER

Not so much is known of Michael Sattler, another of the Swiss Anabaptist martyr singers. His home was in Staufen, Breisgau, and before connecting himself with the reform movement he was a monk. He was arrested by the authorities in Zurich in the latter part of 1525, and was banished from the canton. He was afterward arrested in Strasburg, and May 21, 1527, at Rotenburg on the Neckar, his tongue was torn out, while his body was lacerated with hot tongs and then burned. His character was such that the Strasburg evangelical pastors, after his death, did not hesitate to call him a martyr of Christ,

The seventh hymn in "Auss Bundt," containing thirteen stanzas of four lines, is by Michael Sattler, and has the ring of the martyr spirit ; as, for example, these lines:

> If one ill treat you for my sake,

And daily you to shame awake,

Be joyful, your reward is nigh,

Prepared for you in Heaven on high.

Of such a man fear not the will,

The body only he can kill;

A faithful God the rather fear,

Who can condemn to darkness drear.

O Christ, help thou thy little flock,

Who faithful follow thee, their Rock;

By thine own death redeem each one,

And crown the work that thou hast done.

GEORGE WAGNER

George Wagner was pastor of the Anabaptist church in Munich. He was a man of irreproachable character, and his holy the commended to all about him the Gospel which he delighted to preach. Every possible effort was made to induce him to deny the doctrines he had accepted, but in vain; and at length he was thrown into prison. There he was visited by the Duke who first by means of the Scriptures, and then by means of promises, endeavored to secure his recantation. But Wagner was immovable, and he was at length condemned to death. On his way to execution —it was sometime in 1527,—his wife and children implored him to abandon his heresy and save his immortal soul. All these and other equally earnest entreaties were unavailing. At the stake Wagner lifted his eyes toward heaven and offered this petition: "Father, my Father, there is much in the world that is dear to me, my wife, my children, my life. But dearer than wife, children and life art thou, my Father! Nothing shall separate me from thy love. To thee I consecrate myself wholly as I am in life and in death;" and he added, "I am ready; I know what I am doing." Then joyfully he turned to his executioners and welcomed the flames in which, as in a chariot, his spirit ascended to the skies.

The following is the first stanza of a hymn, 34 in "Auss Bundt," written by Wagner:

We praise our Father, God;

To him hosanuas bring,

Who saves us by the precious blood

Of our atoning King,

The Son whom he has given

To take away our sin,

That faithful as his children here

We heaven at length may win.

CARIUS BINDER

Carius Binder was a cabinet maker in Coburo. Brought at length under the influence of Hans Hut, he was baptized in Stejer, and united with the "Brethren." Evidently possessing gifts which fitted him to become a teacher of the word, he went forth as a bearer of the glad tidings to others. Salzburg seems to have been his field of labor. According to an old chronicle, he and thirty-eight others were shut up in a house which was set on fire, and they all perished in the flames. This was Oct. 25, 1527. The 35th hymn in "Auss Bundt" is ascribed to Jorg Steinmetzer, but according to Dr. Josef Beck, on authorities which he cites, the hymn was written by Binder. It commences,

With all our hearts we thank thee,

Thou holy one and true.

The hymn contains eleven stanzas of eight lines each.

LEONHART SCHIEMER

Prominent among the Anabaptists in Upper Austria was Leonhart Schiemer. He belonged to a good family, and was carefully educated at Vienna and other places. At length he became a monk. After an experience of six years in a monastery of the bare-footed order he made his escape, and, not long after, meeting Hubmeier, and, later, Hans Hut and Oswald Glaidt, who were holding religious services in Vienna in secret, he accepted their teachings and was baptized. At once he began to preach the new evangel, and at Steyer, whither he made his way early in 1527, he baptized a number of converts. Thence he proceeded to other places in Austria and Bavaria, preaching and baptizing. In the Tyrol he was recognized by a Franciscan monk, who betrayed him. Having been arrested, he was brought to trial and sentenced to death. He was beheaded and his body was afterward burned, Jan. 14, 1528, at Rotenburg on the Inn, where, later, seventy of his followers also sealed their faith with their blood.

From a fine hymn, 31 in "Auss Bundt," by Schiemer (here, however, written Schoner), I take the following:

> Thine holy place they have destroyed,
> Thine altars overthrown,
> And reaching forth their bloody hands,
> Have foully slain thine own.
> And we alone, thy little flock,
> The few who still remain,
> Are exiles wandering through the land,
> In sorrow and in pain.
>
> We are, alas, like scattered sheep,
> The shepherd not in sight.
> Each far away from home and hearth.
> And, like the birds of night
> That hid away in rocky clefts,
> We have our rocky hold,
> Yet near at hand, as for the birds.

There waits the hunter bold.

We wander in the forests dark,
With dogs upon our track;
And like the captive, silent lamb
Men bring us, prisoners, back.
They point to us amid the throng.
And with their taunts offend;
And long to let the sharpened axe
On heretics descend.

HANS SCHLAFFER

Another, who has a place among these martyr hymn writers, was Hans Schlaffer. From 1511, to 1526, he was a priest in the Roman Catholic church. Convinced of the errors of that church, he now withdrew from it and united with the Anabaptists. He was well acquainted with the Anabaptist leaders in Augsburg. In Nuremberg he met Hetzer and Denck. In the last days of 1527, he was arrested at Schwatz. A strenuous effort was made to induce him to yield his opposition to infant baptism, but he was immovable. The Scriptures demand, he said, that we believe and be baptized, but there is no command that infants be baptized. He was accordingly sentenced to death and was executed by the sword at Schwatz, early in 1528, with Lienhart Frick, an associate, and nineteen others, all Anabaptists.

JOHN LEOPOLD

John Leopold, who had been a tailor in Augsburg, and was highly esteemed as a citizen, became interested in the new religious movement and united with the Anabaptist church in that city. Later he became a teacher of the word, and aided in the extension at Anabaptist influences. But, with others, he at length fell into the hands of the civil authorities, and was condemned to death. When he was about to be executed, word was brought to him that by the sword he would pass from life to death "No, gentlemen of Augsburg," he replied, "but, if God wills, from death to life." He was executed Apr. 25, 1516.

Hymn 39 in "Auss Bundt" was written by Leopold. The following are the first and last stanzas of this hymn:

My God, thee will I praise
When my last hour shall come,
And then my voice I'll raise
Within the heavenly home.
O Lord, most merciful and kind,
Know strengthen my weak faith,
And give me peace of mind.
To thee in very deed
My spirit I commend,
Help me in all my need,
And let me ne'er offend.
Give to my flesh thy strength,
That I with thee may stand
A conqueror at length.

HANS HUT

Another Anabaptist hymn writer was Hans Hut. He was a native of Hain, in Franken, and during the Peasants War he was found among the followers of Thomas Munzer. Munzer's aims were political rather than religious. He would right the wrongs of the long down-trodden peasants, and so preaching resistance to the rulers, and organizing an armed force, he brought on a revolution. Miserably defeated May 15, 1525, at Frankenhausen, Munzer was made a prisoner, and was subsequently beheaded, with twenty-four of his associates. In this effort of Munzer's the

Anabaptists had no part. They declined to engage in armed resistance to civil authority. They were in sympathy with the oppressed peasants, but would bring about a better state of things, not by revolution, but by restoring primitive Christianity. Beginning in Switzerland the movement extended northward into Germany and among those who connected themselves with it was Hans Hut. Rhegius says he was baptized by John Denck at Augsburg. Like other of the "Brethren" he became at once an apostle of the new doctrine; and he made his way into Silesia, Moravia, and Austria, where, unwearied in his labors, he drew a multitude of followers to the standard of the cross. "One day," says Cornelius, "Hut entered the house of Franz Strigel in Weier, in Franken, drew from his pocket a small book, read the word of God, made known its truths until the head of the house and eight others received baptism. The same night he continued his journey, and no one of those baptized had seen him before or ever saw him again." At length, sometime in 1527, he was arrested in Augsburg and thrown into prison. In Dec, 1528, in an attempt to escape from the prison. Hut lost his life. Though his enemies could not now inflict upon him the punishment they anticipated, they directed that his body should be burned. It was accordingly taken to the place of execution, and there publicly committed to the flames.

The following hymn, 8 in "Auss Bundt," Hut wrote while in the prison at Augsburg. It contains twelve stanzas. Those given below are the seventh, eighth and ninth.

And so God sent his Son, his own,
Who hath to us the truth made known,
His holy way revealing.
The Spirit to us sealing.
And bringing heavenly healing.

He points us to his holy word.
His Testament, in which the Lord
Appears our nature wearing,
His Father's glory sharing,
No one with him comparing.

He man, and also very God,

10

Beneath his feet grim death hath trod,

With truth himself arraying,

His mighty power displaying,

And all our fears allaying.

LUDWIG HETZER

The most prominent of these martyr hymn writers was Ludwig Hetzer. He was a learned man, and early joined the reform movement. We first hear of him in 1523, in connection with the Second Discussion at Zurich, in Switzerland. January 21, 1525, with certain Anabaptists, he was banished from Zurich, and went to Augsburg. This place he was soon compelled to leave, and we next find him in Basel, where he was kindly received by Oecolampadius, whose work on the Lord's Supper he translated and published. Later he made a translation of Malachi, which was published at Basel in 1526. Soon after he appeared at Strasburg, where he fully identified himself with the Anabaptist movement. Here he made the acquaintance of Denck, and became associated with him in a translation of the Old Testament into the German language. In July, 1527, Hetzer was in Nuremberg and Augsburg. In Augsburg he seems to have remained until April, 1528, when he was again banished. We next hear of hunat Bischozell, the home of his youth, if not his birthplace, a village between Constance and St. Gall. Here he devoted himself to the preparation of one or two theological works. In the summer of 1528, he was in Constance, where there was a small circle of Anabaptists. All the other Anabaptist leaders either had died or had been put to death. Toward the end of October Hetzer was arrested, and thrown into prison. His trial occurred Feb. 3, 1529. If his offence had reference to his religious views he could only be imprisoned or banished. The charge brought against him was adultery, which was punishable with death. Of this crime he was adjudged guilty, and sentenced to die.

According to one of the Zwinglian pastors at Constance Hetzer received the announcement of his sentence with indescribable joy. During the night that followed friends were permitted to be with him, and at his request they made the place resound with psalms and hymns. In the morning he addressed the Zwinglian pastors and others, and prayed with them. On his way to the place of execution he referred to his companions—Mantz, Hut, Langenmantel, Sattler, Hubmeier—who had obtained the martyr's crown. Addressing the people, he said "Constance ought not to have God's word in the mouth only, but exhibit it in the life." Thereupon he offered up a fervent prayer, so that many of the people wept with him, and throughout the whole of his progress he was cheerful and unappalled. At the block Hetzer opened his Hebrew Bible, and in a loud, clear voice translated the twenty-fifth Psalm. Then he repeated the Lord's Prayer, ending his supplication with the words, "Through Jesus Christ, the Savior of the world by his blood." After this he laid his head upon the block and received the fatal stroke. "A nobler and more manful death," says John Zwick, a Zwinglian, "was never seen in Constance. We were all with him to his end, and may the Almighty, the Eternal God, grant to me, and to the servants of his word, like mercy in the day when he shall call us home." Thomas Blaurer, another Zwinglian, wrote: "No one has with so much charity, so courageously, laid down his life for Anabaptism as Hetzer. He was like one who spoke with God and died."

It is not strange that recent writers have given no credit to the evidence on which Hetzer was condemned. Keller says the charge is "unproved and unprovable." Those who are corrupt in heart and life are not want to spend their last hours on earth in such tranquil communion with God, or to die so triumphant a death. Hetzer's entire record, and his published writings, are strong witnesses to the purity of his heart and the uprightness of his life. He loved God's word, and he ever insisted upon loyalty to its commands. The Moravian Chronicle states, what will doubtless be the verdict of history, that Hetzer died for "the sake of divine truth," to which he "nobly" bore witness "by his blood." Unquestionably, of all the Anabaptist hymn writers, Hetzer is the first. One of his hymns, included by Wackernagel in his masterly work on German Hymnology, is based on the thirty-seventh Psalm, and contains twenty-three stanzas of eight lines each. The following is the opening stanza:

> Fret not thyself, O pious heart,
> Though evil men surround thee;
> The godless may be richer here,
> But that should not confound thee;

For like the herb in yonder field

They too are long shall wither,

And all their gain shall disappear

Like grass, they know not whither.

Hetzer has also a fine hymn for the strengthening and establishing of faith, and another suggested by the words of Paul (Rom. v. 4), "And patience, experience." The last stanza of the former, in modern dress, is as follows:

Attend, O world, in splendor decked,

Renounce thy works and ways;

Reflect that death will soon cut short

The remnant of thy days.

Repent of sin,

Let Christ within

Redemption work for thee;

When all is past,

With Christ at last,

The kingdom thou shalt see.

GEORGE BLAUROCK

The fifth hymn in "Auss Bundt" was written by George Blaurock. We first hear of him in connection with the discussion concerning infant baptism, Jan. 17, 1525, which was followed by the banishment of Hetzer, Reublin and others. He had been a monk, but had renounced his former faith, and was now arrayed with the Swiss Anabaptists against Zwingli. On account of his oratorical gifts he was called among the "Brethren" the second Paul, and his earnest, active efforts to advance what he believed to be the truth, made him prominent in the new movement. He was soon arrested in Zurich, and thrown into prison. Subsequently he was sentenced to death by drowning. But as he was not a citizen of the canton, he was beaten with rods, and allowed to leave the city after having taken an oath never to return. He seems to have made his way at first into the canton of Appenzell. In 1529, having been arrested in the Tyrol, he was burned at the stake in Claussen.

His hymn in "Auss Bundt" (5) contains thirty-three stanzas of four lines each. "Keep us. Father, through thy truth," he sings; "daily renew us and make us steadfast in persecution. Leave us not, thy children, from now on to the end. Extend to us thy fatherly hand, that we may finish our course." In his death, Blaurock exemplified the truth of one of the stanzas of this hymn: "Blessed," he says, "are those in all tribulation who cling to Christ to the end," and he adds:

> As he himself our sufferings bore
> When hanging on the accursed tree.
> So there is suffering still in store
> O pious heart, for you and me.

MARTIN MALER

In the year 1531, at Gemimden, in Schwabia, Martin Maler, a preacher of the Word, and six others, were condemned to death, and executed. They were first put to the rack, and promised their freedom if they would recant. But they all stood firm. At the place of execution Maler commended himself and his associates to God, asking that he would grant to them a blessed end, and that he would care for the little flock left behind. Maler was the author of the beautiful hymn

> With gladsome voice I sing
> And praise thee, mighty God.

With his imprisoned companions Maler composed hymn 61 in "Auss Bundt,"

> In deep distress I cry to thee;

My prayer, O God, attend.

In an old chronicle Maler is said to be the author of three "beautiful hymns."

PETER RIEDEMANN

Maler recalls another Anabaptist hymn writer, though not a martyr, Peter Riedemann. He was a native of Hirschberg, in Silesia, and died at Protzza, in Hungary, December 1, 1556, when about fifty years of age. He was a highly gifted man, and by his brethren was greatly esteemed for his own and for his works' sake. For preaching the Word he suffered imprisonment several times, first at Gemunden, in 1527, where he remained in prison three years and four weeks, receiving the name of Peter of Gemunden. At Nuremberg he was imprisoned four years and ten weeks; at Marburg, in Hesse, two years. An old chronicle says: "He was rich in divine knowledge, and was as a water fountain which overflows; and he refreshed all those who listened to him. He was the author of numerous works and many excellent hymns. The fine hymn (2) in "Auss Bundt,"

We all believe in one true God,

And love him from our hearts,

which Fusslin erroneously ascribes to John Denck, is ascribed to Riedemann in the hymn books of the Anabaptists. He is also the author of the hymn (37) in "Auss Bundt," wrongly ascribed to Langenmantel, of which the following are the twelfth, fourteenth and sixteenth stanzas:

O Lord, let sin nor guilt

Upon us bring a blot,

Nor terrors of the flesh

Assail us in our lot,

But in thy work through life

May we, whate'er betides,

Ne'er falter in the strife.

In anguish and distress.
Give us the bread of heaven,
And in the pain of death
Let peace to us be given.
Thou Father, full of love.
Who makest rich the poor,
O strengthen from above.

Help us the field to hold.
Our strength thy holy word,
And in our time of need
Protect us by thy sword,
That, heroes of thine own,
We in eternity
May wear the heavenly crown.

HYMNS BY UNKNOWN AUTHORS.

At the close of a volume entitled "Munsterische Geschichten, Sagen und Legenden," are several Anabaptist hymns. The names of the writers are not given. One of these hymns is a part of a hymn (97) in "Auss Bundt." There is nothing to indicate that any of them was written in Munster. The first two are entitled "Old hymns of the Anabaptists." Rev. Franklin Johnson, d. d., of Cambridge Mass., has rendered into English verse the first of these hymns, commencing

Beloved Father, Lord most mild,
Help thou and shield thine every child
Who in these last dread ages
Thy holy battle wages
Where many a serpent rages.

Arm thou with valor each true knight,
And guide and guard him in his fight
With evils old and hoary,
With foeman fierce and gory.
And thus show forth thy glory.

Lord Jesus Christ, beloved King,
Thou who dids't full salvation bring
To men in sorrow lying,
Hear thou thy brethren sighing.
With thirst and hunger dying.

Feed thou our hearts with bread divine,
And let the stream of sweetest wine
That, anguished, thou dids't pour us,
From head to feet flow o'er us.
To cleanse us and restore us.

Then shall we go our way with joy;
The dog shall not our souls annoy
With sword or flood or fire;
Nor shall we fear the ire
Of any monster dire.

Then all the words that thou has said
We glad shall eat, as they were bread.
And march where thou art going.
With warrior trumpets blowing,
The highest walls overthrowing.

Ah, God, thy children wander bare,

Though thou hast might beyond compare;
With raiment cheer their sadness,
That they may preach with gladness
To men in error's madness.

Ye people cleansed with precious blood,
Give thanks and praise alone to God;
He saves when we implore him.
And smites his foes before him,
Till worlds in awe adore him.

If we in trouble trust his name.
We need not fear a world in flame;
Our flesh, the dogs may tear it;
But he will guard the spirit
Through Christ's sufficient merit.

Lord Jesus Christ, strong Son of God,
Remember in these days of blood
Thy walls so breached and battered.
Thy church so sorely shattered.
Thy people peeled and scattered.

We thank and praise thee day by day,
And from our hearts devoutly pray
That thou wouldn't now and ever
Thy prisoners' fetters sever.
And let them perish never.

Dr. Johnson translates:

The church of God, good cheer, good cheer,

So holy here

In days when none bested thee,

Know this thou art Christ's chosen bride,

Who for thee died.

And swift he comes to wed thee;

With raiment fair

And jewels rich and rare

Thy form adorn,

For hastes the morn

When thou shalt eat

This banquet sweet.

And be with endless joy complete.

The stanza Dr. Johnson renders thus:

Oh God of my salvation.

Regard my tears and sighs;

Against thy lowly servant

The violent arise.

'T is for thy word I suffer

These bitter days of pain.

And must lie bound in prison,

And afterward be slain.

These are specimens only of the hymns of the Anabaptists of Switzerland and Germany at the time of the Reformation. The hymns of the Netherland Anabaptists are of a like character. The number of these hymns is large, but their value lies chiefly in this, that in them, as nowhere else, the spirit of the Anabaptist movement of the sixteenth century finds a voice. The term "Anabaptist," until recently, has stood for the revolutionary and fanatical element in the early conflict between Protestantism and Roman Catholicism. But the great majority of the

Anabaptists of the period of the Reformation were law-abiding, peaceable men. Their hymns are a witness to this fact. Liliencron, in his paper, "A Contribution to the Hymnology of the Anabaptists," published by the Bavarian Academy of Sciences (Munich, 1875), says there is in these Anabaptist hymns no trace of anything revolutionary or fanatical. The dogmatical element in them is almost entirely wanting. There is little, even, that is polemical. The Anabaptists believed with all their hearts in the redemption by the blood of Jesus Christ, but they also believed that the work of grace which is wrought by the Spirit in the heart will appear in the life. In these hymns the moral aspects of the Christian life are accordingly made prominent. Faith and love are exalted, and steadfastness in persecution, even unto death, is exhibited as the mark of true discipleship. Some of these hymns, as the preceding pages show, were written in the near prospect of death, and were sung with the block or the fagot in full view. These martyr hymns had their special mission in strengthening fellow disciples for the trial of faith which was sure to come. But there were many Anabaptist hymns which were purely devotional, giving glad if not always beautiful expression to the devout sentiments of truly pious hearts. These and the martyr hymns were the cherished possession in many an Anabaptist home, and next to the Word of God were oftenest on the lips of the scattered members of the Anabaptist host from the Alps to the Baltic and the North Sea, and from Bohemia to the borders of France. That they have been preserved is an occasion for devout gratitude. They are worthy of the recent recognition they have received, and of the place they have already found in the great treasure house of Christian song.

ENGLISH BAPTIST HYMN WRITERS AND THEIR HYMNS

JOHN BUNYAN 1628-1688

It is only a slender tie by which Bunyan is united to the hymn writers of the church. Dr. Belcher is authority for the statement that some lines written by the immortal dreamer of Bedford jail, and found in the Second Part of the "Pilgrim's Progress," have "long been used in some of the Baptist churches in England at the admission of members." They are the words Bunyan puts into the lips of Mercy, as she and Christiana set out on their pilgrimage to the Celestial City.

> Let the Most Blessed be my guide,
> If 't be his blessed will,
> Unto his gate, into his fold,
> Up to his holy hill.
>
> And let him never suffer me
> To swerve or turn aside
> From his free grace and holy ways,
> Whate'er shall me betide.
>
> And let him gather them of mine
> That I have left behind;
> Lord, make them pray they may be thine
> With all their heart and mind.

There are other lines in the Second Part, which the readers of the "Pilgrim's Progress" will recall, especially those which Bunyan puts into the lips of the shepherd boy, commencing

> He that is down needs fear no fall;
> He that is low no pride;
> He that is humble ever shall
> Have God to be his guide.

Those given above, however, so far as I am aware, are the only lines by Bunyan that have been sung. Had Bunyan lived a century later, the treasury of Christian song would doubtless have been greatly enriched by hymns from his pen.

John Bunyan was born in Elstow, near Bedford, in 1628. The record of his christening in Elstow church is as follows: "In 1628, John the son of Thomas Bonnionn, June the 10th of November." His parents were poor, but, as he tells us, " It pleased God to put it into their hearts to put me to school to His parents were poor, but, as he tells us, "It pleased God to put it into their hearts to put me to school to learn both to read and write." His advantages, however, were of the most meagre kind, and not long enjoyed, for he early passed from the school-room to his father's workshop. In his sixteenth year his mother died, and a few weeks later his sister Margaret. His father almost immediately remarried, and thenceforward the home to Bunyan was not what it had been. It is believed that his experience in the army, to which he briefly refers in his "Grace Abounding," belongs to this period. The army was disbanded in 1646, and Bunyan returned to Elstow. Two or three years later he was married. Who his wife was we do not know, but she evidently came from a godly home, and desired to have her own home like that from which she came. The four years that followed their marriage were the years of Bunyan's spiritual conflict, which he has so vividly portrayed. Then, at the end of the struggle, came peace. "The chains fell off," and the new life of blessedness began.

Bunyan united with Mr. Gifford's church in Bedford, in 1653. Two years later he made Bedford his home. Here his wife soon died, and Bunyan was left to be both father and mother to his four children. His pastor, Mr. Gifford, also died not long after Bunyan's removal to Bedford, and Bunyan, by request of his brethren who had discovered his gifts, began to preach. Wherever he went the people "came to hear the word by hundreds, and that from all parts, though upon Sunday and from divers accounts." His right to preach was frequently questioned, and in November, 1660, he was arrested, and soon after tried for "devilishly and perniciously abstaining from coming to church to hear divine service, and for being a common upholder of several unlawful meetings and conventicles, to the great disturbance and distraction of the good subjects of this kingdom, contrary to the law of our sovereign lord, the king." Then followed his twelve years' imprisonment in Bedford jail, from 1660 to 1672. Three years of liberty succeeded. Then, in the winter and early spring of 1675-76, Bunyan was again in prison, and it was during this time that he wrote the "Pilgrim's Progress", continuing his career as an author, upon which he entered not long after he began to preach. The "Pilgrim's Progress" has been sold in many editions and in untold numbers of copies, in all English-speaking lands, and has been translated into between seventy and eighty languages and dialects, and is continually appearing in new forms and new languages. Rufus Choate once called the speech of Mr. Standfast, near the close of the Second Part, "the most mellifluous and eloquent talk that was ever put together in the English language." Of Bunyan's "Holy War," Lord Macaulay says, "If the ^Pilgrim's Progress' did not exist, it would be the best allegory that ever was written."

Bunyan's last years were years of busy work as a writer and a preacher. Wherever he went crowds came together to listen to his words. His death occurred in London, August 31, 1688, and lie was buried in Bunhill Fields.

BENJAMIN KEACH 1640-1704

Benjamin Keach was born in Stokehaman, Buckinghamshire, Feb. 29, 1G40. Converted in his fifteenth year, he united with a neighboring Baptist church, and three years later he began to preach. In 1662, the Act of Uniformity was passed, and at one of his meetings Keach was seized by four troopers who threatened to trample him to death under their horses feet, but he was providentially rescued by one of their officers. In 1664, Mr. Keach published "The Child's Instructor, or a New and Easy Primer." For this he was indicted and brought to trial at the Aylesbury Assizes, which began October 8, before Lord Chief Justice Hyde, afterward Lord Clarendon, who instructed the jury to bring in a verdict of guilty. This they did, and Mr. Keach was sentenced to be imprisoned for a fortnight; then to stand the next Saturday upon the pillory at Aylesbury, in the open market from eleven o'clock till one, with a paper on his head bearing this inscription: "For writing, printing and publishing a schematical book"; the next Thursday to stand in the same manner and for the same time in the market at Winslow; then to have his book burned by the common hangman. He was also required to forfeit to the King's majesty the sum of twenty pounds, and to remain in jail until he could find sureties for good behavior and appearance at the next assizes; and lastly, to renounce his doctrines, and make such public submissions as should be required. "I hope," said Keach to his lordship, "I shall never renounce the truth which I have written in that book," and this part of the sentence was not insisted upon.

In 166S, Mr. Keach accepted an invitation to become pastor of a small Particular Baptist church, which met in a private house in Tooley Street, London. After the Declaration of Indulgence enacted in 1672, a meeting-house was erected at the corner of Goat Street, Horsley-down, Southwark. Here his services were attended by large audiences, and it became necessary to enlarge the house again and again. Up to this time Baptists in England were opposed to singing as a part of worship, but Mr. Keach now with the consent of his church, introduced the practice of singing a h\min at the Lord's Supper. Later, there was singing in the church on Thanksgiving days. Finally, about the year 1690, the church, only a few dissenting, voted to sing a hymn every Lord's day, after the sermon, so that those who were opposed to this part of the service could "go freely forth." In 1691, Mr. Keach published a work in favor of the new practice, entitled "The Breach" repeated in God's Worship, or Singing of Psalms, Hymns and Spiritual Songs proved to be a holy ordinance of Jesus Christ."

Mr. Keach was a voluminous writer. His two most popular works were - Tropologia, or a Key to Open Scripture Metaphors," and "Gospel Mysteries Unveiled, or an Exposition of the Parables." He was also the author of some poetical compositions, the most important of which were "Zion in Distress, or the Groans of the Protestant Church." first published in 1666, and his "Distressed Zion Relieved, or the Garment of Praise for the Spirit of Heatless," published after the Revolution. He also published in 1691, a collection of hymns entitled "Scriptural Melody," containing nearly three hundred hymns. None of them are now in use. The following is number 15.

> The Lord, he is our sun and shield.
> Our buckler and safeguard,
> And hence we stand and will not yield,

Though enemies press hard.

Like as a shield the blow keeps off
The enemy lays on,
So thou keeps off all hurt from us,
And saves us every one.

Let foes strike at us as they please,
On the head or the heart;
This precious shield which we do use
Secures us every part.

From sin, from satan and the world
No art we need to fear.
Since thou art such a shield to us,
O God and Savior dear!

Our shield and our great reward.
To thee all praise be given;
Who with thy saving help afford
Until we come to heaven.

Mr. Keach remained pastor of the church at Horsley down until his death, which occurred July 18, 1704. His funeral sermon was preached by Rev. Joseph Stennett.

JOSEPH STENNETT 1665-1713

The name of Stennett has a prominent place in English Baptist history, and also in Baptist hymnology. Joseph Stennett was the author of the hymn, and many other good hymns which are still in use. His grandson, Samuel Stennett, was the author of

On Jordan's stormy banks I stand,

and other hymns of equal merit. Joseph Stennett was the son of Rev. Edward Stennett, a dissenting minister, who enthusiastically espoused the cause of the Parliament and the Commonwealth. After the Revolution, with other Nonconformists who had been conspicuous in the important events that preceded, he suffered persecution and for a short time imprisonment. Removing at length to Wallingford, without abandoning the work of the ministry, he engaged in the practice of medicine in order to support his family. Of his three sons, two became ministers and one a physician.

Joseph was born at Abingdon, in 1663. In early life he made a profession of faith, and united with his father's church. Under the guidance of skillful instructors he acquired a good knowledge of philosophy and theology, also of the French, Italian, Hebrew and other languages. When twenty two years of age he went to London, where he accepted an appointment as a teacher. In 1688, he married Susanna, daughter of George Guill, a French Protestant refugee, whose estates had been confiscated in 1685, at the time of the Revocation of the Edict of Nantes, and who was now engaged in mercantile pursuits in London. In the following year Mr. Stennett was called to the pastorate of the Seventh Day Baptist church, then worshiping in a hill in Devonshire Square, London, of which his father had for a while been pastor; afterward removed to Pinner's Hall. He preached for other churches on Sunday, but of this Seventh Day Baptist church he remained pastor until his death. His cultivated intellect, polished manners, and high Christian character gave him a commanding position, and he was greatly esteemed in all denominations. At the request of his brethren he prepared and presented to William III, an address with reference to his deliverance from the "Assassination Plot."

In 1712, Mr. Stennett published twelve hymns, entitled "Hymns for the Celebration of the

Holy Ordinance of Baptism." These were long in use in Baptist churches. Among them were

"The great Redeemer we adore,"

"Thus was the great Redeemer plunged."

The hymn beginning

Another six days' work is done

contained fourteen stanzas in its original form. Of these, the 1st, 10th, 11th and 13th stanzas only are generally retained. In Rippon's "Selection" six stanzas are given. In Rippon, also, the following sacramental hymn by Stennett is inserted (482):

Lord, at thy table I behold
The wonders of thy grace;
But most of all admire that I
Should find a welcome place, —

I, that am all defiled with sin,
A rebel to my God;
I, that have crucified his Son,
And trampled on his blood.

What strange, surprising grace is this,
That such a soul has room
My Savior takes me by the hand,
My Jesus bids me come.

Eat, O my friends, the Savior cries.
The feast was made for you;
For you I groaned, and bled, and died.
And rose, and triumphed too.

With trembling faith, and bleeding hearts,

Lord, we accept thy love;

'T is a rich banquet we have had.

What will it be above?

Ye saints below, and hosts of heaven,

Join all your praising powers;

No theme is like redeeming love.

No Savior is like ours.

Had I ten thousand hearts, dear Lord,

I'd give them all to thee;

Had I ten thousand tongues, they all

Should join the harmony.

In the English "Baptist Hymnal" this hymn is included, with the omission of the second stanza.

Prominent among Stennett's prose writings was a reply, which, in 1704, he made to David Russen's "Fundamentals without a Foundation, or a True Picture of the Anabaptists." So successful was he in this work that he was requested to write a history of the Baptists. He commenced to collect materials for such a work, but did not live long enough to execute his purpose. He died July 11, 1713. Among his last words were, "I rejoice in the God of my salvation, who is my strength and God." He left a widow and four children, and was buried in the churchyard of Hitchenden, Buckinghamshire. The epitaph on his tombstone was written by Dr. Ward, of Gresham College. His complete prose and poetical works (except his reply to Russen) were published in four volumes, in 1732.

JAMES FANCH 1764-1767

Rev. James Fanch of Romsey, who was associated with Rev. Daniel Turner in the production of the hymn

Beyond the glittering starry globe,

was born in 1704, and died December 12, 1767. Rev. S. B. Brown, pastor of the Baptist church at Romsey, in a letter to Mr. Francis Jennings of Philadelphia, dated June 23, 1870, says of Mr. Fanch: "At the close of the year 1750, during the time he was pastor of the Baptist church at Romsey, a spiritual movement commenced in the neighboring village (five miles away) of Lockerly. Those whose hearts were specially influenced, not finding the bread of life in the parish church of Lockerly, repaired to Romsey to hear the Rev. J. Fanch, a faithful minister of Christ, and a man of classical accomplishments. In 1751, a house was licensed for preaching at Lockerly. Mr. Fanch preached to them on Sunday evenings; much good resulted from his services, and soon afterward he had the pleasure of baptizing sixteen persons at the neighboring village of Broughton, which possessed a baptistery. Shortly after, five more were baptized and in 1753, they were formed into a church, which continued for some time a branch of that at Romsey. Mr. Fanch was acknowledged their pastor, and preached a sermon at the foundation of the church from Phil, 1. 27, which he afterward printed, with others, in a volume of sermons. Mr. Fanch continued to administer the ordinances to them till his death. He also frequently visited and preached at Southampton, which at that time had no Baptist church."

Mr. Fanch was the author of "Free Thoughts on Practical Religion" (1761), "A Paraphrase on a Select Number of the Psalms of David, done from the Latin of Buchanan, to which are added some Occasional Pieces" (1764), and "Ten Sermons on Practical Subjects," (1767). The first of these works contains occasional hymns.

In Rippon's "Baptist Annual Register," Vol. 3, p. 471, is Fanch and Turner's hymn.

Beyond the glittering starry globe.

The following are the stanzas by Mr. Fanch:

Beyond the glittering starry globe
Far o'er the eternal hills,
There, in the boundless worlds of light,
Our great Redeemer dwells.

Immortal angels, bright and fair,
In countless armies shine,
At his right hand, with golden harps,
To offer songs divine.

Hail! prince, they cry, forever hail
Whose unexampled love
Moved thee to quit these glorious realms
And royalties above

While thou dids't condescend on earth
To suffer rude disdain,
They cast their honors at thy feet,
And waited on thy train.

Thro' all thy travels here below,
They did thy steps attend;
Oft gazed, and wondered when at last
The scene of love would end.

They saw thy heart tranfixed with wounds,
Thy crimson sweat and gore;
They saw thee break the bars of death,
As none ever brake before.

They brought thy chariot from above,

To bear thee to thy throne;

Clapped their triumphant wings and cried

"The glorious work is done."

DANIEL TURNER 1716-1798

Mr. Turner was born at Blackwater Park, near St. Albans, Hertfordshire, March 1, 1710. In early he united with the Baptist church at Hemel-Hemp-Stead, in the neighborhood of his birth-place. Having received a good classical education, he devoted himself (1738) to the work of teaching. In 1741, he became pastor of the Hosier Lane Baptist Church at Reading, on the Thames. In 1748, he removed to Abingdon, Berkshire, having accepted a call to the pastorate of the Baptist church in that place, a position which he held during the remainder of his long and useful life. He died September 5, 1798.

Of his prose writings, the more important are "A Compendium of Social Religion" (1758), "Letters Religious and Moral" (1766), "Short Meditations on Select Portions of Scripture" (1771), "Dissertations on Religion" (1775), "Essays on Religion" (1780), and "Expositions on Scripture" (1790). His poetical writings were "Divine Songs, Hymns and other Poems" (1747), and "Poems, Devotional and Moral" (1794). Of his hymns four marked "D. T." appeared in the "Collection of Hymns" (1769) compiled by Dr. John Ash and Dr. Caleb Evans, viz.:

"With thee, great God, the star of light,"

"Welcome, blessed morning to our eyes,"

"Jesus, full of all compassion,"

"Faith adds new charms to earthly bliss."

The last two are still in use, and the first of the two, as given in this early collection, is as follows:

Jesus, full of all compassion,
Hear thy humble suppliant's cry;
Let me know thy great salvation,
See, I languish, faint, and die.

Guilty, but with heart relenting,
Overwhelmed with helpless grief,
Prostrate, at thy feet repenting,
Send, Oh send me quick relief.

Whither should a wretch be flying,
But to him who comfort gives?
Whither, from the dread of dying,
But to him who ever lives?

While I view thee, wounded, grieving,
Breathless, on the cursed tree.
Fain I'd feel my heart believing.
That thou suffered thus for me.

With thy righteousness and spirit,
I am more than angels blest,
Here with thee, all things inherit
Peace, and joy, and endless rest.

Without thee, the world possessing,
I should be a wretch undone;
Search through heaven, the land of blessing,
Seeking good, and finding none.

Hear then, blessed Savior, hear me,
My soul cleaveth to the dust;
Send the Comforter to cheer me,
Lo! in thee I put my trust.

On the word thy blood hath sealed.
Hangs my everlasting all.
Let thine arm be now revealed.
Stay, Oh stay me, less I fall!

In the world of endless ruin,
Let it never, Lord, be said,
"Here 's a soul that perished, suing,
For the boasted Savior's aid!"

Saved — the deed shall spread new glory
Through the shining realms above;
Angels sing the pleasing story.
All enraptured with thy love

Of Turner's hymns, nine appeared in Rippon's "Selection." In a note to the 442d hymn, Dr. Rippon says: "For the alterations made in this and several of the following hymns on baptism, I am indebted to my venerable friend, the Rev. Mr. Turner of Abingdon."

JOHN NEEDHAM

Concerning Mr. Needham's early life we have no information. His father was pastor of the Baptist church in Hitchen, Hertfordshire, and the son entered upon the work of the ministry, but where I have not learned. Probably for a time he aided his father, who supported himself in part by teaching. In 1746, Mr. Needham removed to Bristol, where he was associated with Rev. John Beddome in the pastorate of the Baptist church in the Pithay. He was ordained co-pastor May 10, 1750. Rev. W. R. Stevenson says: "Mr. Beddome was at this time old and infirm, and two years later resigned the pastorate altogether; but as the church had important branches, the services of two ministers were absolutely required. A Mr. Tommas was invited to become assistant to Mr. Needham, but would only accept an invitation as co-pastor on an official equality with the other minister. To this Mr. Needham and a number of his friends objected. True, the church had been accustomed from time immemorial to have two pastors, but the plan had not worked well, so that in 1750, when Mr. Needham was ordained co-pastor, the church came to a resolution, recorded on their minute-book, never again to have two pastors, excepting when, as in that case, one should be partially disabled through age or infirmity. But the majority of the church had set their hearts upon Mr. Tommas, and determined to have him upon his own terms. An unhappy conflict ensued, and in the end the majority passed a resolution pronouncing Mr. Needham to be no longer either a minister or member of the church which for years he had faithfully served.

"There was in Bristol at that time another Baptist church, worshiping in a part of the city called Callowhill. A Mr. Foot was their pastor. Mr. Needham and his friends applied to the Callowhill church for the use of their meeting-house on one part of the Lord's-day, which was granted; and from November, 1752, to June, 1755, the two congregations occupied the same building at different hours. But at the date last mentioned the two churches united, Mr. Foot and Mr. Needham becoming joint pastors, and administering the Lord's Supper alternately. It is known that this arrangement continued up to the year 1784; but the history of both church and pastors after that date is almost a blank. All that can be stated is that in 1787, the second of the two pastors died, and the church at Callowhill became extinct; but which it was, Mr. Foot or Mr. Needham who survived the other, is unknown."

Mr. Needham was the author of a large number of hymns. In 1768, he published a volume entitled "Hymns, Devotional and Moral, on Various Subjects, Collected Chiefly from the Holy Scriptures, and Suited to the Christian State and Worship." Of the 263 hymns in this collection some are still in use, and highly esteemed.

The following hymn, also by Needham, is in the English "Baptist Hymnal" (283):

When some kind shepherd from the fold
Has lost a straying sheep,
Through vales, o'er hills, he anxious roves,
And climbs the mountain steep.

But O, the joy, the transport sweet,
When he the wanderer finds!
Up in his arms he takes his charge,
And to his shoulder binds.

Homeward he hastes to tell his joys,
And make his bliss complete;
The neighbors hear the news, and all
The joyful shepherd greet.

Yet how much greater is the joy
When but one sinner turns,
And with a humble, broken heart,
His sins and errors mourns.

Pleased with the news, the saints below
In songs their tongues employ;
Beyond the skies the tidings go,
And heaven is filled with joy.

Angels rejoice in louder strains,
And seraphs feel new fire;
"A sinner lost is found," they say.
And strike the sounding lyre.

BENJAMIN WALLIN 1711-1782

Benjamin Wallin was born in 1711, in Southwark, London, where his father, Rev. Edward Wallin, became pastor of the church at Maze Pond in 1703. A cripple from infancy through the carelessness of a nurse, he devoted himself assiduously to study, and was placed under the tutorship of Rev. John Needham. For a while he engaged in business, and then directed his attention to the work of the Christian ministry. In 1780, he preached his first sermon, and in the following year, became pastor of the church which his father had served, and continued in the pastorate, honored for his many Christian virtues, until his death, February 19, 1782.

Besides many occasional sermons, he published several essays on Practical Religion, "Lectures on Primitive Christianity," "Lectures on the Epistle to the Church at Sardis," "Lectures on the Faithful in the Days of Malachi." He also published (1750) a volume of "Evangelical Hymns and Songs, in Two Parts: The First, composed on Various Views of the Christian Life and Warfare; The Second, in Praise of the Redeemer, Published for the Comfort and Entertainment of True Christians, with Authorities at large from the Scriptures." Two of these hymns, considerably modified, Wallin contributed to the Gospel Magazine for June, 1776. Toplady transferred both of them to his "Psalms and Hymns," published that year. One of them Rippon used in his " Selection" (77), from which it was transferred to the supplement (89) of "Wincheli's Watts" and the "Psalmist" (337), viz.:

Hail mighty Jesus how divine
Is thy victorious sword!
The stoutest rebel must resign
At thy commanding word.

How deep the wounds these arrows give!
They pierce the hardest heart.

Thy smiles of grace the slain revive,
And joy succeeds to smart.
Still gird thy sword upon thy thigh;
Ride with majestic sway;
Go forth, great Prince, triumphantly,
And make thy foes obey.

And when thy victories are complete,—
When all the chosen race
Shall round the throne of glory meet
To sing thy conquering grace, —

Oh may my humble soul be found
Among that glorious throng;
And I with them thy praise will sound
In heaven's immortal song.

ANNE STEELE 1716-1778

More than one hundred of Miss Steele's hymns are found in our modern compilations. Of no other Baptist hymn writer can this be said. Indeed, as Dr. Hatfield remarks, "No one of the gentler sex has so largely contributed to the familiar hymnology of the church as the modest and retiring, but gifted and godly, Anne Steele. She may well be styled the female 'Poet of the Sanctuary.' "She was the eldest daughter of William Steele, a timber merchant, who for thirty years was a deacon and occasional preacher in the Baptist church at Broughton, and for a like period was the beloved pastor of the church, without salary. Born at Broughton in 1716, she became in early life a member of her father's church. From childhood she was an invalid, and at times a great sufferer. When she was twenty one years of age, the young man to whom she was engaged to be married was drowned while bathing, the day before the wedding was to take place.

She could say with the Psalmist, "All thy waves and thy billows are gone over me." Yet heart-broken, she did not yield to despair, but made herself a ministering spirit, devoting her life to deeds of love and mercy. Many of her hymns, written to lighten her own burdens, give beautiful expression to the sweetness of her Christian character, and the depth of her Christian experience. The death of her greatly venerated father, Sept. 10, 1769, is said to have hastened her own death, which occurred in November, 1778, at the age of sixty-one.

The closing scenes in Miss Steele's life are thus described by Dr. Evans: "Having been confined to her chamber for some years, she had long waited with Christian dignity for the hour of her departure. And when the time came, she welcomed its arrival; and though her feeble body was excruciated with pain, her mind was perfectly serene. She took a most affectionate leave of her weeping friends around her, and at length, the happy moment of her dismission arriving, she closed her eyes, and with these words upon her dying lips, 'I know that my Redeemer live,' gently fell asleep in Jesus."

Miss Steele's first publication appeared in 1760, in two volumes, under the title "Poems, on Subjects Chiefly Devotional," by "Theodosia." The following entry in her father's diary, under date November 29, 1757, seems to have reference to this publication: "This day Nanny sent part of her composition to London to be printed. I entreat a gracious God, who enabled and stirred her up to such a work, to direct in it, and bless it for the good of many. I pray God to make it useful, and keep her humble." October, 1759, he wrote: "Her brother brought with him her poetry, not yet bound. I earnestly desire the blessing of God upon that work, that it may be made very useful."

After her death these two volumes of her "Poems," with a third prepared by herself, were published (1780), by Rev. Caleb Evans, d.d., of Bristol. It is said it was in a collection of hymns compiled by Dr. Evans and Dr. John Ash, published in 1769, that Miss Steele's hymns were first made available for general use in religious worship.

The most familiar of her hymns is that commencing In its original form this hymn contains ten stanzas, as follows:

When I survey life's varied scene,
Amid the darkest hours,
Sweet rays of comfort shine between,
And thorns are mixed with flowers.

Lord, teach me to adore thy hand,
From whence my comforts flow,
And let me in this desert land
A glimpse of Canaan know.

Is health and ease my happy share?
Oh may I bless my God;
Thy kindness let my songs declare.
And spread thy praise abroad.

While such delightful gifts as these
Are kindly dealt to me,
Be all my hours of health and ease
Devoted, Lord, to thee.

In griefs and pains thy sacred word
(Dear solace of my soul!)
Celestial comforts can afford.
And all their power control.

When present sufferings pain my heart.
Or future terrors rise.
And light and hope almost depart
From these dejected eyes,

Thy powerful word supports my hope.

Sweet cordial of the mind,

And bears ray fainting spirit up.

And bids me wait resigned.

And oh, whate'er of earthly bliss

Thy sovereign hand denies.

Accepted at thy throne of grace,

Let this petition rise;

"Give me a calm, a thankful heart,

From every murmur free;

The blessings of thy grace impart,

And let me live to thee.

"Let the sweet hope that thou art mine,

My path of life attend

Thy presence through my journey shine,

And bless its happy end."

BENJAMIN BEDDOME 1717-1795

For fifty-two years Benjamin Beddome was the beloved pastor of the Baptist church at Bourton-on-the-Water, in the eastern part of Gloucestershire. He was born at Henley-in-Arden, a market town near Warwick, January 23, 1717. In 1724, his father, Rev. John Beddome, removed to Bristol, where he became a co-pastor of the Pithay Baptist church. Here Benjamin Beddome spent his youth, and in due time he was apprenticed to a surgeon and apothecary. His conversion occurred in connection with a sermon which was preached August 7, 1737, by Rev. Mr. Ware, in his father's church at Bristol, from the text, Luke xv. 7, "Likewise joy shall be in heaven over one sinner that repenteth," etc. At the expiration of his apprenticeship he entered upon a course of study preparatory to the work of the Christian ministry, first under Mr. Bernard Foskett, then tutor in the Baptist Academy, Bristol, and afterward at the Independent Academy in London, under the learned Rev. John Eames. He was baptized in London, September 27, 1739, by Rev. Samuel Wilson, and united with the Baptist church in Goodman's Fields. By this church he was called to preach. The church in Bourton was at that time pastorless, and Mr. Beddome was invited to supply the pulpit. His labors were acceptable, and he preached both at Bourton and Warwick. At length, in answer to repeated solicitations, he accepted the pastorate of the church at Bourton, and he was ordained September 23, 1743. Dr. Joseph Stennett preached the sermon from the text, "Obey them that have the rule over you," etc., Heb. xiii. 17. December 27, 1749, he married Elizabeth Boswell, a daughter of one of his deacons.

By his faithful ministrations Mr. Beddome greatly endeared himself to his people. After the death of Rev. Samuel Wilson, Mr. Beddome was invited to become Mr. Wilson's successor. Call after call was sent to him, and declined. At length, so importunate were the brethren in London that Mr. Beddome asked the people to make the decision for him. They sent a prompt refusal to London, and Mr. Beddome remained at Bourton until his death.

He seems to have exercised his poetical gift throughout his ministry. It was his custom to prepare a hymn to be sung after his morning's sermon each Lord's-day. A promising son, who had just completed his medical studies, died in Edinburgh, January 4, 1778. That day, not knowing of his son's death, not having been informed even of his sickness, he preached from Psalms xxxi. 15, "My times are in thy hand." The hymn which he had composed for the day was the now familiar one, commencing

My times of sorrow, and of joy,

Great God, are in thy hand,

My choicest comforts come from thee,

And go at thy command.

One of his best hymns Mr. Beddome wrote after recovering from a severe illness. He had first written a hymn of gratitude for his restoration to health. On further reflection he wrote these lines:

> If I must die, O let me die
> Trusting in Jesus' blood!
> That blood which hath atonement made.
> And reconciles to God.
>
> If I must die, then let me die
> In peace with all mankind.
> And change these fleeting joys below
> For pleasures more refined.
>
> If I must die, as die I must.
> Let some kind seraph come,
> And bear me on his friendly wing
> To my celestial home!
>
> Of Canaan's land from Pisgah's top
> May I but have a view!
> Though Jordan should overflow its banks,
> I'll boldly venture through.

Mr. Beddome lived to a ripe old age, and died after a long illness, September 3, 1795, having been engaged in writing a hymn only a few hours before his departure. Beside a Circular Letter of the Midland Association for 1765, his only publication was a "Scriptural Exposition on the Baptist Catechism by way of Question and Answer," which appeared in 1752. A second edition was printed in 1776. Ten years after his decease two volumes of his sermons were published, and a third volume appeared in 1835.

Of Beddome's hymns, Montgomery says they are "very agreeable as well as impressive, being for the most part brief and pithy. A single idea, always important, often striking, and sometimes ingeniously brought out, not with a mere point at the end, but with the terseness and simplicity of the Greek epigram, constitutes the basis of each piece."

The honorary degree of a.m. was conferred upon Mr. Beddome in 1770, by Rhode Island College, now Brown University.

EDMUND JONES 1722-1765

The well known hymn, commencing

Come, humble sinner, in whose breast,

is ascribed by Dr. Joseph Belcher to Rev. Edmund Jones, "a highly popular Welsh Baptist preacher of the last century," who resided at Trevecca, Wales. This is an error its author was an esteemed English Baptist pastor of the same name. The hymn first appeared in Rippon's "Selection" (1787), ascribed to Edmund Jones, and in a foot note Dr. Rippon says: "The Rev. Mr. Jones was a truly worthy pastor of the Baptist church at Exon, Devon. His successor, was my very amiable friend, the Rev. Mr. Thomas Lewis, to whose memory this page is sacred." Rev. Wm. Parkinson introduced this hymn into his "Selection of Hymns and Spiritual Songs" (New York, 1809), and in a note referring to the hymn, following Dr. Rippon, he says: "Mr. Jones was a truly worthy pastor of the Baptist church in Exeter, Devon."

Rev. Edmund Jones was a son of Rev. Philip Jones, and was born in 1722, at Cheltenham, Gloucestershire. His boyhood, for the most part, was spent at Upton-on-Severn, Worcestershire, where his father had become pastor of the Baptist church. Of this church, at an early age, Edmund became a member. Later he was sent to the Baptist College at Bristol, where he entered upon a course of study preparatory to the work of the Christian ministry. In 1741, he was invited to supply the pulpit of the Baptist church in Exeter. His services were so acceptable that in 1743, he was ordained as pastor of the church. In this position he remained until his death, April 15, 1765.

Like many of the Baptist churches in England; the church at Exeter, when Mr. Jones became its pastor, did not make singing a part of the Sunday service. Mr. Jones succeeded in bringing about a change, and the service of song was introduced in 1759. The hymn above referred to was doubtless one of others which Mr. Jones composed for this service. In Rippon's "Selection" it is entitled, "The Successful Resolve—I will go in unto the King. Esther iv. 16," and is as follows:

Come, humble sinner, in whose breast
A thousand thoughts revolve,
Come, with your guilt and fear opprest,
And make this last resolve.

"I'll go to Jesus, thou my sin
Hath like a mountain rose;
I know his courts, I'll enter in,
Whatever may oppose.

"Prostrate I'll lie before his throne,
And there my guilt confess,
I'll tell him I 'm a wretch undone
Without his sovereign grace.

"I'll to the gracious King approach,
Whose scepter pardon gives.
Perhaps he may command my touch
And then the suppliant lives.

"Perhaps he will admit my plea,
Perhaps will hear my prayer;
But if I perish I will pray.
And perish only there.

"I can but perish if I go,

I am resolved to try;

For if I stay away, I know

I must forever die."

In an article in the New York Evangelist, Rev. Henry A. Nelson, d.d., says : " In some editions this hymn is printed ' come, trembling sinner,' and in some, 'come, humble sinner.' In either form it is a precious hymn to me, but I rather prefer the first, ' come, trembling sinner.' My first recollection of the hymn goes back to a solemn hour, when I surely was a 'trembling sinner,' whether a 'humble' one or not. How vividly I remember it! I was sitting in the chimney corner of the big farm-house fireplace, used for the family cooking, as well as for warmth of the family room. I was a sad and sorrowful little boy. Conviction of sin had smitten me. Faithful parental teaching and faithful preaching had been energized by God's spirit, bringing home God's condemning law to my quickened conscience. 'Sin revived and I died.' I knew I was wicked, I knew that ' God is angry with the wicked every day.' I shuddered with fear of the wrath to come.' Much kind and sympathetic instruction had been given life but kind sympathy had not been allowed to prevent fidelity. Very searching had been the instruction given me at home and at church. I feared the deserved wrath of God. I trembled in anticipation of his judgment. I sat silent and gloomy by the fireside. My sister, a few years older, had recently found the Savior. She had tasted and seen that the Lord is gracious. She was a thoughtful, loving, not talkative girl. She was busy before the fire with some culinary work. She saw her little brother's countenance sad. She knew what ailed him. She did not try to talk to me. She opened her little hymn-book, Nettleton's ' Village Hymns,' to the place where that hymn was printed, and silently handed it to me. I remember no sermon, no talk, which helped me more than that. The dear form and face on which that firelight shone in the old farm-house have remained vividly pictured in my memory more than half a century, and if I shall ever come to look on them again where they now are, with the angels, I think as likely as not the sight will first of all remind me of that look of sisterly pity which lighted the way of that hymn to my heart."

SAMUEL STENNETT 1727-1795

Samuel Stennett was the great grandson of Rev. Edward Stennett, a grandson of Rev. Joseph Stennett, author of the hymn

Another six days' work is done

and a son of Rev. Joseph Stennett, d.d., for many years pastor of the Baptist church in Exeter, where Samuel was born m 1727. Ten years later his father removed to London, having accepted a call to the pastorate of the Baptist church in Little Wild Street, Lincoln's Inn Fields. Of this church Samuel early became a member. His studies were pursued first under Rev. John Hubbard, an eminent theological instructor at Stepney, and afterward under the celebrated linguist, Dr. John Walker, of the Academy at Mile End. "He was formed by nature and grace," says a writer in Rippon's "Register", "for the distinguished figure he afterward made. To the strength of natural faculties, vigor of imagination, and acuteness of judgment, of which he was possessed, he had added, from his earliest years, so close an attention to reflection and study that there was scarcely a topic in science or literature, in religion or even politics, but he seemed to have investigated; and so habitual was it to him to arrange his ideas on the different subjects, in a manner peculiar to himself, and yet quite natural, that when a question, which to others was new, unusual, or perplexed, had been proposed to him, they were surprised to find how familiarly he was acquainted with it."

In 1747, Mr. Stennett became his father's assistant, and after the death of his father he was ordained as his successor in the pastorate of the church in Little Wild Street, June 1, 1758. "The Baptist denomination lay particularly near his heart, and his concern for it ran uniformly through his whole life."

In 1767, he received a call from the Sabbatarian Baptist church, of which his grandfather was pastor; but though he did not accept the call, he preached for the church every Saturday morning for twenty years. In 1769, he published his volumes of "Discourses on Practical Religion." He was also the author of a work entitled "Remarks on the Christian Ministers' Reasons for Administering Baptism by Sprinkling," published in 1772. In 1775, he published "An Answer to the Christian Ministers' Reasons for Baptizing Infants." This was followed in 1783, by "Discourses on Domestic Duties"; in 1786, by "Discourses on the Parable of the

Sower"; and in 1790, by "Discourses on the Divine Authority, and Various Uses of the Holy Scriptures." All of his writings were marked by great elegance of style. His scholarship was recognized by King's College, Aberdeen, which; in 1763, conferred upon him the degree of Doctor of Divinity. He enjoyed the personal friendship of George III, and, like his grandfather, could have held a high position in the church of England if he had been willing to renounce his Nonconformist principles.

The following hymn is the first in Rippon's "Selection," and one of the best of Dr. Stennett's compositions:

To God, the universal King,
Let all mankind their tribute bring:
All that have breath your voices raise
In songs of never-ceasing praise.

The spacious earth on which we tread,
And wider heavens stretched o'er our head,
A large and solemn temple frame,
To celebrate its Builder's fame.

Here the bright sun, that rules the day,
As through the sky he makes his way,
To all the world proclaims aloud
The boundless sovereignty of God.

When from his courts the sun retires.
And with the day his voice expires,
The moon and stars adopt the song.
And through the night the praise prolong.

The listening earth with rapture hears
The harmonious music of the spheres;

And all her tribes the notes repeat.

That God is wise, and good, and great.

But man, endowed with nobler powers,

His God in nobler strains adores;

His is the gift to know the song,

As well as sing with tuneful tongue.

Dr. Stennett was honored with the friendship of the philanthropist, John Howard, who was accustomed to attend his meeting when in London. In a letter written at Smyrna, August 11, 1786, Mr. Howard says: "With unabated pleasure I have attended your ministry; no man ever entered more into my religious sentiments, or more happily expressed them. It was some little disappointment when any one occupied your pulpit. Oh, sir, how many Sabbaths I ardently long to spend in Little Wild Street: on those days I generally rest, or, if at sea, keep retired in my cabin. It is you that preach, and I bless God I attend with renewed pleasure. God in Christ is my rock, the portion of my soul. I have little more to add—but accept my renewed thanks. I bless God for your ministry. I pray God reward you a thousand-fold."

Dr. Stennett died August 24, 1795, and was buried in Bunhill Fields. John Gadsby, in his "Memoirs of Hymn Writers and Compilers," says: "The death of his wife greatly afflicted him, and seemed to deaden him to the world. He appeared to have no further desire to live in it. Just before he was confined to his bed, he prayed earnestly in his family that God might give him an easy passage out of life; and God granted him that which he requested."

JOHN FELLOWS

The time and place of Mr. Fellows' birth are unknown. In early life he resided at Bromsgrove, Worcestershire, and Dr. Belcher speaks of him as a "shoemaker." Dr. Watts, in the "Bibliotheca Britannica," and Allibone, in his "Critical Dictionary of English Literature," call him a Methodist. He was connected with the Calvinistic Methodists a large part of his life, but in his later years he made his residence in Birmingham, and there in 1780, according to Dr. Hatfield, he was baptized by Rev. Mr. Turner, and united with the Baptist church in Cannon street. He had been a Baptist in sentiment, however, for many years, as his hymns, dated 1773, show, and as there is no record of his baptism at Birmingham,—in fact, in the column of " Baptized," there is a blank,—it is possible that he simply transferred his church relations in that year. He died July 30th, 1785, not November 2, as some writers affirm.

Mr. Fellows was the author of a large number of works, mostly in verse among them "Grace Triumphant, a Sacred Poem in Nine Dialogues" (1770); "Bromsgrove Elegy, in Blank Verse, on the Death of the Rev. G. Whitefield" (1771); "An Elegy on the Death of Dr. Gill" (1771); "Hymns on Believers' Baptism" (1773); "Eloquent and Noble Defense of the Gospel, in his three Celebrated Speeches, Paraphrased in Blank Verse " (1775); "Hymns in a Great Variety of Meters, on the Perfection of the Word of God and the Gospel of Jesus Christ" (1776); "The History of the Holy Bible, Attempted in Easy Verse" (1777); "A Fair and Impartial Enquiry into the Rise, etc., of the Church of Rome, in a Series of Familiar Dialogues" (1779); and "A Protestant Catechism."

Great God, now condescend
To bless our rising race;
Soon may their willing spirits bend
The subjects of thy grace.

O, what a pure delight
Their happiness to see!
Our warmest wishes all unite
To lead their souls to thee.

O, grant thy spirit Lord,
Their hearts to sanctify;
Remember now thy groans;

Our hope on thee rely.

Draw forth the melting tear,
The penitential sigh;
Inspire their hearts with faith sincere,
And fix their hopes on high.

These children now are thine;
We give them back to thee;
O, lead them, by thy grace divine,
Along the heavenly way.

This hymn, in a modified form, is found in the "Calvary Selection of Spiritual Songs" (801), and in the "Baptist Hymnal" (574).

WILLIAM TUCKER 1731-1814

William Tucker was born at Chard, Somerset, March 27, 1731. Here he served an apprenticeship, and then removed to London, where he came under the influence of George Whitefield; and returning to his native place, he brought with him the better purposes he had formed. In 1764, he engaged in business as a cutler and ironmonger. By study of the Scriptures he was led to adopt Baptist views, and in 1765, he was baptized, and united with the Baptist church in Chard. With this church his membership continued forty-eight years, and to the last he adorned the profession he had made. He died February 2, 1814, in the eighty-third year of his age.

Amidst ten thousand anxious cares,
The world and Satan's deep-laid snares.
This my incessant cry shall be,
"Jesus, reveal thyself to me!"

"When Sinai's awful thunder rolled,
And struck with terror all my soul,
No gleam of comfort could I see
Till Jesus was revealed to me.

When by temptations sore oppressed.
Distressful anguish fills my breast.
All, all is grief and misery
Till Jesus is revealed to me.

When various lusts imperious rise,
And my unguarded soul surprise,
I 'm captive led, nor can get free
Till Christ reveals himself to me.

When darkness thick as beamless night
Hides the loved Savior from my sight,
Nothing but this my ardent plea,
"Jesus, reveal thyself to me!"

'It is he dispels the dismal gloom,
Gives light and gladness in its loom.
Then have I joy and liberty
As Christ reveals himself to me.

CHARLES COLE 1733-1813

Rev. Charles Cole was born in Wellow, Somersetshire, May 20, 1733. His parents died when he was six years of age. For awhile he was cared for by his relatives; and having early learned to weave broadcloth, he went to Freshford, near Bradford, Wilts. At Bradford he witnessed the administration of the ordinance of baptism by Mr. Harris, pastor of the Baptist church in Bradford. Such an impression was made upon his mind at this time that he was led after a while, against his inclinations, to attend Mr. Harris' services. Soon after he accepted Christ as his Savior, and in February, 1756, he was baptized, and united with the Bradford church. Two years later he was called by the church to the work of the ministry. He preached his first sermon at Whitechurch, in May, 1758, and was inedited by the church to supply the pulpit that year. At the close of the year he received a unanimous call to the pastorate. His ordination Occurred June 6, 1759. The Lord greatly blessed his labors, and the church was enlarged fourfold under his ministry, which continued until his death, December 3, 1813, a period of more than half a century.

In 1789, he published a volume entitled "A Three-Fold Alphabet of New Hymns. I. On the Public Ministry of the Word. II. On Baptism. III. On the Lord's Supper. To which is added a Supplicatory Supplement." Number 8 of the Supplement is as follows:

Lord, in thy churches ever dwell,
Let them enjoy thy tender care;
Do Zion good in thy good will,
And grant thy choicest blessings there.

Let thy salvation be proclaimed
By such as know and love the same;
Nor let thy servants be ashamed
To shout thy great and glorious name.

Let sinners hear the Gospel, Lord,
And let them feel its power, too;
That to thy praise they may record
What thy victorious grace can do.

Let Zion's gates with glory shine;
There let thy joyful presence rest;
Let love and peace and pleasure join,
And prosper those whom thou hast blest.

The Lord is good; let Israel hope,
For his good will is toward them;
The Lord is good, and buildeth up
The walls of his Jerusalem.

JAMES NEWTON 1733-1790

Concerning the early life of Mr. Newton, little is known. He was born in Chenies, Buchinghamsture, in 1733, and from pious parents he received a careful Christian training. When seventeen years of age, he went to London, where he united with the Baptist church at Maze Pond, then under the pastoral charge of Rev. Benjamin Wallin. Possessing a studious turn of mind and an ardent thirst for knowledge, he was at length persuaded to devote himself to the work of the Christian ministry. His preparatory studies were pursued under the direction of Dr. Thomas Llewellyn, and about the year 1757, he accepted an invitation from the Baptist church in the Pithay, Bristol, to become the colleague of Rev. John Tommas, and with this church he remained until his death. In 1770, at the formation of the Bristol Education Society, an organization for the education of candidates for the ministry, he was chosen classical tutor in the Baptist College at Bristol, being associated with Dr. Caleb Evans and Rev. Hugh Evans. For this position he was admirably fitted. With the Latin and Greek classics, the Hebrew Scriptures, and the writings of the Talmudists, he was intimately acquainted, and he continued to teach as well as to preach, until the close of life. He died April 8, 1790, greatly lamented by his flock as well as by all those who had shared his instructions.

He left in manuscript a volume of original hymns, which Dr. Belcher, in his notice of

Newton, says he placed in the library of Regents Park College, London. In the "Collection of Hymns" compiled by Dr. John Ash and Dr. Caleb Evans, and published at Bristol in 1769, is the following baptismal hymn (371) by Mr. Newton:

"Proclaim," said Christ, my wondrous grace,
To all the sons of men;
He that believes, and is baptized
Salvation shall obtain."

Let plenteous grace descend on those
Who, hoping in thy word,
This day have publicly declared
That Jesus is their Lord.

"With cheerful feet may they go on,
And run the Christian race;
And in the troubles of the way,
Find all sufficient grace.

BENJAMIN FRANCIS 1734-1799

Of the early life of Benjamin Francis, little is known. He was a Welshman, and was born in 1734. At fifteen years of age he united with the Baptist church in his native town, and three years later he entered Bristol College with the purpose of preparing himself for the work of the Christian ministry. Having completed his studies, he preached a short time at Sodbury. In 1757, he accepted a call to the pastorate of the Baptist church in Shortwood (Horsley), Gloucestershire, and was ordained in the following year. Under his unwearied labors and earnest preaching the church greatly prospered, and thrice it was found necessary to enlarge the meeting-house. One of his hymn

Great King of glory, come,

was written for the rededication, September 18, 1774, of his meeting-house after one of its enlargements. He preached also in surrounding villages, and as his fame increased he was summoned to minister in distant places. Calls came to him from London and elsewhere, but in his affection for the people among whom he was ordained, he was immovable, and he made Shortwood his home until his death, December 14, 1799. A few days before his death he said, "If I could mention nothing of former experiences, I can at this moment go to Jesus as a poor sinner, longing; for salvation in his own sovereign way." His life was one of usefulness and honor from its beginning to its close.

Ye objects of sense and enjoyments of time,
Which oft have delighted my heart,
I soon shall exchange you for views more sublime,
And joys that shall never depart.

One of the best known of his hymns is the following:
My gracious Redeemer I love,
His praises aloud I'll proclaim,
And join with the armies above,
To shout his adorable name.
To gaze on his glories divine
Shall be my eternal employ;
To see them incessantly shine,
My boundless, ineffable joy.

He freely redeemed, with his blood,
My soul from the confines of hell,
To live on the smiles of my God,
And in his sweet presence to dwell,
To shine with the angels of light,
With saints and with seraphs to sing,
To view, with eternal delight,

My Jesus, my Savior, my King.

In Meshech, as yet, I reside,
A darksome and restless abode!
Molested with foes on each side,
And longing to dwell with my God.
O, when shall my spirit exchange
This cell of corruptible clay,
For mansions celestial, and range
Thro' realms of ineffable day.

My glorious Redeemer; I long
To see thee descend on the cloud,
Amidst the bright numberless throng,
And mix with the triumphing crowd;
O, when wilt thou bid me ascend.
To join in thy praises above.
To gaze on thee, world without end,
And feast on thy ravishing love.

Nor sorrow, nor sickness, nor pain,
Nor sin, nor temptation, nor fear,
Shall ever molest me again,
Perfection of glory reigns there.
This soul and this body shall shine
In robes of salvation and praise,
And banquet on pleasures divine.
Where God his full beauty displays.

Ye palaces, scepters, and crowns.
Your pride with disdain I survey;

Your pomps are but shadows and sounds,

And pass in a moment away;

The crown that my Savior bestows,

Yon permanent sun shall outshine;

My joy everlastingly flows,

My God, my Redeemer, is mine.

ROBERT ROBINSON 1735-1790

Few hymns in the English language have more frequently given expression to the desires of pious hearts than the one commencing

Come, thou fount of every blessing.

Its author, Robert Robinson, was born in Swaffham, Norfolk, September 27, 1735. In his eighth year his parents removed to Scarning, in the same county, where he received excellent instruction in an endowed grammar school. In his fourteenth year, the death of his father reduced the family to poverty, and Robert was apprenticed to a hairdresser in London. He had acquired a love of learning, however, and his fondness for books followed him. By early rising he continued his study of the classics, and was more ready to give attention to such books as came in his way than to business.

May 24, 1752, in his seventeenth year, he went to hear Whitefield preach. In a letter to Whitefield, written six years later, he says: "I confess it was to spy the nakedness of the land I came —to pity the foil of the preacher, the infatuation of the hearers, and to abhor the doctrine." Whitefield's text was Matt. iii. 7. Of the sermon Mr. Robinson says: "Mr. Whitefield described the Sadducean character this did not touch me. I thought myself as good a Christian as any man in England. From this he went to that of the Pharisees. He described their exterior decency, but observed that the poison of the viper rankled in their hearts. This rather shook me. At length, in the course of his sermon, he abruptly broke off, paused for a few moments, then burst into a flood of tears, lifted up his hands and eyes, and exclaimed, 'Oh, my hearers, the wrath's to come!' the wrath's to come. These words sank into my heart like lead in the waters. I wept, and when the sermon was ended retired alone. For days and weeks I could think of little else. Those awful words would follow me wherever I went." They followed him two years and seven months before peace came to his troubled soul. December 10, 1755, to use his own words, he "found full and free forgiveness through the precious blood of Jesus Christ."

For some time after completing his apprenticeship, he continued at his employment in London. After hearing Wesley and Whitefield, and associating with them in Christian work, while visiting friends at Mildenhall, in Norfolk, in 1758, he was requested to preach, by some Christians there "who had the word preached but now and then." He yielded to their earnest solicitations, and subsequently preached in Norwich. The people flocked in crowds to hear him, and his preaching was in demonstration of the spirit and with power.

At this time he had not formally separated from the church of England, and a rich relative made liberal inducements to him if he would leave the "Methodists" and take orders in the Established Church ; but he declined. About this time doubts were awakened in his mind concerning infant baptism. These led to an examination of the subject, and as a result of his investigations he became a Baptist. Not long after he was invited to preach by the Baptist church in Cambridge, though he did not accept the pastoral office until nearly two years later. He was ordained June 11, 1761. At Cambridge his success was marvelous. "Members of the University, and other hearers, who had never in their lives entered a Baptist meeting-house, became regular attendants. In 1764, a new edifice, capable of seating six hundred persons, was built and paid for. While thus prospering in his ministry in this University town, he enlarged the circle of his influence by extensive village preaching in the surrounding country, and wherever he went 'the common people heard him gladly.'"

In the year 1770, he entered upon an extended literary career. In 1774, he published his "Arcana; or the Principles of the late Petitioners to Parliament for Relief in the Matter of

Subscription." This was a masterly defense of the principles of nonconformity. A translation of "Saurin's Sermons," in five volumes, with a "Memoir of Saurin and the French Reformation," followed in 1775-1782. In 1776, he published "A Plea for the Divinity of our Lord Jesus Christ"; in 1777, "An Essay on the Composition of a Sermon"; in 1778, "A Plan of Lectures on the Principles of Nonconformity"; in 1780, "The General Doctrine of Toleration applied to the Particular Case of Free Communion"; in 1782, his "Political Catechism"; and in 1786, a volume of "Village Sermons." In 1781, at the request of the Baptists in London, he commenced a "History of the Baptists," but the work proved to be a greater one than he was able to perform. As the result of his labors, however, we have his "History of Baptism," which was published in 1790, and "Ecclesiastical Researches," which appeared in 1792, two years after his death.

Robinson was the author of two well known hymns. One, commencing

Mighty God, while angels bless thee,

had this origin, according to Dr. Joseph Belcher: "It was composed for the use of Benjamin Williams, deacon of the Baptist church at Reading. Benjamin was a favorite of Robinson when a boy. One day the poet took the boy into his lap, and under the influence of that affectionate feeling which a child's love inspires, he wrote:

Mighty God, while angels bless thee,
May an infant praise thy name?
Lord of men as well as angels,
Thou art every creature's theme.

So far the poet's mind seems to have been influenced by the child he was holding. But a warm glow of religious feeling was awakened within him, and the second stanza was one of remarkable fervor and power:

Lord of every land and nation,
Ancient of eternal days,
Sounded through the whole creation,
Be thy just and lawful praise.

After completing the whole hymn, he read it to the child, and put it playfully into his hand. Well do we remember," adds Dr. Belcher, "the deep feeling with which Dean Williams described to us the scene, as we sat with him by his own fireside."

The remainder of this hymn is as follows:

> For the grandeur of thy nature,
> Grand beyond a seraph's thought;
> For created works of power,—
> Works with skill and kindness wrought;
>
> For thy providence, that governs
> Thro' thine empire's wide domain;
> "Wings an angel, guides a sparrow;
> Blessed be thy gentle reign.
>
> But thy rich, thy free redemption,
> Dark through brightness all along;
> Thought is poor, and poor expression,
> Who dare sing that awful song?
>
> Brightness of the Father's glory,
> Shall thy praise unuttered lie?
> Fly, my tongue, such guilty silence!
> Sing the Lord who came to die.
>
> Did archangels sing thy coming?
> Did the shepherds learn their lays?
> Shame would cover me ungrateful,
> Should my tongue refuse to praise.
>
> From the highest throne in glory,

To the cross of deepest woe;

All to ransom guilty captives;

Flow my praise, forever flow.

Go, return, immortal Savior!

Leave thy footstool, take thy throne;

Thence return, and reign forever,

Be the kingdom all thine own.

SAMUEL MEDLEY 1738-1799

The author of the well known hymn

O could I speak the matchless worth

was born June 23, 1738, at Chestnut, Hertfordshire, where his father, a friend of Sir Isaac Newton, kept a boarding-school. When fourteen years of age he was apprenticed to an oil-dealer in London, but at seventeen years of age, becoming dissatisfied with his employment, he availed himself of the privilege of completing his apprenticeship in the royal navy. He entered the service as a midshipman, and in a short time was promoted to the position of master's mate. In a sea fight off Cape Lagos, August 18, 1759, he was severely wounded. On the return of the fleet he was carried to the house of his grandfather, then deacon of the Baptist church in Eagle Street, which was under the pastoral care of Rev. Andrew Gifford, d.d. The young officer had thus far led a wild life, but the pious efforts of his grandfather to induce him to choose "the good part" were crowned with success, and in December, 1760, he united with Mr. Gilford's church.

Though promotion was promised to him, he now abandoned the naval service, and having married in 1762, he opened a school in King Street, Soho, and devoted himself to the study of the classics and sacred literature. In August, 1766, he was licensed to preach, and in the following year he became pastor of the Baptist church in Watford, Hertfordshire, where he remained until 1772, when he accepted a call to the pastorate of the Baptist church in Liverpool. His ministry here was greatly blessed, and he continued to serve this church until his death, July,

1799, in the sixty-first year of his age. He never forgot the experiences of his early sailor life, and its familiar imagery was present with him to the last. "I am a poor shattered bark just about to gain the blissful harbor," he said one day, just before his death; "and oh! how sweet will be the port after the storm! But a point or two more, and I shall be at my heavenly Father's home."

Like other preachers of his time, he was accustomed to write hymns to aid in enforcing the lessons of the sermon. Miller, says: "Thirty-six of his hymns were printed as leaflets between 1786 and 1790. I have, however, a copy of 'Hymns on Select Portions of Scripture,' by Mr. Medley, 2d Edition, Bristol, 1785." In 1789, by request, Mr. Medley published a volume of his hymns, and another and larger volume in 1794. Doubtless it was from this edition of 1787 that Rev. John Stanford, in his "Collection of Evangelical Hymns," New York, took fifteen of Medley's hymns, their first introduction, probably, into this country. An enlarged edition, containing 230 hymns, was published in 1800, the year following his death. It was entitled "Hymns. The Public Worship and Private Devotions of True Christians Assisted in Some Thoughts in Verse; Principally Drawn from Select Passages of the Word of God." His memoir, compiled by his son, was published the same year.

The following fine hymn (133) is certainly worthy of a place with these:

Dearest of names, our Lord, our King!
Jesus thy praise we humbly sing;
In cheerful songs will spend our breath.
And in thee triumph over death.

Death is no more among our foes,
Since Christ the mighty conqueror rose;
Both power and sting the Savior broke,
He died, and gave the finished stroke.

Saints die and we should gently weep;
Sweetly in Jesus' arms they sleep;
Far from this world of sin and woe,

Nor sin, nor pain, nor grief they know.

Death no terrific foe appears,
An angel's lovely form he wears;
A friendly messenger he proves
To every soul whom Jesus loves.

Death is a sleep; and O, how sweet,
To souls prepared its stroke to meet!
Their dying beds, their graves are blessed.
For all to them is peace and rest.

Their bodies sleep, their souls take wing,
Uprise to heaven, and there they sing
With joy, before the Savior's face,
Triumphant in victorious grace.

Soon shall the earth's remotest bound
Feel the archangel's trumpet sound;
Then shall the graves' dark caverns shake,
And joyful, all the saints shall wake.

Bodies and souls shall then unite,
Arrayed in glory strong and bright;
And all his saints will Jesus bring,
His face to see, his love to sing.

O, may I live with Jesus nigh,
And sleep in Jesus when I die!
Then joyful, when from death I wake,
I shall eternal bliss partake.

JOHN FAWCETT 1739-1817

The date of Dr. Fawcett's birth, as given above, is old style, but according to our present reckoning, he was born January 17, 1740. Rev. W. R. Stevenson, of Nottingham, who has given much attention to Baptist hymnology, writes: "This I learn from a valuable book sent me by Dr. Fawcett's grandson, — a life of Fawcett by his son who assisted him in his school. I found it necessary to allow for the change of style, in order to understand statements made in the book concerning Dr. Fawcett's age at certain periods. In the book itself, the date is given thus '1739 — 1740 (O. S.)' The elate usually given, in sketches of Dr. Fawcett's life, is January 6, 1739."

Dr. Fawcett's birthplace was Lidget Green, near Bradford, Yorkshire. His father died when he was eleven years of age, leaving a widow and several children in humble circumstances. When John was thirteen years old, he was apprenticed to a trader in Bradford, with whom he remained six years. During his apprenticeship, when sixteen years old, he was converted under the preaching of a sermon by George Whitefield, from the text, John iii. 14: "And as Moses lifted up the serpent in the wilderness, even so must the Son of man be lifted up." Referring to this sermon afterward, he wrote, "As long as life remains I shall remember both the text and the sermon." For a while after his conversion, he attended the services of the church of England, but early in 1758 he united with the Baptist church in Bradford, which had just been organized.

He at once made himself useful in church work, and soon the question came before him concerning his duty to preach the gospel. No unworthy motives should influence his decision. He wrote in his diary: "Lord, I know not what to do, but my eyes are upon thee. If in thy wise counsel thou hast fixed upon me to bear thy name to Gentile sinners, I earnestly implore that thou wouldst give me a right spirit, and bestow upon me every needful qualification for that most difficult and important work. If thou dost not call me to do it, Father, not my will, but thine be done." The decision was at length made, and in 1763, at the request of his pastor, he began to preach. In the following year, February, 1764, he became pastor of the small Baptist church at Wainsgate, near Halifax, West Riding, of Yorkshire, where he was ordained July 31, 1765.

It was to commemorate this incident in his life that Fawcett wrote his well known hymn:

Blest be the tie that binds
Our hearts in Christian love;
The fellowship of kindred minds
Is like to that above.

Before our Father's throne
We pour our ardent prayers;
Our fears, our hopes, our aims are one,
Our comforts and our cares.

We share our mutual woes;
Our mutual burdens bear;
And often for each other flows
The sympathizing tear.

When we asunder part,
It gives us inward pain;
But we shall still be joined in heart,
And hope to meet again.

This glorious hope revives
Our courage by the way;
While each in expectation lives.
And longs to see the day.

From sorrow, toil and pain.
And sin, we shall be free;
And perfect love and friendship reign
Through all eternity.

In 1772, Fawcett published "The Christian's Humble Plea for his God and Savior; in answer to several Pamphlets lately published by the. Rev. Dr. Priestly." In 1774 appeared "The Sick Man's Employ." In 1777 a new chapel, which would seat six hundred people, was built for him at Hebden Bridge, near Wainsgate. His residence was at Brearley Hall, in the village of Midgley, in the same neighborhood, where he opened a boarding-school, subsequently removed to Ewood Hall, which he continued through life as an aid in the support of his growing family. In 1778 he published his "Advice to Youth, on the Advantages of Early Piety," which passed through several editions. His hymn book appeared in 1782. It was entitled "Hymns adapted to the Circumstances of Public Worship and Private Devotion." It contained one hundred and sixty-six hymns. Many of them were written to be sung after the sermon to which they had reference, and were composed in the midnight hours preceding the Sabbath. An "Essay on Anger" appeared in 1788. "The Cause of Christ; the Christian's Glory," and "Considerations in favor of the newly organized Missionary Society," followed in 1793, the "Life of the Rev. Oliver Heywood" in 1796, and "Christ Precious to those that Believe" in 1799. Dr. Fawcett was also the author of "The History of John Wise," a book for children.

It is an evidence of Dr. Fawcett's high reputation as a scholar and an educator that in 1793, after the death of Dr. Caleb Evans, he was invited to succeed the latter as President of the Baptist Academy at Bristol, an honor which he declined. In 1811, he published, as the fruit of his ripe biblical knowledge, his "Devotional Family Bible." His life was one of suffering as well as of toil, and his sufferings grew heavier rather than lighter in the closing years of his life. A paralytic stroke, in February, 1816, was the occasion of his relinquishment of pastoral work, and he died July 25, 1817, having as the end drew near devoutly exclaimed, "Come, Lord Jesus, come quickly!"

Dr. Belcher gives the following account of Dr. Fawcett's last public service: "Let us take our last look at this excellent minister of Jesus Christ. He has ascended the pulpit at an association in Yorkshire. A thousand eyes are fixed on him in love and admiration, and all present express their conviction by words and smiles, that a spiritual feast has been provided for them. As a good soldier of Christ, he has endured hardness for more than half a century. His praise has been in all the churches, his ministry has been greatly prized through the whole of that populous district, and his usefulness has been honored at home and abroad, in the college and in the place itself. He has now come to bear his dying testimony to the doctrine of the cross, and to bid farewell to the ministers and friends with whom he has been so long associated. Many of them have a strong presentiment that they shall see his face no more, and are prepared to receive his message as from the lips of a man who has finished his course, and now stands at the entrance of heaven. As he rises in the pulpit, a deathlike silence overspreads the crowded congregation, and all ears are opened to catch the words of inspiration. With a tremulous voice, and with deep emotions, he reads the text; 'This day I am going the way of all the earth,' Josh, xxiii. 14, and long before he finished his discourse the place became a Bochim—the house of God — the gate of heaven. The sermon, which was committed to the press by the agency of its hearers, yet exists as a monument to his love of truth, his holy affection, and his zeal for the extension of the doctrines of sovereign mercy."

JOHN LANGFORD

The following hymn, found in many collections, has long been ascribed to Rev. John Langford:

Now begin the heavenly theme,
Sing aloud in Jesus' name!
Ye, who his salvation prove,
Triumph in redeeming love.

Ye, who see the Father's grace
Beaming in the Savior's face,
As to Canaan on ye move.
Praise and bless redeeming love.

Mourning souls, dry up your tears;

Banish all your guilty fears;
See your guilt and curse remove,
Canceled by redeeming love.

Ye, alas I who long have been
Willing slaves of death and sin,
Now from bliss no longer rove;
Stop and taste redeeming love

Welcome all by sin opprest,
Welcome to his sacred rest;
Nothing brought him from above,
Nothing but redeeming love.

When his spirit leads us home,
When we to his glory come,
We shall all the fullness prove
Of our Lord's redeeming love.

He subdued the infernal powers,
Those tremendous foes of ours
From their cursed empire drove.
Mighty in redeeming love.

Hither, then, your music bring,
Strike aloud each cheerful string!
Mortals, join the host above.
Join to praise redeeming love.

It is now generally believed, however, that the authorship of this hymn is erroneously ascribed to Langford. The hymn is found in a collection of "Hymns and Spiritual Songs," published by Langford in 1776. In a second edition he marked with an asterisk the hymns which he had himself composed, and this hymn is not so marked. It is to be found, too, in earlier collections—in the Appendix to Madan's "Selection" (1763), and in "A Collection of Hymns, by John Edwards, Minister of the Gospel, Leeds, York. Second Edition, 1769." As a writer of hymns, however, Langford has a place in this volume.

Concerning John Langford, but little is now known. He became pastor of the Baptist church in Blocksfields, Southwark, in 1775. There he remained twelve years, and then removed to Rose Lane, Ratcliff, and subsequently to Bunhill Row. He preached a sermon on the death of Whitefield. His story seems to have been a sad one. It is said that through an act of imprudence he was compelled to retire from the ministry, and that having inherited a fortune from a relative, he squandered it in extravagance, and ended his days in beggary.

JOHN DRACUP

Miller says: "Rev. John Dracup was for seventeen years pastor of a Congregational church at Steep Lane, Yorkshire. He afterward continued his ministry at Rodhillena, near Todmorden, and at Rochdale. In 1784, having become a Baptist, he returned to his first congregation at Steep Lane, and presided over them for eleven years, till his death. May 28, 1795." That an English Baptist minister should become pastor of a Congregational church is not a thing unknown in English ecclesiastical history, so that there is nothing in the fact above stated that leads us to question what Mr. Miller says. But Rippon, in his "Register," Vol. 3, puts Steep Lane in his list of "Baptist Churches in England," and in a note, referring to the church at Steep Lane, he says: "In our list of 1794, the name of Mr. John Dracup stood as pastor here. This aced and much esteemed servant of Christ finished his course with honor and tranquility in the latter end of May, 1795. And on the day his funeral [sermon] was preached, his aged widow also expired. They had lived happily together for a long course. After his death Mr. William Wrathall, formerly at Wainsgate [this was a Baptist church], became their pastor, but removed from them to Bolton-le-Moor [also a Baptist church], in Lancashire, about the close of August, 1798. They are now supplied by a young man of Mr. Fawcett's Academy," unquestionably a Baptist. As Rippon prepared this note in 1798, there can be little doubt, it would seem, but that Miller is mistaken.

Dracup published in 1787 his "Hymns and Spiritual Songs," some of which had previously appeared in Lady Huntingdon's "Select Collection." One of these hymns, somewhat altered, is to be found in "The Hymn Book" edited by Rev. Andrew Reed, d.d., 1841, 19th Ed., 1868:

Thanks to thy name, O Lord, that we
One glorious Sabbath more behold;
Dear Shepherd, let us meet with thee
Among thy sheep, in this thy fold.
Now Lord, among thy tribes appear,
And let thy presence till the throng;
Thy awful voice let sinners hear,
And bid the feeble heart be strong.

Gather the lambs into thine arms,
And satisfy their every want;
Those that are weak defend from harm,
And gently lead them, lest they faint.

Put forth thy shepherd's crook, and stay
Thy erring sheep, and bring them back;
O bring the wandering home today,
And save them for thy mercy's sake.

Dear tender-hearted Shepherd, look.
And let our wants thy pity move;
And kindly lead thy little flock
To the sweet pastures of thy love.

GEORGE KEITH, R. KEENE

In Rippon's "Selection" (1787) first appeared the following well known hymn, afterward somewhat abbreviated

How firm a foundation, ye saints of the Lord,
Is laid for your faith in his excellent word;
What more can he say than to you he hath said?
You, who unto Jesus for refuge have fled.

In every condition, in sickness, in health,
In poverty's vale, or abounding in wealth;
At home and abroad, on the land, on the sea,
As thy days may demand, shall thy strength ever be.

Fear not, I am with thee, be not dismayed,
I, I am thy God, and will still give thee aid;
I'll strengthen thee, help thee, and cause thee to stand,
Upheld by my righteous, omnipotent hand.

When thro' the deep waters I call thee to go.
The rivers of woe shall not the overflow;
For I will be with thee, thy troubles to bless,
And sanctify to thee thy deepest distress.

When thro' fiery trials thy pathway shall lie,
My grace all sufficient shall be thy supply;
The flame shall not hurt thee, I only design
Thy dross to consume, and thy gold to refine.

Even down to old age, all my people shall prove

My sovereign, eternal, unchangeable love;

And when hoary hairs shall their temples adorn.

Like lambs they shall still in my bosom be borne.

The soul that on Jesus hath leaned for repose,

I will not, I will not, desert to his foes;

That soul, though all hell should endeavor to shake,

I'll never — no never—no never forsake."

A note to the last line says, "Agreeable to Dr. Doddridge's Translation of Heb. xiii. 5."

The only designation of authorship attached by Dr. Rippon to this hymn is the letter " K." By some the hymn has been ascribed to Thomas Kirkham, who published a volume of hymns in 1788; but the hymn is not in this collection. By others it has been ascribed to Caroline Keene, and by yet others to Rev. William Kingsbury. According to the late D. Sedgwick, the well known hymnologist, it was written by George Keith, a London book publisher, and a son-in-law of Dr. Rippon, who is said to have been a writer of hymns, and to have led the singing in Dr. Rippon's church for many years. Accordingly, for some time and in many collections, this hymn has been ascribed to George Keith. But of late this claim has been denied by prominent hymnologists. It is said that according; to Wilson's "Dissenting Churches of London," George Keith died in 1775. Why then should Dr. Rippon, in 1787, have hesitated to affix his son-in-law's name to this hymn, and the others in his collection marked "K.," if Keith was the author? But is it true that George Keith, the publisher, died in 1775? I have a volume of Fawcett's "'Hymns," printed by G. Wright & Son, Leeds, York, in 1782, "and sold by G. Keith, Grace Church Street," London. The references to George Keith in Wilson's volumes are to persons who evidently cannot be identified with George Keith, the publisher, in Grace Church Street, London.

Rev. H. L. Hastings, editor of the "Christian," Boston, in May, 1887, made the following suggestion in his paper: "In preparing hymns and music for 'Songs of Pilgrimage,' we were led to go over not only Dr. Rippon's hymn-book, but also his 'Tune Book,' edited by Thomas Walker, who for a time led the singing in Dr. Rippon's church. We noticed that over the hymn in question was placed the name of a tune to which it was to be sung, which was 'Geard.' On looking up that tune in the book, we found it was composed by R. Keene. There being but two tunes of that meter in the entire book, the thought arose, was the 'K.' of the hymn the same person as the ' R. Keene,' to whose tune it was to be sung Examining both hymn and tune they seemed to be made for each other, and the evidence seemed to point to R. Keene as the author of the hymn; and we accordingly inserted it in 'Songs of Pilgrimage,' with the original tune, and placed under it the name of R. Keene, with a query, to indicate uncertainty as to its origin.

Mr. Hastings thinks that for various reasons a musician and choir-master might put his name to a tune which he had composed, while modesty, or other considerations, might cause him to append his initial only to a new hymn. While there is force in Mr. Hastings' suggestion as to the authorship of this well known hymn, therefore, the mystery is not wholly removed. There are those who still believe that "How firm a foundation," was written by George Keith. Evidently it was written by a Baptist, and has a place here.

The late Rev. S. W. Duffield, in his notes on this hymn in "English Hymns," says: "One peculiarity is noticeable in the last line of the closing verse. The very singularly repetitious grouping of words reminds US that a similar style of expression is found in the passage of Scripture (Heb. xiii. 5), upon which the hymn is in some measure constructed. There are, in the Greek text, five negatives grouped in a single sentence. In our language, the rule says: 'Two negatives are equivalent to an affirmative.' Not so here: each adds its meaning with all the intensity of a cumulative force. 'I will never leave thee, nor forsake thee,' as in the common version, is strengthened much in the New Revision, so that it stands: 'I will in no wise fail thee, neither will I in any wise forsake thee.'"

"Once in the old Oratory at evening devotion, in Princeton Seminary," as Dr. C. S. Robinson relates, "the elder Hodge, then venerable with years and piety, paused as he read this hymn, preparatory to the singing, and in the depth of his emotion was obliged to close his delivery of the final lines with a mere gesture of pathetic and adoring wonder at the matchless grace of God in Christ; and his hand silently beat time to the rhythm instead:

"I'll never— no, never—no, never forsake!"

Rev. James Gallaher, in the "Western Sketch Book," in an account of a visit to Gen. Jackson at the Hermitage in September, 1843, says: "The old hero was then very frail, and had the appearance of extreme old age; but he was reposing with calmness and confidence on the promise and covenant of God. He had now been a member of the church for several years." During the conversation which took place. Gen. Jackson turned to Mr. Gallaher, and remarked: "There is a beautiful hymn on the subject of the exceeding great and precious promises of God to his people."

W. AUGUSTUS CLARKE

Gadsby says that Mr. Clarke "was ordained by a Greek bishop, but afterward joined the Baptists, and became pastor of Redcross Street about 1773. In 1780, in consequence of the part he took with the mob against increasing the liberties of the Papists, he had to leave, when he opened a room in Bunhill Row. There he remained only three months and then went to Ireland, and from Ireland to America. He returned to England about 1797, and went to Petticoat Lane, but that place being taken down, he again went to Bunhill Row, in 1801. I have no account of his death."

Mr. Clarke in 1788 published "a Book of Hymns, with Spiritual Remarks on each Hymn, which work," as he tells us, "under the sweet operations of the Divine Spirit, was made a blessing to many precious souls in England, Ireland and America." In 1801, he published his "Hymns, Doctrinal and Experimental, for the Free-Born Citizens of Zion, who know their Election of God, and glory in the Evangelical Truths comprised in the Gospel of a Finished Salvation." The collection, which was dedicated to his own flock, contained 261 hymns. The following is hymn 166:

Almighty lover, now appear,

And make thy mercy known;

Subdue our unbelieving fear.

And this our meeting crown.

Lord, never let us silent be

Respecting things divine;

But sweetly love and talk of thee,

And feel thy glory shine.

O, may thy love and reigning grace,

Be our delightful theme,

Till we behold thy lovely face.

Without a cloud between.

Let orient beams upon us shine,

Come, set our hearts on tire;

With ardent love to thy dear name.

Lord, grant us our desire.

SAMUEL DEACON 1746-1816

The son of a General Baptist minister, Samuel Deacon was born at Ratby, February 6, 1746. When fifteen years of age he was apprenticed to a watchmaker, and in 1771, having married, he engaged in business for himself at Barton. But he had qualities, it was thought, that fitted him for the work of the gospel ministry, and having commenced to preach in 1777, he was ordained as associate pastor with his father in 1779. He had a useful ministry, and died March 2, 1816.

He was the author of several prose and poetical works. Among the former was his "Comprehensive Account of the General Baptists," and "A Father's Advice to a Son." In verse he published "An Attempt to Answer the Important Question ' What must I do to be Saved?'" Also "Prudence and Evangelicus," and " A Cabinet of Jewels for the Children of God." His hymn book was first published in 1785. The second edition, which appeared in 1797, entitled "Barton Hymns" had an appendix containing thirty four hymns on Baptism.

RICHARD BURNHAM
1749-1810

He was born in 1749, at Guilford, Surry. His father, Rev. Richard Burnham, died when he was three years of age, and his early years were devoted to pleasurable pursuits. At length, while attending a "Wesleyan Chapel, he was led to accept Christ as his Savior, and he commenced at once, as a preacher, to tell "the old, old story." Not long after, he adopted Baptist views, and united with a Particular Baptist church at Reading. Later, having removed to Staines, Middlesex, on the Thames, he organized a Baptist church. In 1780 he went to London to obtain funds for his church, and while engaged in this service he was invited to remove to the metropolis, and establish a new interest there. He consented, and a church was organized at Greenwalk, Surry, near Blackfriar's Bridge, and to this church, several times removed, he continued to minister until his death, which occurred October 30, 1810. He was buried in Tottenham Court Road church cemetery, and the epitaph on his monument describes him as "endowed with an ardent zeal for the Redeemer's interest, an acute penetration, and vigor of mind seldom equaled. His ministry was remarkably owned to the conversion of many,"

The hymn by which he is best known is the following:

Jesus I thou art the sinner's friend;
As such I look to thee;
Now, in the fullness of thy love,
O Lord I remember me.

Remember thy pure word of grace, —

Remember Calvary;
Remember all thy dying groans,
And then remember me.

Thou wondrous Advocate with God I
I yield myself to thee;
While thou art sitting on thy throne,
Dear Lord 1 remember me.

Lord! I am guilty, —I am vile,
But thy salvation's free;
Then, in thine all-abounding grace,
Dear Lord! remember me.

In 1783, Burnham published "New Hymns on Divine Subjects." The volume contained 141 hymns, which in subsequent editions were increased to 452 hymns. The above hymn appeared in the first edition. As now printed, it is in an amended form. In 1796, John Asplund published in Boston an American edition of these "New Hymns." It is not a little strange that the best known of Burnham's compositions,

Jesus, thou art the sinner's friend,

is not found in this collection, which contains 320 of Burnham's hymns. In his preface Mr. Asplund says: "Without flattery, I think they are the best hymns I have ever seen, or been acquainted with, and therefore venture to recommend them to others."

JOHN RIPPON 1751-1836

Dr. John Rippon was the compiler of Rippon's "Selection of Hymns," and was born in Tiverton, Devonshire, April 29, 1751. When sixteen years of age he was converted, and united with the Baptist church in Tiverton. In the following year, with a purpose to enter upon the work of the Christian ministry, he entered the Baptist College at Bristol, where he had as instructors Rev. Hugh Evans and his son Rev. Caleb Evans. In 1772, on the completion of his studies at Bristol, he was invited to preach in the pulpit of the Baptist church in Carter Lane, Tooley Street, London, which had been made vacant by the death of the celebrated Dr. John Gill in the autumn of the preceding year. The result was that he received a call to the pastorate, and he was ordained pastor of the church November 11, 1773. The church had been under the pastoral care of Dr. Gill fifty-four years, and Dr. Rippon retained the pastorate until his death, December 17, 1836, a period of sixty-three years. He had not the learning of his predecessor, but he possessed popular gifts of a high order, and his ministry was eminently a successful one. At the time of the erection of the present London Bridge, compelled to seek a new location, the church erected a house of worship in New Park Street. It was to this church of Gill and Rippon that Mr. Spurgeon was called when he began his work in London.

The first edition of Rippon's "Selection" appeared in 1787. It was entitled "A Selection of Hymns from the Best Authors, intended to be an appendix to Dr. Watts' Psalms and Hymns." Of this collection of hymns, more than thirty editions were published in England, and many in this country. Dr. Rippon was a great admirer of Dr. Watts, and in 1798, "in consequence of the numerous errors which have crept into almost all the late editions of Dr. Watts' Psalms and Hymns," Dr. Rippon published an improved edition of Dr. Watts' productions. "An Arrangement of the Psalms Hymns and Spiritual Songs of the Rev. Isaac Watts, D.D.," followed in 1801, in which the division into first, second and third books disappeared, and the contents were disposed according to subjects, as in his own "Selection." In the announcement it was stated that the profits of this "arranged edition" would be "applied to the encouragement of village preaching, among the different denominations of Christians, to assist ministers of a small income, and to other benevolent purposes." Dr. Hatfield says. "It is probably the most accurate edition of Dr. Watts' book ever published." When Rev. James M. Winchell prepared his " Arrangement of the Psalms, Hymns and Spiritual Songs of the Rev. Isaac Watts, D.D.,"—a work used in Baptist churches in this country very extensively before the publication of the "Psalmist," —he acknowledged his indebtedness to Dr. Rippon's earlier work. In 1810, Dr. Rippon published "An Index of all the Lines in Watts' Hymns and Psalms."

Of Dr. Rippon's other works mention should be made of his edition of Dr. John Gill's "Exposition of the Old and New Testaments," with a memoir prefixed, and also of his "Baptist Annual Register," from 1790 to 1802.

Here, Lord, my soul convicted stands
Of breaking all thy ten commands;
And on me justly might not thou pour
Thy wrath in one eternal shower.

But, thanks to God! its loud alarms
Have warned me of approaching harms;
And now, O Lord! my wants I see;
Lost and undone, I come to thee.

I see, my fig-leaf righteousness
Can ne'er thy broken law redress;
Yet in thy gospel plan I see
There's hope of pardon even for me.

Here I behold thy wonders, Lord!
How Christ hath to thy law restored
Those honors, on the atoning day,
Which guilty sinners took away.

Amazing wisdom, power and love,
Displayed to rebels from above!
Do thou, O Lord! my faith increase
To love and trust thy plan of grace.

JOHN ADAMS 1751-1835

John Adams was a native of Northampton, where he was born in 1751. In early life he was apprenticed to an ironmonger. When eighteen years of age he united with the Baptist church in Northampton, of which Rev. John Collett Ryland was pastor. In middle life, on account of a change of views, he was excluded from the church. Later, having retired from business, he removed to London, and subsequently to Olney and Newton Blossomville. Subsequently he returned to Northampton, where he died May 15, 1835.

Jesus is our great salvation,
Worthy of our best esteem!
He has saved his favorite nation;
Join to sing aloud to him;
He has saved us,
Christ alone could us redeem.

When involved in sin and ruin
And no helper there was found,
Jesus our distress was viewing,
Grace did more than sin abound;
He has called us.
With salvation in the sound.

Save us from a mere profession I
Save us from hypocrisy;
Give us. Lord, the sweet possession
Of thy righteousness and thee;
Best of favors!
None compared with this can be.

Let us never, Lord, forget thee;
Make us walk as pilgrims here;

We will give thee all the glory

Of the love that brought us near;

Bid us praise thee.

And rejoice with holy fear.

JOHN RYLAND, D.D. 1753-1825

Early in Benjamin Beddome's ministry at Bourtonon-the-Water, occurred the conversion of a farmer's son, a young man of eighteen, John Collett Ryland. Young Ryland studied at Bristol, then entered the Christian ministry, and after a pastorate of thirteen years at Warwick, became pastor of the Baptist church in Northampton, where he labored with great success twenty-seven years. His son, John Ryland, was born January 29, 1753, during the Warwick pastorate. John Collett Ryland was a good scholar, and like many of his brethren in the ministry, he supported himself in part by receiving into his family a number of students. He was also the tutor of his son. In August, 1764, he thus writes concerning him: "John is now eleven years and seven months old. He has read Genesis in Hebrew five times through; he read through the Greek New Testament before nine years old. He can read Horace and Virgil. He has read through Telemachus in French. He has read through Pope's Homer, in eleven volumes; read Dryden's Virgil in three volumes. He has read Rollins' Ancient History, ten volumes octavo, and he knows the Pagan mythology surprisingly."

September 11, 1767, the elder Ryland had the pleasure of baptizing his son. The latter seems to have had his thoughts early directed to the work of the Christian ministry, and he commenced preparatory studies under the direction of his father. He preached his first sermon on Sunday, January 27, 1771, two days before he completed his eighteenth year. For ten years he assisted his father in the family school he had established on coming to Northampton, and preached each Sabbath, either in Northampton or in some one of the surrounding villages. June 8, 1781, he was ordained, and became his father's assistant in the pastorate of the Northampton church. When his father removed to Enfield, near London, November 11, 1785, John Ryland became sole pastor of the church. His ministry at Northampton was greatly blessed. In company with Carey, Andrew Fuller and others, he aided in the organization of the Baptist Missionary Society, at Kettering, October 2, 1792. His is the first name appended to the resolutions adopted that day, and he was one of those whose subscriptions for the work then commenced amounted to £13 2s. 6d.

In April, 1792, Mr. Ryland received an invitation to the pastorate of the Broadmead Baptist church, Bristol, and also to the presidency of the Baptist college there, as the successor to Dr. Caleb Evans. It seems to have been difficult for him to break the ties that bound him to Northampton, for it was not till 1794, that he accepted the call to Bristol, and removed to that place. Here he did a work honorable to himself and most useful to his brethren. His influence was widely felt. In addition to his other labors he was appointed secretary of the Baptist Missionary Society on the death of Andrew Fuller, and he discharged the duties of this office several years. He died May 25, 1825, after uttering the words, "No more pain." His funeral sermon was preached by the celebrated Robert Hall.

In a tribute to his memory John Foster says: "He excelled very many deservedly esteemed preachers in variety of topics and ideas. To the end of his life he was a great reader, and very far from being confined to one order of subjects, and he would freely avail himself of these resources for diversifying and illustrating the subjects of his sermons. The readers of the printed sketches of his sermons, who never heard him, can have no adequate idea of the spirit, force and compulsion on the hearer's attention, with which the sermons were delivered."

In 1792, Mr. Ryland received the honorary degree of Doctor of Divinity from Brown University. Of his published works, which for the most part consist of occasional discourses, mention should be made of his "Memoirs of the Rev. R. Hall, of Arnsby," "A Candid Statement of the Reasons which induce the Baptists to Differ in Opinion and Practice from so many of their Christian Brethren," and "The Work of Faith, the Labor of Love, and the Patience of Hope Illustrated in the Life and Death of the Rev. Andrew Fuller, of Kettering."

JOHN DEACON 1757-1821

About the middle of the last century, there lived at Ratby, in Leicestershire, not far from Charnwood Forest, an agricultural laborer, whose name was Samuel Deacon. He was converted to God through the instrumentality of one of Lady Huntingdon's itinerating preachers. He became pastor of a church at Barton, near Market Bosworth, which was the mother of nearly all the General Baptist churches in the midland counties of England. This Samuel Deacon, sometimes called the elder, had two sons, Samuel and John, half brothers, who both became preachers and hymn writers. Of Samuel an account has already been given.

John Deacon was born 1757, in what month is unknown. He joined the church at Barton in early life, and was taught the business of clock and watch making; but developing gifts for the ministry, he was sent to London to study under Dan Taylor, the most learned minister at that time among the General Baptists. At the completion of his studies, he became pastor of the church in Friar Lane, Leicester, a post which he occupied, with one brief, unhappy interval, very usefully, until his death, March 10, 1821. During his last illness he was frequently visited by the celebrated Robert Hall, then minister in Leicester, and was much refreshed by his conversation and prayers. In 1800, Mr. Deacon compiled and published a hymn book, which, with some additions and alterations, was extensively used in the General Baptist churches until 1851. In the editions which appeared subsequently to 1804, eleven of his own hymns were included, all intended for use at Sunday-school anniversaries. He left in manuscript about thirty others, which had been sung at his own chapel on special occasions. None of his hymns, however, have been introduced into other collections. The following is founded on Psalm viii. 12:

> Eternal Sovereign of the skies,
> How wondrous is thy name;
> Through earth and heaven thy glories rise,
> And spread thy matchless fame.

> The sons of Adam, old and young,
> Shall own thy boundless sway;

And babes, with feeble, artless tongue,

Their cheerful tribute pay.

Children shall in thy temple crowd,

And shout with loud accord,

Hail, Son of David, Son of God!

Hosanna to the Lord!

ALICE FLOWERDEW 1759-1830

Mrs. Alice (not Anne, as in some collections) Flowerdew, was a native of England, but nothing is known concerning her birthplace or early life. Her husband, Daniel Flowerdew, held a government position in Jamaica a few years, and late in the last century returned to England with his wife, where he died in 1801. Mrs. Flowerdew then established a boarding school for young ladies at Islington, near London. Her "Poems on Moral and Religious Subjects" appeared in 1803, third edition in 1811. In the preface to the first edition she says that these poems were "written at different periods of life—some indeed at a very early age, and others under the very severe pressure of misfortunes, when my pen had frequently given that relief, which could not be derived from other employments." She attended the ministry of Rev. John Evans, d.d., pastor of the General Baptist church in Worship Street, and is said to have shared his Arian views. From Islington, in 1814, she removed her boarding-school to Bury Street, Edmunds, and subsequently to Ipswich, where she died. She was buried at Whitton, a few miles from Ipswich, The following is the inscription upon her tomb: "Sacred to the memory of Mrs. Alice Flowerdew, who died September 23, 1830, aged 71 years."

The hymn by which she is best known, and which is still found in many collections, is the following harvest hymn, sometimes erroneously ascribed to John Needham:

Fountain of mercy! God of love I

How rich thy bounties are!

The rolling seasons, as they move,
Proclaim thy constant care.

When in the bosom of the earth
The sower hid the grain,
Thy goodness marked its secret birth,
And sent the early rain.

The Spring's sweet influence was thine,
The plants in beauty grew;
Thou gave refulgent suns to shine,
And mild refreshing dew.

These various mercies from above
Mature the swelling grain;
A yellow harvest crowns thy love.
And plenty fills the plain.

Seed time and harvest. Lord, alone
Thou dost on man bestow;
Let him not then forget to own
From whom his blessings flow!

Fountain of love! our praise is thine;
To thee our songs we'll raise,
And all created Nature join
In sweet harmonious praise.

JAMES UPTON 1760-1834

James Upton was born at Tunbridge Wells, September 15, 1760. At the age of sixteen he removed to Waltham Abbey, Essex, where he soon came under religious influences, and at the age of eighteen he united with the Baptist church in that place. Among the helps to a Christian life which were blessed to him he makes especial mention of Watts' "Psalms and Hymns." He seems early to have devoted himself to the work of the Christian ministry, and February 20, 1785, he preached his first sermon at Waltham Abbey, from 1. Cor. xv. 10. June 27, 1786, he was ordained pastor of the Baptist church in Greenwalk, afterward Church Street, Blackfriars, London. The membership of the church at that time was only twelve, and the congregation very small, but the work of the new pastor was greatly blessed, and in 1800, the membership of the church had increased to about two hundred and ninety, and made the work of enlarging the meeting house a necessity, there not being room for the members comfortably to sit down at the Lord's table. Mr. Upton, greatly beloved and honored, remained pastor of the church until his death, September 22, 1834, a period of forty-eight years.

In 1798, he published "A Serious Address on Certain Important Points of Evangelical Doctrine and of Christian Duty," and in 1814, "A Collection of Hymns, designed as a New Supplement to Dr. Watts' Psalms and Hymns," consisting of 422 selections from various authors, including some originals. One of these (277), generally attributed to him, is the following:

Come, ye who bow to sovereign grace,
Record your Savior's love;
Join in a song of grateful praise
To him who rules above.

Once in the gloomy grave he lay,
But by his rising power,
He bore the gates of death away;
Hail, mighty Conqueror!

Here we declare in emblem plain,
Our burial in his grave;

And since in him we rose again,

We rise from out the wave.

JONATHAN FRANKLIN 1760-1833

Rev. Jonathan Franklin was born November 10, 1760. His first settlement as pastor was at Croydon, where he served the Baptist church until 1808, when he removed to London, and became pastor of the Red-Cross-Street Chapel. Here he remained until his death, which occurred May 3, 1833. Mr. Franklin was the author of a large number 'of hymns (he published "Hymns and Spiritual Songs" in 1801), of which the best known is the following:

In mounts of danger and of straits,

My soul for his salvation waits;

Jehovah-jireh will appear,

And save me from my gloomy fear.

He in the most distressing hour.

Displays the greatness of his power;

In darkest nights he makes a way.

And turns the gloomy shade to day.

Jehovah-jireh is his name;

From age to age he proves the same;

He sees when I am sunk in grief,

And quickly flies to my relief.

JOSEPH SWAIN
1761-1796

Rev. Joseph Swain was born in Birmingham in 1761. Left an orphan in early life, he was apprenticed to an engraver in London, where he was subjected to evil influences by worldly associates. Serious thoughts, however, at length took hold of his mind, and having bought a Bible, he was led by reading the Scriptures to choose the better part. Finding a new joy in Christian song, he began to write hymns in order to give expression to his own devout sentiments. May 11, 1783, he was baptized by Dr. John Rippon, and having become a member of Dr. Rippon's church in Carter Lane, Southwark, he devoted himself to active service for his Master. Thus were developed gifts which gave promise of usefulness in the Christian ministry, and he entered upon a course of preparation for that work. June 2, 1791, he was called to take charge of a mission in East Street, Walworth, London. The mission grew into a church, which was organized in December following. Mr. Swain's ordination occurred in Dr. Rippon's church, February 8, 1792. In Rippon's "Register," Vol 1, p. 522, is the following quaint account of this service:

"After singing, Mr. Upton, of Greenwalk, prayed. Mr. Timothy Thomas described a Gospel church, made some very candid remarks on the imposition of hands in ordinations, and proposed the usual questions to the church and the ministry. These being satisfactorily answered, Mr. Swain read his confession of faith, Mr. Booth prayed the ordination prayer, laying on hands with Dr. Rippon, Mr. Smith, of Eagle Street, etc. Mr. Rippon gave the charge, Mr. Button addressed the church from Eph. v. 15: 'See then that ye walk circumspectly,' etc. Mr. Smith prayed the last prayer. Mr. John Giles conducted the praises of God, at proper intervals, by lining out two or three verses at a time, from different hymns, also part of Dr. Watts' 132nd Psalm, and the whole 410th hymn of Mr. Rippon' s 'Selection,'

Let Zion's watchmen all awake."

Mr. Swain's ministry was greatly blessed, and in a short time the membership of the church was increased from twenty-seven to two hundred. But his career of ministerial influence was brief. He died after a two weeks' illness, April 14, 1796, in the thirty-fifth year of his age.

JOB HUPTON 1762-1849

In a village on the borders of Needwood Forest, near Burton-on-Trent, Staffordshire, Mr. Hupton was born in March, 1762. In early life he received deep religious impressions from the teachings of a pious mother, yet he would not allow them to influence his life. On the contrary, he hardened his heart against them. From his early years, working at a forge, he passed his leisure hours in the society of evil companions; but the prayers of his mother followed him. When twenty-two years of age, while in a public house, his conscience was awakened, and he was led to see his lost condition. Shortly after, at Walsall, near Birmingham, the truth was "still more deeply impressed upon him by a sermon preached by Rev. John Bradford, curate of Frilsham, Bedfordshire, one of Lady Huntingdon's preachers; but still he did not find acceptance with God. Anxious days followed, but at length, while at his forge, the darkness passed from his mind as he was meditating upon the words of Isaiah, "Arise, shine, for thy light is come."

With his conversion there came a call to the Gospel ministry, and he spent a few months at Lady Huntingdon's college in Trevecca, Wales. For several years he devoted himself to evangelical work in different parts of the country. In September, 1794, having adopted Baptist views, he accepted a call to the pastorate of the Baptist church in Claxton, Norfolk. Here he had a long and useful ministry. He died October 19, 1849, having been a preacher of the Gospel more than sixty-four years.

From 1803, to 1809, he wrote much in poetry and prose for the Gospel Magazine. A few years before his death his prose contributions to the Magazine were brought together in a volume entitled "The Truth as it is in Jesus." His "Hymns and Spiritual Poems," with a brief memoir, were collected and published in 1861, by Mr. Daniel Sedgwick. "Some of his poetry," says Dr. Hatfield, "has great merit." Only one of his hymns has found its way into general use. This is herewith given, as altered by Dr. John Mason Neale in the Christian Remembrancer, No. 121. It is part of the "Hymn of Praise to the Redeemer," consisting of thirteen stanzas, beginning, "Come, ye saints, and raise an anthem."

Come ye faithful, raise the anthem,
Cleave the skies with shouts of praise;
Sing to him who found the ransom,

Ancient of eternal clays;

God Eternal, Word Incarnate,

Whom the Heaven of heavens obeys!

Ere he raised the lofty mountains,

Formed the sea, or built the sky,

Love eternal, free and boundless,

Forced the Lord of Life to die;

Lifted up the Prince of princes

On the throne of Calvary.

SAMUEL PEARCE 1766-1799

On the coast of England, at Plymouth, in Devonshire, Samuel Pearce was born, July 20, 1766. When fifteen years of age he was deeply impressed with his need of a Savior, and a year later a sermon which he heard deepened these impressions, and he was led to Christ, the sinner's friend. Subsequently, having forgotten the source of his strength, he went astray, but he was again led to the cross, and reverently, in an everlasting covenant, he gave himself to the service of his Master. Having decided to study for the ministry, he went to Bristol, where he entered the Baptist College, devoting himself, as opportunity offered, to evangelistic work in and around Bristol. In 1790, he became pastor of the Cannon Street Baptist church in Birmingham, where he was ordained August 18. Rev. Andrew Fuller offered the ordaining prayer. Dr. Caleb Evans, of Bristol, delivered the charge, and the sermon was preached by Rev. Robert Hall, senior, of Arnsby, from Deut. i. 38: "Encourage him." Mr. Pearce labored in Birmingham with great zeal and success until his death, October 10, 1799.

With Carey, Fuller and Ryland, Mr. Pearce was an earnest advocate of foreign missions, and his name is affixed to the resolutions adopted at the meeting of ministers at Kettering, October 2, 1792. He was also one of the contributors that day to the funds of the "Baptist Society for Propagating the Gospel among the Heathen," then and there organized. It was his desire to go to India with Carey, and so strong were his convictions of duty, and on the other hand so strong were the objections of his people, that he decided to leave with the Board the question whether he should go or remain. It was their opinion that he would be more useful to the cause of missions in England than in India, and they advised him to continue in his pastorate in Birmingham. Yielding to the judgment of his friends, he labored so long as life lasted, with untiring energy, to arouse in his brethren in England and Ireland a deeper interest in mission work among the heathen. In 1794, in a letter to Dr. Rogers, of Philadelphia, he urged the formation of an American Baptist Foreign Missionary Society. Though cut down in the prime of manhood, he left the record of a well-spent life, and his influence was long felt, not only in Birmingham, but in many parts of England.

JOHN FOUNTAIN 1767-1800

But little is known concerning Mr. Fountain's early years. It is thought that London was his birth-place. He was a member of the Eagle Street Baptist church in that city, and in January, 1796, was recommended by the church to the committee of the Baptist Missionary Society for appointment under their auspices. He sailed from Gravesend, near the close of April, 1796, and joined William Carey in his mission work at Mudnabatty, Bengal, Carey having reached Bengal three years earlier. Mr. Fountain began to preach in Ben Bali in June, 1798. The same year he translated a hymn written in Bengali by William Carey, commencing

Jesus now have pity on me.

This hymn was published in England in Rippon's "Register," Vol. 3, p. 170. The East India Company refusing in October, 1799, to allow Mr. Marshman and his associates who had just arrived from England to join Carey and Fountain at Mudnabatty, which was about four hundred miles from the coast, the latter came down to Serampore and placed themselves under Danish protection. Here they established their mission, receiving many kindnesses from the Governor, Col. Bie. Writing from Serampore, May 14, 1800, Mr. Fountain said:

"Somebody must make a beginning, and to us it appears no small grace, that Jehovah hath appointed us to this work. We shall lay the foundation, and our successors will see the building rise. How soon so ever death may put a period to my labors, it will surely yield some consolation to my soul in its departing moments, that I have borne witness for Christ among the heathen, and assisted in translating the word of life into the language of Bengal."

JOSHUA MARSHMAN 1768-1837

Dr. Marshman was bora at Westbury Leigh,Wiltshire, April 20, 1708. In early life he evinced a fondness for books and study. In 1794, he accepted the charge of a school connected with the Broadmead Baptist church, Bristol, and not long after he was baptized, and united with the church. At the same time he entered the theological seminary at Bristol, and de voted himself to the Hebrew, Syriac, and other languages. Becoming interested in Dr. Carey's work in India, he and his wife, in 1799, offered themselves for missionary service, and sailed May 29, for India. They landed at Serampore October 18, and the mission was established there, Dr. and Mrs. Marshman opening a boarding-school to aid them in the prosecution of their work. In 1806, Dr. Marshman commenced the study of the Chinese language for the purpose of translating the Scriptures into that tongue. In 1814, he published his "Key to the. Chinese Language," and in fifteen years from the time he commenced his study of the language he completed the publication of the first portion of the Scriptures in the Chinese language, consisting of the book of Genesis, the four Gospels, and Paul's Epistles to the Romans and Corinthians. In 1826, he visited England, and returned to India in 1829.

His principal works, aside from those already mentioned, are a "Dissertation on the Characters and Sounds of the Chinese Language" (1809), "The Works of Confucius, containing the Original Text, with a Translation" (1811), and "A Defense of the Deity and Atonement of Jesus Christ" (1822). He also assisted Dr. Carey in the preparation of a "Sanskrit Grammar," and a "Bengalee and English Dictionary." An abridgement of the latter he published in 1827.

He died December 5, 1837, and was buried in the cemetery at Serampore, by the side of his illustrious colleagues, Carey and Ward. In 1811, Brown University conferred upon him the honorary degree of Doctor of Divinity.

Hail, precious book divine I
Illumined by thy rays,
We rise from death and sin
To speak the Savior's praise;
The shades of error, dark as night,
Vanish before thy radiant light.

We bless the God of grace,
Who hath his word revealed
To earth's bewildered race.
So long in darkness held.
His love designs; his people pray;
His providence prepares the way.

Now shall the heathen learn
The glories of our King;
And from their idols turn
Jehovah's name to sing;
Diffusing heavenly light around,
This book shall Satan's power confound.

Deign, gracious Savior, deign
To smile upon thy word;
Let millions now attain
Salvation from the Lord;
Nor let its growing conquests stay,
Till earth exult to own thy sway.

WILLIAM WARD 1769-1823

One of the celebrated triumvirate at Serampore, Mr. Ward was born at Derby, England, October 10, 1769. He learned the printer's trade in his native town, and subsequently became editor of the Derby Mercury. Afterward he edited papers in Stafford and Hull. In August, 1796, during his residence in Hull, he united with the Baptist church there. It was believed that he could best promote the cause of his master by devoting himself to the work of the Christian ministry, and a benevolent friend offered to pay his expenses during his preparatory course. He accordingly renounced journalism and gave himself to theological study under the direction of Rev. Dr. Fawcett, at Ewood Hall, Yorkshire. A few months afterward, learning that the Baptist Missionary Society wished to secure a missionary printer, in order to publish the Bengalee translation of the Scriptures, Mr. Ward offered his services for that purpose, together with the preaching of the Gospel to the heathen, as opportunity offered; and May 29, 1799, in company with Joshua Marshman, William Grant, Daniel Brunsdon, and their families, he sailed for India. Grant died at Serampore, October 31, 1799, soon after their arrival, and in Rippon's " Register," Vol. 3, pp. 225, 226, Mr. Ward, in verse, pays a tribute to the memory of his companion, who, it seems, had once been a scoffer at Christianity; but grace had subdued his heart. From it these lines are taken:

No longer now he doubts the word of God,
Normally tramples on the Savior's blood;
He feels the power and majesty divine
Which shine in every page, in every line;
Wonders he never beheld the scene before,
And longs to bear the news to every shore.

To prove the change divine, his prayer is heard;
To India's shore he bears the heavenly word;
Jesus accepts the soul his grace has won;
On India's plains arrived, his work is done;
Content, the way to heathen lands is shown.

He follows Mercy to the world unknown.

Mr. Ward printed, at Serampore, the Bengalee New Testament and other translations, and wrote "An account of the Writings, Religion, and Manners of the Hindoos," which was published at Serampore in 1811, and was reprinted in England and America. It was a work of great value, and such it still remains. In 1819, Mr. Ward visited England, where lie was most heartily welcomed as the first missionary who had returned to tell the story of the triumphs of the cross in India. He also visited Holland, and subsequently the United States, where he spent three months, deepened the missionary interest in the churches, and received for the college at Serampore contributions to the amount of ten thousand dollars. He returned to India in 1821, and died, after a short illness, March 7, 1823, aged fifty-three years.

HENRY PAICE

The earliest mention of Henry Paice is in Dr. Rippon's "Register," in an account of his ordination, May 13, 1795, as pastor of the Particuhir Baptist church at Waddesdon Hall, Bucks. Five years afterward he had removed to Aylesbury, in the same county, but the church there being unable to support him, Mr. Paice, in 1800, accepted an invitation to Broseley, in Shropshire. July 29, 1824, he was recognized as pastor at High Wycombe, Bucks, from which place he removed, a few years later, to Pimlico, London. His subsequent history cannot now be traced.

During his residence at Broseley he published a collection of one hundred and sixty-nine hymns, chiefly selected from the periodicals of that day, but including eight with the letter P. affixed, which are believed to be his own. Mr. Paice's book has no date, but was printed and sold by William Smith, at Ironbridge, which is near Broseley, and sold also by the editor at Broseley. The probable date is about 1804.

The only one of Mr. Paice's hymns which has found a place in other collections, is one commencing

Great source of uncreated light.

The last three stanzas, with the first word altered, appear as a short hymn in the "Selections" of Gadsby, Denham and Stevens. A better selection, perhaps, would have been the following:

O be not angry, Lord,
And I, though dust, will speak;
If thou, ere long, dost not return,
This wounded heart will break.

Within thy sacred courts,
With rapture have I heard
The whispers of thy love, and felt
The comforts of thy word.

But ah I those days are fled,
And I begin to fear,
Lest those sweet gentle sounds of thine
No more should charm mine ear.

Creatures can ne'er supply
His presence whom I love;
Had I the utmost they could give,
My soul would empty prove.
Scatter this darkness, Lord,
And bid these shadows flee;
And deign, thou Sun of Eighteousness,
Again to shine on me.

Thus shall my soul, revived.
Confess thy saving power;

96

Shall tune her long-neglected harp,

Her Jesus to adore.

WILLIAM GADSBY 1773-1844

Rev. William Gadsby was born in Attleborough, Warwickshire, about January 3, 1773. His parents were poor, and he was apprenticed to a ribbon weaver when thirteen years of age. An execution which he witnessed in 1790, impressed him deeply, and he abandoned his previous course of life. Having passed through various experiences, he was baptized in 1793, and united with the Baptist church at Coventry. In 1798, he commenced to preach, and two years later a chapel was built for him at Hinckley, In 1805, he accepted the pastorate of the Baptist church in St. George's Road, now called Rochdale Road, Manchester, where he ministered until his death, January 27, 1844. His labors were abundant in all the country around, and he is said to have preached twelve thousand sermons.

In 1814, he published his "Nazarene Songs," and also his "Selection of Hymns." In 1838, a new edition of the latter, with a supplement, appeared. In 1846-7, all of Hart's hymns which were not included in earlier editions, were added, and in 1849-50, a second supplement, by Mr. Philpot, was added, increasing the whole number to more than eleven hundred. Mr. Gadsby also published a "Selection of Hymns for Sunday Schools."

JOHN BURTON 1773-1822

This writer is known as John Burton, senior, to distinguish him from another hymn writer of the same name, who was born in 1803. He was probably a native of Nottingham, and was born February 26, 1773. He seems early to have become interested in Sunday school work, and his first hymns were written for the school in which he was a teacher. A volume of his hymns was published in 1802, under the title, "The Youth's Monitor in Verse. In a Series of Little Tales, Emblems, Poems, and Songs, Moral and Divine." His "Hymns for Sunday-schools, or Incentives to Early Piety," in two parts, followed, the second in 1806. The first contained thirty-six hymns, and the second sixty. In 1810, he published a collection of hymns adapted for Sunday-schools, containing one hundred and twenty-one hymns, some of which were his own. The Nottingham collection reached its twentieth edition in 1861. Ten of his hymns are found in "The Voice of Praise," published by the London Sunday school Union. Mr. Burton was the author of "The Nottingham Sunday-school Union Spelling Book," "The Young Plantation," in verse, "The Shrubbery," and other works for the young.

He removed to Leicester about the year 1813, and there enjoyed the friendship of Robert Hall, who wrote the preface to one of his books. He died June 24, 1822, leaving an unpublished volume of hymns for village worship.

One of his hymns, commencing

Holy Bible! book divine!
Precious treasure! thou art mine,

first appeared in the Evangelical Magazine for 1805, and was signed "J. B. Nottingham." A son, born in 1808, relates that he was taught this hymn by his father before he was able to read.

One of his best known hymns is the following:

Time is winging us away
To our eternal home;
Life is but a winter's day,—
A journey to the tomb.
Youth and vigor soon will flee,
Blooming beauty lose its charms;
All that's mortal soon shall be
Enclosed in death's cold arms.

Time is winging us away
To our eternal home;
Life is but a winter's day,

A journey to the tomb;
But the Christian shall enjoy
Health and beauty soon above,
Where no worldly griefs annoy,
Secure in Jesus' love.

Another favorite hymn by the same writer begins
O thou that hearest prayer.
Attend our humble cry.
And let thy servant share
Thy blessing from on high;
We plead the promise of thy word;
Grant us thy Holy Spirit, Lord.

WILLIAM W. HORNE 1773-1826

Not much is known concerning this hymn writer. He was born at Gissing, Norfolk, in 1773. Having devoted himself to the work of the Gospel ministry, he became pastor of the Baptist church at Yarmouth, and afterward at Leicester. About 1806, he removed to London, where he preached to two churches in the eastern part of the metropolis. These churches, shortly before his death, were united in the Ebenezer Chapel, Commercial Road. He died July 27, 1826, aged fifty-two.

Death is no more a frightful foe.
Since I with Christ shall reign;
With joy I leave this world of woe,
For me to die is gain.

To darkness, doubts and fears, adieu!

Adieu, thou world so vain;
Then shall I know no more of you;
For me to die is gain.

No more shall Satan tempt my soul.
Corruptions shall be slain,
And tides of pleasure o'er me roll;
For me to die is gain.

Nor shall I know a Father's frown,
But ever with him reign.
And wear an everlasting crown;
For me to die is gain.

Sorrow for joy I shall exchange,
Forever freed from pain.
And o'er the plains of Canaan range;
For me to die is gain.

Fain would my raptured soul depart,
Nor longer here remain,
But dwell, dear Jesus, where thou art;
For me to die is gain.

JOHN STEVENS 1776-1847

John Stevens was born at Aldwinkle, Northamptonshire, June 8, 1776. When about the age of sixteen, to improve himself in his business as a shoemaker, he went to London, where he began to attend the ministry of Rev. R. Burnham, of Grafton Street, Soho. There he was baptized, and not long afterward he was called by the church to preach. In 1797, he became minister at Bundle, in his native county. Thence he removed to St. Neot's, and subsequently to Barton, in Lincolnshire. In 1811, after the death of Mr. Burnham, he was invited to succeed him at Grafton Street. The place became too small, and after a temporary removal to another building in 1824, a new chapel was erected in Meard's Court, where Mr. Stevens continued to minister until his death, October 6, 1847.

Mr. Stevens belonged to the High Calvinistic school of theology, had popular gifts as a preacher, and was a keen controversialist. When at St. Neot's he wrote a book entitled " Help for the True Disciples of Immanuel," in opposition to the views of Andrew Fuller. In 1809, he published a work entitled "Doctrinal Antinomianism Refuted, and the Old Law Established in a New Relation." This was in opposition to Mr. William Gadsby. But his most famous book was a treatise entitled "A Scriptural Display of the Triune God and the Early Existence of Jesus' Human Soul," published soon after his settlement as pastor at Grafton Street. Of the Pre-Existence theory, as it was termed, he was a warm advocate.

In 1809, Mr. Stevens published a "New Selection of Hymns, including also several original Hymns never before offered to the Public." This selection went through a number of editions (8th, 1847), and was enlarged from time to time. In the form in which it is now used, it contains nine hundred and seventy hymns, and was edited by J. S. Anderson, of Zion Chapel, New Cross Road, London. Thirty-four of the hymns were composed by Mr. Stevens. Most of them embody High Calvinistic views of election and the atonement, but a few of the hymns on Baptism and the Lord's Supper would be acceptable to most Baptists. The following is number 710 in Stevens' "Selection":

Around this social board,
In sweetest bonds of love,
We take our seats before the Lord
In hope to meet above;

Memorials of our Priest
Before our eyes appear,
With pleasure may we keep the feast,
Since Jesus Christ is here.

Ye hungry, thirsty, come I
Draw near and freely take;
Your Savior kindly said, "Here's room;'
Make free for Jesus' sake.

There's room by Jesus' side,
And room beneath his feet, —
Room for the humble to abide,
"Where his redeemed meet.

THOMAS COLES 1779-1840

In the eastern part of the picturesque county of Gloucester stands an old-fashioned English village, having a rather large number of comfortable looking houses, with fronts covered with ivy or other climbing plants, and a stream of clear swiftly running water flowing through it. The houses are on both sides of the water, and the stream, four or five yards wide, is spanned by several bridges. Hence the name of the place, Bourton-on-the-Water. Here for fifty-two years Benjamin Beddome was the Baptist pastor. Here, too, the celebrated essayist, John Foster, found his wife, and spent the first nine years of his married life.

Thomas Coles, who was born at Rowell, near Winchcomb, Gloucestershire, August 31, 1779, early in life removed to Bourton, and here, when about sixteen years of age, he united with the Baptist church. His baptism took place only a month before the death of his venerable pastor,

Mr. Beddome, the officiating minister being Rev. Benjamin Francis, of Horsley, also famous as a hymn writer. Shortly afterward, Thomas Coles proceeded to Bristol to study for the ministry, under Dr. Ryland, and two years later to the University of Aberdeen, where in due time he took his degree of master of arts. The services of Mr. Coles were sought for by important churches in Birmingham and London, both Samuel Pearce and Abraham Booth desiring to have him as assistant. But, in 1801, he accepted the earnest invitation of his friends at Bourton-on-the-Water to become their pastor, a position which he held with honor and usefulness to himself until his death, September 23, 1840.

Mr. Coles will probably be best known to posterity as the successor of Beddome and the friend and correspondent of John Foster. As a hymn writer, he is known by one hymn only, the 372d, in the "Selection" enlarged. One who has read the description given above of Bourton-on-the-Water will not fail to observe in this hymn how the clear, ever-running village brook reminded the author of that "river, the streams whereof make glad the city of God," as well as of "the fountain open for sin and uncleanness."

Indulgent God I to thee I raise
My spirit, fraught with joy and praise;
Grateful I bow before thy throne,
My debt of mercy there to own.

Rivers descending, Lord I from thee,
Perpetual glide to solace me;
Their varied virtues to rehearse
Demands an everlasting verse.

And yet there is beyond the rest,
One stream—the widest and the best —
Salvation I lo, the purple flood
Bolls rich with my Redeemer's blood

I taste — delight succeeds to woe;

I bathe —no waters cleanse me so;

Such joy and purity to share,

I would remain enraptured there

Till death shall give this soul to know

The fullness sought in vain below; —

The fullness of that boundless sea

Whence flowed the river down to me.

My soul, with such a scene in view,

Bids mortal joys a glad adieu;

Nor dreads a few chastising woes

Sent with such love, so soon to close.

JOHN LAWSON 1787-1825

After his decease this devoted servant of Christ was generally known by his friends as "the beloved Lawson." There is in these words a beautiful testimony to the gentle, affectionate spirit of the man. He was born at Trowbridge, Wiltshire, July 24, 1787. Displaying a genius for wood carving, he was sent to London, in 1803, to be articled to a wood engraver. In 1806, he joined the Baptist church in Eagle Street, and shortly afterward, his thoughts being directed to the subject of Christian Missions, it occurred to him that in matters connected with his own calling he might be of use in the mission field. He offered himself to the Baptist Missionary Society, and in 1810, he set sail for America, on his way to India. Various circumstances detained him in the United States for more than a year, during which time he preached in many churches with great acceptance. Arriving at Serampore in 1812, he soon rendered essential service in the printing office and school. Subsequently he became pastor of Baptist churches in Calcutta, and devoted much of his time to the work of education. He was well skilled in music, and composed a number of tunes, which became popular in England and America, as well as in India. His knowledge of natural history was extensive. But his favorite recreation was poetical composition. Between the years 1820, and 1825, he published four works of this kind, "Orient Harping," "Female Influence," "The Lost Spirit," and "Roland." Beside these, he left behind him a manuscript volume of miscellaneous poems, afterward printed. During the last three years of his life Mr. Lawson acted as agent of the American Baptist Board of Foreign Missions. He died in Calcutta, October 22, 1825.

Two hymns by Mr. Lawson are in the Comprehensive edition of Rippon's "Selection":
While in the howling shades of death,

and the following:

> Europe, speak the mighty name,
> Loud the eternal Three proclaim;
> Let thy deep, seraphic lays
> Thunder forth the echoing praise.
> Asia, bring thy raptured songs;
> Let innumerable tongues
> Swell the chord from shore to shore,
> Where thy thousand billows roar.

> Sable Africa, aid the strain,
> Triumph o'er the broken chain;
> Bid thy wildest music raise
> All its fervor in his praise.
> Shout, America, thy joys,
> While his love thy song employs;
> Let thy lovely wilderness
> High exalt his righteousness.
> All as one adore the Lord —
> Father, Spirit, and the Word;

Hail, thou glorious Three in one,

Worthy thou to reign alone.

Praise him, all ye nations, praise;

Saints in heaven, your anthems raise;

Angels, join the solemn chord —

Reign, forever, holy Lord.

JOHN HOWARD HINTON 1791-1873

Mr. Hinton was the son of Rev. James Hinton, pastor of the Baptist church in Oxford, where he was born March 24, 1791. His mother was a daughter of Isaac Taylor, an eminent engraver, and a friend of the philanthropist, John Howard. As the latter was about to leave England on his last journey, he said to his friend's daughter, "I have now no son of my own; if ever you have one, pray call him after me." She remembered his words, and her eldest son received the name, John Howard. During his student life Mr. Hinton devoted himself at first to medicine, but having decided to enter the Christian ministry, he connected himself with Bristol College, where he remained two years. In 1813, he entered the University at Edinburgh. Having finished his university course, he accepted a call, in 1816, to the pastorate of the Baptist church in Haverford-west, Pembrokeshire. About the year 1820, he removed to Reading. In 1837, he became pastor of the Baptist church in Devonshire Square, Bishopsgate, London. His influence, already widely felt in the denomination, was greatly extended during this pastorate, which continued until 1863. The foreign missionary enterprise had in him a most earnest friend and advocate. The interests of the Baptist Union were also greatly fostered by him.

Among his numerous works are "Athanasia; or Four Books on Immortality"; "Letters Written in Holland and North Germany"; "Memoirs of William Knibb"; "A History of the United States of North America"; "Inspiration"; "An Exposition of the Epistle to the Romans on the Principle of Scripture Parallelism"; "Theology, or an Attempt toward a Conservative View of the Whole Counsel of God"; " On the Work of the Holy Spirit in Conversion"; "Elements of Natural

History"; "Individual Effort, and the Active Christian"; "The Harmony of the Religious Truth and the Human Reason"; "On Man's Responsibility"; "On Acquaintance with God"; "On God's Government of Man"; "On Redemption," etc., beside numerous sermons and pamphlets. His theological works he brought together, and published in seven volumes, in 1864-5.

It was also the author of several hundred hymns, prepared for the most part for use in connection with his sermons. His "Hymns by a Minister," a collection of one hundred and sixteen original hymns, appeared in 1833; some were printed in connection with his Theological Lectures.

Father of all, before thy throne,
Grateful, but anxious parents bow;
Look in paternal mercy down,
And yield the boon we ask thee now.

'T is not for wealth, or joys of earth,
Or life prolonged we seek thy face;
'T is for a new and heavenly birth,
'T is for the treasures of thy grace.

'T is for their souls' eternal joy,
For rescue from the common woe;
Do not our earnest suit deny.
We cannot, cannot, let thee go.

WILLIAM GROSER 1791-1856

He was born in London, August 12, 1791. His parents were members of the Eagle Street Baptist church, and his father some years later having been licensed to preach by that church, he removed with his family to Watford, where he entered upon the pastorate of the Baptist church in that place. Like many another Baptist pastor of his day, he eked out his support by keeping a school, in which he had the assistance of his son. The latter was converted when about nineteen years of age, and commenced a course of study preparatory to the work of the Christian ministry. He preached his first sermon in 1811, and two years later he was invited to take the pastoral charge of the Baptist church at Princes Risborough. In 1819, he removed to Battle, Sussex, and a year later he set tied at Maidstone, where he remained nineteen years. He then went to London, where he edited the Baptist Magazine, and engaged in other literary labors. In 1848, he became pastor of the Baptist church in Chelsea, but resigned in 1851, to take the secretaryship of the Irish Society. He died August 6, 1856, after a useful and laborious life, and greatly beloved by a wide circle of friends.

GEORGE FRANCIS

I have been able to glean only a few facts concerning Mr. Francis. He was pastor of the Baptist church in Snow's Fields, Southwark, London, and had a large following in his time. In his doctrinal position he is said to have occupied like grounds with John Stevens and Dr. Gill. In 1824, he published a collection of hymns, principally for the use of his own congregation. Sixteen of the eight hundred and eight hymns in this collection were by Mr. Francis, including the following (127):

Cast on this earth a feeble worm,
Where grief and pain in varied form,
Hard press on every side;
My only refuge from despair.
Is the assurance God is near.
And surely will provide.

Should darkness all his steps surround,
My feeble reason quite confound.

And his deep counsels hide;
He in the whirlwind and the storms,
His righteous, sovereign plan performs,
And will for me provide.

Ye poor, who live upon his care,
Like birds that wing the ambient air,
Whate'er may you betide;
Distrust not his all-bounteous hand,
The weak you are a chosen band;
He will for you provide.

When clouds and rains and threatening skies,
At distance place pure harvest joys,
In heavenly love confide;
His truth is firm and will prevail,
Nor seed, nor harvest time shall fail,
Jehovah will provide.

Yes, days of clouds and rain are gone,
The sun delights his course to run.
And pour his glories wide;
Hence from this present joyful hour,
My faith. shall rest upon that Power,
Who can and will provide.

CORNELIUS ELYEN 1797-1873

Mr. Elyen was born at Bury St. Edmunds, Suffolk, February 12, 1797. His parents were

Congregationalists, but having adopted Baptist principles, he was baptized May 6, 1821, and united with the Baptist church in his native place. Two years later, on the retirement of the pastor, he was called to the pastorate of the church, and was ordained in July, 1823. For nearly forty-nine years he ministered to this people, greatly beloved by all, and an earnest friend of every good cause. During this time, his church increased from forty members to over six hundred. He was warmly attached to Mr. Spurgeon, occasionally preached for him, and at the time of Mr. Elven's death, Mr. Spurgeon paid a worthy tribute to his memory. He died August 10, 1873, among the people for whom he had so long labored.

In January, 1852, there was a revival in Mr. Elven's church, and among other hymns which he wrote to be used at the services, were the following stanzas, which have found their way into many recent collections:

With broken heart and contrite sigh,
A trembling sinner, Lord, I cry;
Thy pardoning grace is rich and free;
O God, be merciful to me.

I smite upon my troubled breast,
With deep and conscious guilt opprest;
Christ and his cross ray only plea;
O God, be merciful to me!

Far off I stand with tearful eyes.
Nor dare uplift them to the skies;
But thou dost all my anguish see;
O God, be merciful to me.

And when, redeemed from sin and hell,
With all the ransomed throng I dwell,
My raptured song shall ever be,
God hath been merciful to me!

JOSEPH HARBOTTLE 1798-1864

Joseph Harbottle was born at Tottlebank, Ulverton, in North Lancashire, September 25, 1798. His father was pastor of the Baptist church at Tottlebank between forty and fifty years. He was baptized and united with his father's church in 1819. In early life he was very fond of classical literature, and made great progress in the acquisition of Latin, Greek and Hebrew. Rev. Dr. Steadman was then tutor in the Baptist college at Horton, near Bradford, and in 1822, Mr. Harbottle, having begun to preach, went to reside in Dr. Steadman's family, and for a time acted as classical teacher to the students. In 1823, he became pastor of the Baptist church at Accrington, a position he filled with honor and usefulness for many years. In 1840, Rev. D. Griffiths and himself became co-pastors of the church, and tutors of a Baptist college, which was commenced at Accrington, Mr. Harbottle being classical and Hebrew tutor. But in 1848, this college was given up, and Mr. Harbottle accepted a pastorate at Oswaldtwistle, near Accrington, and for more than a year ministered to a newly formed church. He died January 19, 1864.

EDWARD STEANE 1798-1882

Only one hymn written by Dr. Steane, appears in any printed collection, but that is a hymn of so much merit, that for its sake alone he should be included among Baptist hymn writers. Edward Steane, d.d., was born in Oxford, March 23, 1798. He was baptized by Rev. James Hinton, of whose church his father was a deacon, and by whom he was encouraged to devote himself to the Christian ministry. After receiving a very complete education at Bristol and Edinburgh, he became, in 1823, pastor of a newly formed church at Camberwell, in the suburbs of London. This pastorate he retained about forty years, although from 1858, onward, when strength began to fail, most of its active duties were discharged by his honored colleague. Rev. Charles Stanford.

Dr. Steane was for many years one of the secretaries of the Baptist Union, and indeed there was scarcely any denominational movement of importance in which he did not take a leading part. He was one of the committee engaged in the preparation of the hymn book called the "New Selection" (1828), in which first appeared the hymn above mentioned. He was one of the originators of the Bible Translation Society, and for a long period was first its secretary and then its treasurer. The Evangelical Alliance owed its existence partly to him, and for some years he was editor of the Alliance organ, "Evangelical Christendom." Many of his occasional sermons were printed, and toward the close of life he published a volume on "The Doctrine of Christ Developed by the Apostles."

In 1862, Dr. Steane went to reside at New House Park, near Rickmansworth, and there he died. May 8, 1882. He was buried, amidst many tokens of love and honor, in Norwood Cemetery, southeast London.

The following is Dr. Steane's hymn:

Prophetic era! blissful day
We catch thy warm, inspiring ray,
Which gleams o'er India's plains;
We hail the dawn of morning light
That breaks upon the gloomy night,
Where superstition reigns.

We hasten thy advance to meet;
With vivid joy the sign we greet,
That brightens in the sky, —
The peaceful sign of heavenly love.
Which like the holy mystic dove,
Declares Messiah nigh.

Behold! he comes in triumph now;

Before him see the mountains bow,

And all the valleys rise;

He comes with majesty and grace.

To sanctify the human race.

And raise them to the skies.

We'll aid thy triumphs, mighty King!

The glories of thy cross well' sing.

And shout salvation round;

Till every nation, every laud,

From Greenland's shore to Africa's strand

Shall echo back the sound.

Let earth commence the lofty praise;

Let heaven prolong the enraptured lays;

Swell every tuneful lyre;

Bright seraphs! chant the immortal song.

And pour the bounding notes along,

From heaven's eternal choir.

BAPTIST W. NOEL 1799-1873

Hon. and Rev. Baptist Wriothesley Noel, a younger son of Sir Gerard Noel Edwardes, Bart., and Diana, daughter of Charles Middleton, the first Baron Barham, also brother of the Earl of Gainsborough, was born at Leithmont, near Leith, July 10, 1799. His education he received at Trinity College, Cambridge, where he was graduated in 1826. Having received ordination in the Church of England, he took charge of St. John's Chapel, Bedford Row, London, where he won distinction as a preacher. He received also an appointment as one of the Queen's chaplains. In 1848, having become convinced of the scripturalness of Baptist views, he withdrew from the

Church of England, and was baptized in London, August 9, 1849. The reasons for this step he gave in two works, "Essay on the Union of Church and State" (1848), and "Essay on Christian Baptism" (1849). In the Church of England he had occupied a prominent position, and his influence was wielded for the best interests of Christianity. In his new relations he occupied a no less prominent position, and his influence was greatly extended. Soon after his withdrawal from the established church he was called to the pastorate of the John Street Baptist Chapel, London, and his Sunday services were thronged with eager hearers. Plain, winning, impressive, he was a preacher whom all delighted to hear. He was active also in advancing the interests of various religious and benevolent organizations. Retiring from his pastorate in 1868, his text for the day was Gal. vi. 14: "God forbid that I should glory, save in the cross of our Lord Jesus Christ." He died Sunday afternoon, January 19, 1873, in his seventy-fifth year.

It was written by an older brother, Rev. Gerard Thomas Noel. One of the best of Baptist Noel's hymns is the following:

There's not a bird with lonely nest
In pathless wood or mountain crest,
Nor meaner thing, which does not share,
O God, in thy paternal care.

Each barren crag, each desert rude.
Holds thee within its solitude;
And thou dost bless the wanderer there.
Who makes his solitary prayer.

In busy mart or crowded street,
No less than in the still retreat,
Thou, Lord, art near, our souls to bless
With all a parent's tenderness.

And every moment still doth bring
Thy blessings on its loaded wing;

Widely they spread through earth and sky
And last through all eternity

And we, wherever our lot is cast,
While life and thought and feeling last,
Through all our years, in every place,
Will bless thee for thy boundless grace.

ROBERT GRACE

Rev. Robert Grace, the author of "Original Hymns, particularly adapted to Prayer-meetings, and Special Occasions," and others which have appeared from time to time in the magazines of the day, was born in the Isle of Wight, July 19, 1799. He was converted at a very early age, and was baptized by the late Rev. Thomas Tilley, of Forton, near Gosport. Before he was eighteen years of age he was encouraged by the church to exercise his talents for preaching, and after a course of study under pastoral guidance, he entered upon his prolonged ministry. After laboring for a short time as an agent of the Home Mission at Niton, Isle of Wight, he accepted the pastorate at Addlestone, Surrey, whence he removed to Battle, Sussex, where he served the church many years. His last pastorate was at Winchcombe, Gloucester. He is now a resident of London.

GILL TIMMS

Of this hymn writer very little is known, or can now be ascertained. He was living in 1838, — was a deacon of the Baptist church in Eagle Street, London, and was for some time one of the editors of the "Baptist Magazine," to which he occasionally contributed pieces in prose and verse. In 1819, he published a volume entitled, "Remarks on God's Foreknowledge, together with some papers from the Baptist Magazine." Two of Mr. Timms' hymns appeared in the "New

Selection" (1828), from which they have been transferred to other collections. Short poems, also written by him, and with his initials appended, are found in the Baptist Magazine, with the following titles and dates: "The Vanity of Literary Attainments without Religious Knowledge"(1832); "The Poverty of Christ" (1833), and "Submission under Affecting Domestic Bereavements" (1833).

The first, in full, is as follows:

Happy the men whose bliss supreme
Flows from a source on high;
And flows in one perpetual stream,
When earthly springs are day.

Contentment makes their little more,
And sweetens good possessed,
While faith foretastes the joys in store,
And makes them doubly blest.

If Providence their comforts shrouds
And dark distresses lower,
Hope paints its rainbow on the cloud,
And grace shines through the shower.

What troubles can these hearts overwhelm,
Who view a Savior near?
Whose Father sits and guides the helm,
Whose voice forbids their fear?

JAMES LINGLEY 1868 (circa)

In the English Baptist collection, known as "Psalms and Hymns" (1860), is a sweet hymn (772) for a Lord's-day morning service, commencing

Once more we leave the busy road.

The writer was James Lingley, a man in humble circumstances, originally a member of the Baptist church at Bury St. Edmunds, but transferred, in 1826, to the Baptist church in Cotton Street, Poplar, at the east end of London. He was accustomed to lead the Sunday morning prayer-meeting, and for some time was a very active church member. The hymn was first printed in the Baptist Magazine for 1829. About the year 1868, he lay very ill in Grey's Hospital, and was there visited by Rev. J. T. Wigner. It is believed that Mr. Lingley died shortly after the date mentioned. He told Mr. Wigner that he had "tried his hand" at a few other hymns, but that this hymn was the only one that had lived. Notwithstanding diligent inquiry, it has been found impossible to obtain the date of his birth and death. The hymn mentioned above is as follows

Once more we leave the busy road
Of worldly toil and care,
To worship our Redeemer, God,
In his own house of prayer.

As strangers in a land of woe
We pass our mortal days;
Yet now and then rejoicings know
In God's own house of praise.

Ye mourning Christians, join the song,
Your harps once more employ;
Remember, as ye pass along.
This is the house of joy.

Dear Savior! in thy temple shine.
Then shall our souls be blest;
And know and prove the truth divine,
Thine is a house of rest.

An emblem of our future bliss,

Thy temple. Lord, we love;

While we anticipate in this

Our Father's house above.

AMOS SUTTON 1802-1854

This devoted missionary of Christ, of humble parentage, was born at Seven oaks in Kent, January 21, 1802. When his school life was over, he was placed in a large business establishment in the metropolis, but the temptations of a great city proved too strong for him. Returning to his home in the country, the faithful ministry of his pastor was blessed to his conversion, and he was baptized, and joined the Baptist church at Sevenoaks. Soon he was actively employed in Sunday-school teaching, and other works of Chris tian usefulness. In 1823, he offered himself as a candidate for missionary service to the General Baptist Foreign Missionary Society, and after a period of preparatory study, he left England for India in August, 1824. His field of labor was the province of Orissa, to the west of the Bay of Bengal, and here, with intervals of furlough spent in his native land and in America, he toiled most diligently and faithfully until his death, August 17, 1854.

Dr. Sutton compiled an Orissa-English Dictionary, prepared the first Orissa hymn book, some of the hymns being his own composition, and translated a number of useful English books into the Orissa Language. He also wrote for English readers "A Narrative of the Orissa Mission," and other works. The honorary degree of Doctor of Divinity was conferred upon him by Waterville College (now Colby University), at Waterville, Maine, U. S. A. In 1833, he visited the United States, and while there awakened so much interest in the missionary cause as to prompt the Freewill Baptists to commence their mission to northern Orissa.

Dr. Sutton's second wife, to whom he was married in India in 1826, was an American lady, who survived him many years. He was an able and good man, whose memory will long be fragrant.

JOHN E. GILES 1805-1875

John Eustace Giles was a son of Rev. W. Giles, and was born April 20, 1805, at Dartmouth, where his father was pastor of the Baptist church. His early education he received in the private school of Rev. James Hinton, at Oxford. In his twentieth year he was baptized by his father, and became a member of the Baptist church at Chatham, of which his father was at that time pastor. Soon after he entered the Baptist College at Bristol, and commenced a course of study preparatory to the work of the Christian minis try. At the conclusion of his studies, he preached a short time at Haverford-west. He then became pastor of the Salter's Hall Chapel, London, where he was ordained in September, 1830. From 1836, to 1846, he was pastor of the Baptist church at South Parade, Leeds. During his pastorate in Leeds, with Dr. Acworth, he visited Hamburg in behalf of Dr. Oncken and the persecuted Baptists there. Later, with Rev. Henry Dawson, he went to Denmark to plead with the king in behalf of the Baptists in that kingdom. He also took an active part in the Anti-Corn-Law struggle. At the close of his labors in Leeds he was settled for a short time in Bristol. Then, from 1847, for fourteen years, he was pastor of the Baptist church in Sheffield. He was afterward pastor at Rathmines, Dublin, whence he removed to London, where he was pastor of the church at Clapham Common until his death, June 24, 1875. He possessed pulpit talents of a very high order, and his life was one of very great usefulness.

Among his published works were "A Funeral Sermon on the Death of Robert Hall,"

"Lectures on Socialism," "A Lecture on Popery," "A Circular Letter on the Spirit of Faith." He was also a contributor to the Eclectic Review.

JOHN T. WIGNER

Rev. John Thomas Wigner, one of the most respected ministers of the Baptist denomination in England, was born in or about the year 1815, at Harwich, in Essex, where his father was a tent and sail maker. When a youth he removed to Burnham, in Essex, and there in his sixteenth year he was baptized, and joined the Baptist church. In 1836, he became a student at Stepney College (now Regent's Park), and in 1840, he entered upon the pastorate of the Baptist church in Lynn, Norfolk. On his fiftieth birthday a great sorrow came to him, and that day, to use his own words, has been to him a no dies ever since, and is never referred to. Hence the indefinite expression used above concerning the date of his birth. From Lynn, Mr. Wigner removed, in 1866, to Brockley, where shortly afterward a new chapel and school rooms were built for him, and where he still ministers to a large and attached congregation.

Mr. Wigner was one of the company of ministers who, in 1860, brought out the now well-known Baptist hymn book, entitled "Psalms and Hymns." A supplement to this book was published in 1881, of which Mr. Wigner was the editor. He also edited, in 1882, a hymn book for the young, which has a large circulation among Baptist churches. It is entitled "Psalms and Hymns for School and Home." Mr. Wigner is the author of two hymns which have a place in the publications named.

W. POOLE BALFERN 1818-1887

Rev. W. Poole Balfern was born at Hammersmith, near London, September 4, 1818. His first pastorate was at Bow, near London, where he entered upon his labors in September, 1855. Here he remained seven years, and then resigned on account of ill health. After a two years' rest, though far from being well, he opened a chapel at Springvale, Ham, for the poor near his home. Some years later, and while thus engaged, he received an invitation from the church at Norlands Chapel, Noting-hill, in the same neighborhood. The church was burdened with a heavy debt, and was unable to pay for the support of a stated pastor. He accepted the invitation, and entered upon the pastorate of the church, taking with him the church he had gathered. Here he remained two years, when, his health again failing, he was obliged to resign. For a change and rest, he went to Brighton, and after a while he was called to the pastorate of the Sussex Street Baptist church, then in a very low condition. There he labored ten years, when age and brain prostration compelled him to resign. He died at his home in Brighton, July 3, 1887.

Mr. Balfern used his pen in the preparation of many works in prose and verse. Among them are "Glimpses of Jesus, or Christ Exalted in the Affections of his People"; "Lessons from Jesus, or the Teachings of Divine Love"; "The Sheltering Blood, or Sinner's Refuge"; "The Pathos of Life "; " The Beauty of the Great King, and other Poems for the Heart and Home"; "Lyrics for the Heart "; "Gethsemane, or Incidents of the Great Sorrow"; "Heart Fellowship with Christ, with Meditations and Prayer for each Sunday in the Year"; "The Way of Peace." He was also a frequent contributor to religious journals. Mr. Balfern's hymns are found in his published works and the religious journals, from which some of them have been transferred to "The Baptist Hymnal" and other collections. Some of his hymns are also in various Sunday-school hymn books. The following is from the English "Baptist Hymnal" (900):

> Say not, O wounded heart,
> Thy love can find no home;
> Behold the Bridegroom of thy soul,
> And hear him whisper, "Come!"

> No falsehood dwells in him.
> His heart no change hath known;
> The faith which rests upon his word,
> Makes all his love its own.

With watchful love he waits
To welcome to his breast
Each wanderer who, with weary feet,
Would seek his perfect rest.

The sighs of Penitence
He hears, and counts her tears;
And when she leans upon his breast,
Forgives the sins of years.

Turn then, O soul, and lived
In Christ's own heart find peace;
Now let assurance of his love
Bid all thy conflicts cease.

The London Baptist says of Mr. Balfern: "He was singularly unselfish and loving in personal character, and his tone in writing was an index to the true spirituality of his mind."

JOSEPH TRITTON 1819-1887

Mr. Tritton was from 1869, until the time of his death, treasurer of the Baptist Missionary Society. He took a deep, practical interest in foreign missionary work, and at different times contributed largely for missionary purposes. To other purposes, also, he devoted his means on a liberal scale. He was for some time treasurer of the Baptist Irish Society, of the Surrey Mission, and of the Institution now known as the Asjdum for Fatherless Children.

Mr. Tritton was born at Battersea, September 21, 1819. His father's family, including himself, were in earlier years members of the church at Battersea, under the pastoral care of Rev. Joseph Hughes, one of the founders of the British and Foreign Bible Society, and a friend of

John Foster. He was educated partly at private schools and partly at the Charter House, For upward of forty years he was a partner in the well known banking house of Barclay, Bevan, Tritton & Co. He died May 1, 1887.

EMMA TURKEY 1819-1851

In "Psalms and Hymns for School and Home," are two hymns for children, sweet and tender in their simplicity, to which are appended the signatures "E. Turney," and "E. T." It cannot be affirmed with certainty, but all the facts make it extremely probable, that the writer of these hymns was Mrs. Emma Turney, nee Emma Bolwell, who was born at Aldeburgh, Suffolk, December 17, 1819, and May 13, 1842, became the wife of Mr. G. L. Turney, a deacon of the General Baptist church in Borough Road, Southwark. Mrs. Turney, before her marriage, had been engaged in tuition, and was an accomplished Christian lady. She died September 10, 1851. Number 351 in the above collection begins

Come to Jesus, little one.

The following is number 372:

The darkness now is over,
And all the world is bright;
Praise be to Christ, who keep
His children safe at night

We cannot tell what gladness
May be our lot today,
What sorrow or temptation
May meet us on our way;

But this we know most surely,
That through all good or ill,

God's grace can always help us
To do his holy will.

Then, Jesus, let the angels,
Who watch us through the night
Be all day long beside us
To guide our steps aright.

And when the evening cometh,
We'll kneel again to pray,
And thank thee for the blessings
Bestowed throughout the day.

BENJAMIN W. PROVIS

Benjamin Wilmot Provis is a good specimen of a class of men happily to be found in many Non-conformist churches in the smaller towns of England; intelligent, godly laymen, pillars in the communities to which they belong. Mr. Provis was born at Chippenham, Wiltshire, November 15, 1822, but for many years past he has resided at Coleford, Gloucestershire, where he is engaged in business. He is a member of the Baptist church in that place, and for the last thirty years he has been superintendent of the Sunday-school and leader of the choir. He has written a number of hymns, chiefly for use in the Sunday-school, or on anniversary occasions. Most of these are unknown beyond his own locality, but two have been introduced into popular hymn books,—

"No tie so strong or sweet below,"
"Bright and joyous be our lay."

The first of these is herewith given as amended by the author:
No tie so strong or sweet below
That time doth not dissever;

But in the Father's home there waits
This recompense forever—
No parting there, no parting there,
No parting there forever.

Our cords of joy are cleft in twain.
Not one remains unbroken;
Yet heaven relinks eternally,
For so the Lord hath spoken.
No parting there, etc,
Why mourn we gaps which years have made?

Why grieve for the departed?
Since Christ shall reunite in heaven,
And heal the broken-hearted.
No parting there, etc.

Yea, in the Paradise of God
The sorrows of life's story
Shall be resolved in psalms of praise
And everlasting glory.
No parting there, etc.

Sing we today; the night draws on I
Come night of mortal slumber!
To-morrow clasp we waiting hands
Of hosts no man can number.
No parting there, etc.

JOHN H. BETTS

Rev. John Henry Betts was born June 16, 1825, at Great Yarmouth, Norfolk, where his father was for many years pastor of the Baptist church. He commenced his own ministry in 1847, and has labored successfully in London, Edinburgh, Manchester, Darlington, and Newcastle-upon-Tyne. Since 1881, he has been pastor at Rye Hill Chapel, in the important city last named.

In early life Mr. Betts published a volume of poems entitled "Early Blossoms," consisting of hymns and translations from the Greek and Latin classics. While in London and Edinburgh he also published three small volumes of sermons and lectures, now out of print. For several years he was editor of the Primitive Church Magazine. He is also the compiler of a collection of hymns for Sunday-schools, entitled "The Children's Hosanna." Several of these hymns were written by Mr. Betts, and are to be found in Mayor's "Book of Praise," a collection of hymns for the young, which has had a large circulation in Great Britain. One of these is the following:

Beautiful Star, whose heavenly light
Cheers a guilty world of night;
Thou shed thy glories from afar,
Star of the Christian, beautiful star.

Beautiful Star, whose kindly ray
Brings to earth a glorious day;
With steady, heaven enkindled flame,
Thou shinest, evermore the same.

Beautiful Star, thy pilot spark
Leads the traveler in the dark.
Through all his journey to the skies,
He lifts to thee his gladdened eyes.

Beautiful Star, when o'er the deep
Wildest storms of sorrow sweep,
The sailor feels and fears no ill.

For overhead thou shinest still.

Beautiful Star, the darksome tomb
In thy light shall lose its gloom;
O let me find thy presence there.
And even in death I'll feel no fear.

JOHN COMPSTON

Probably no man in England has done more to popularize the great temperance movement by the aid of music and song, than Rev. John Compston. True, no hymns of his are sung in the ordinary worship of the churches, but at Band of Hope meetings and other temperance gatherings his stirring verses are familiar favorites, and some of them contain so much of the religious as well as the lyrical element that their author may well have a place in this volume. Mr. Compston was born at Smallbridge, near Rochdale, Lancashire, January 9, 1828, his father, Samuel Compston, being a Congregational minister. John Compston became a Baptist, and beginning to preach in the year 1852, he accepted a call to the pastorate of the Baptist church, Inskip, near Preston. He labored subsequently at Bramley (now Leeds), Barnsley, York Road, Leeds; and, in 1878, removed into Somersetshire to become pastor of the United churches of Fivehead and Isle Abbots, near Taunton, a post he still occupies. While at Leeds he discharged the duties of organizing secretary to the Yorkshire Band of Hope Union.

His first work in connection with hymns was the publication of a popular little book known as "Lancashire Sunday-school Songs," afterward incorporated in a larger book entitled "Sacred Songs for Home and School," of which Rev. J, Lees was co-editor. A hymn for the young, composed by Mr. Compston, commencing

Joseph, a lovely youth,

appeared in both of these collections, and has been reprinted elsewhere. In 1857, and 1863, music for these sacred songs was published by Mr. Compston, in the latter instance with the title

"Popular Sacred Harmonies." In 1881, he edited a more important work, which has passed through several editions, and is entitled "The National Temperance Hymnal." In this work words and music are combined. Of the five hundred compositions contained in it, twenty are by Mr. Compston.

DAWSON BURNS

Dawson Buens, d.d., was born in Southwark, London, December 22, 1828, and is the younger son of Jabez Burns, d.d., widely known in his day as a preacher and author, and especially as a speaker and lecturer in behalf of temperance reform and other philanthropic movements. Dawson Burns studied for the ministry at the General Baptist College then located at Leicester; and, in 1851, commenced public work in Manchester. After a time he became assistant, and eventually successor to his father as minister of the General Baptist Chapel, Church Street, Marylebone, London. This position he resigned a few years ago in order to devote himself more entirely to literary and organizing work in connection with the temperance cause. In 1868, he published, with Dr. F. Lees as co-editor, the "Temperance Bible Commentary"; in 1872, "Bases of the Temperance Reform"; in 1875, "Christendom and the Drink Curse"; in 1883, "Temperance Ballads"; beside numerous contributions, year by year, to periodicals, congresses, etc.

But in the midst of this almost incessant work of advocacy and controversy Dr. Burns has not ceased, in the quiet of his home, to practice the art of poetry. In 1884, he published "Rays of Sacred Song" (London, S. W. Partridge & Co.), a volume containing nearly forty hymns, and many short poems, chiefly on Scripture subjects. In 1886, appeared from his pen "Oliver Cromwel!, and Other Poems." The following is from the English "Baptist Hymnal" (783):

> Gladsome we hail this clay's return;
> In God's great name again we meet;
> Our hearts once more within us burn,
> And our communion shall be sweet.

We bless thee, Lord, for all the good
Thy liberal hand has freely given,
For grace by which our feet have stood
In ways that lead the soul to heaven.

For all the mercies of the past
We join in songs of filial praise,
Around us now thy favor cast,
Thou Guide and Guardian of our days.

It was by thy Spirit-kindling flame
Thy servants felt their bosoms glow,
And in thy all sustaining name,
They still with hallowed ardor go.

More strength we crave, more love, more zeal.
That we may follow Christ; and live
To labor for our brethren's weal,
And unto thee the glory give.

JAMES F. SMYTHE

Mr. Smythe was born in Bristol, October 29, 1830, and studied for the ministry at the Baptist college in that city. In 1858, he entered upon public life as minister at Worstead, in the agricultural county of Norfolk. It was afterward his lot to be the first Baptist pastor in modern times in the ancient city of York. Subsequently he labored in Canterbury and Bolton, and is now pastor of the General Baptist church at Berkhampsted. Mr. Smythe's first poetical production appeared in the Baptist Magazine in the year 1856, and was entitled "God and the Soul." Since then he has written a considerable number of hymns and short poems, which have appeared in the Sword and Trowel, the General Magazine, and other religious periodicals. The following, from "Psalms and Hymns for School and Home" (128), is from his pen:

O Jesus I meek and lowly,
Who once did sojourn here;
O Jesus! pure and holy,
Thy gentle voice I hear!
It speaks from out the pages
Of thine own Book divine;
It comes all down the ages,
To weary hearts like mine.

O Jesus! meek and lowly,
Of comforters the best;
O Jesus! pure and holy,
To me thou offer'st rest;
Best from all mental anguish,
The rest of sin forgiven.
Rest when I fail and languish,
The perfect rest of heaven.

O Jesus I meek and lowly,
I look to thee alone;
Jesus I pure and holy,
To thee for rest I come;
I trust, and so believe thee,
I seek thy blessed face;
Receive me, oh, receive me.
Within thy kind embrace!

CHARLES H. SPURGEON

Few men are so widely known as Charles Haddon Spurgeon. He was born June 19, 1834, at Kelvedon, Essex, where his father was pastor of an Independent church. At an early age he was placed under the care of his grandfather, also an Independent minister, who lived at Stambourne, in the same county. Later he attended a private academy at Colchester, which had become his father's residence. When fifteen years of age he studied a year at an agricultural college at Maidstone. Afterward he was an assistant in a school at Newmarket. In the autumn of 1850, he became deeply interested in his religious welfare, and a few months later, at the Primitive Methodist Chapel at Colchester, he heard a sermon from the text, "Look unto me, and be ye saved, all ye ends of the earth." The preacher's words reached his heart, and then and there, according to his own glad testimony, he gave himself to the Lord Jesus Christ. When considering the duty of publicly confessing his allegiance to his Master, he decided to unite with a Baptist church, and May 3, 1851, he was baptized at Isleham, near Newmarket.

For awhile he devoted himself to the work of tract distribution and Sunday-school teaching. He then removed to Cambridge, where he found employment as usher. Here he united with the Baptist church in St. Andrews Street, of which Robert Robinson and afterward Robert Hall had been pastors, and engaged in religious work as opportunity offered. His first sermon he preached at Teversham, when sixteen years of age, having received a license as a lay preacher. In 1852, he was called to the pastorate of the little Baptist church at Waterbeach. Here crowds flocked to hear him. His fame soon reached London, and, in the autumn of 1853, the deacons of Dr. Rippon's old church in New Park Street invited him to come to London, and supply the pulpit. The invitation was accepted, and the impression which the young preacher made by his sermons was such that he at once received a call to the pastorate. This he accepted, and removing to London he entered upon his work in the metropolis under very bright prospects. Crowds attended his preaching services, and within a year it became necessary to enlarge the church edifice. Meanwhile Exeter Hall was hired, and overflowing congregations greeted him there. The enlarged chapel proved inadequate to seat the throngs that assembled to hear him, and, in 1856, Mr. Spurgeon commenced preaching in the Music Hall in Surry Gardens, which had accommodations for seven thousand people. To meet the wants of the rapidly growing church, the Metropolitan Tabernacle was erected, the corner-stone of which was laid in August, 1859. The building was completed in 1861, at a cost of one hundred and fifty thousand dollars. Here Mr. Spurgeon has since preached to large congregations, the house having seats for fifty-five hundred people, and standing-room for one thousand more. When the church took possession of the Tabernacle it had a membership of eleven hundred and seventy-eight; the membership is now upward of five thousand. Connected with the church are "The Pastor's College," for the training of young men for the ministry, and many benevolent institutions, including almshouses and orphan asylums. Since 1868, Mr. Spurgeon's brother, Rev. James A. Spurgeon, has been associated with him as assistant pastor.

Mr. Spurgeon's sermons have been published each week, and very widely circulated, either in the preacher's own tongue or in translations. He has also published many valuable works, of which especial mention should be made of his "Commentary on the Psalms," in seven volumes, entitled "The Treasury of David." In 1866, he published "Our Own Hymn Book, a Collection of Psalms and Hymns for Public, Social and Private Worship." In this admirable collection two hundred and twenty authors are represented by eleven hundred and twenty-nine hymns. Mr. Spurgeon's own contributions were fourteen psalms and ten hymns, with three which he had altered.

EDWARD H. JACKSON

Rev. Edward H. Jackson was born in Birmingham, April 12, 1838, his father being a civil engineer in the employ of the Government. He was brought up a Congregationalist, but became a Baptist in 1856, and a Baptist minister, in the General Baptist section of the denomination, in 1859. His first station was in Liverpool for two years. Since then, he has been pastor at Billesdon and Castle Donnington, in Leicestershire, at Ripley, in Derbyshire, and at South, in Lincolnshire.

Mr. Jackson has been a frequent lecturer in behalf of the Society for the Liberation of Religion from State Patronage, etc. Most of his hymns have been written for Sunday-school anniversaries. Three were first published in the "Baptist Hymnal," and seven others in the "School Hymnal" (London, 1880). Several have been introduced into other collections of hymns for the young. The following is 301 in the "School Hymnal":

The Golden Land is shining
Beyond the azure sky,
Its pearly gates are massive
Its jasper walls are high;
Its warders are the angels,
And evermore they keep
The splendors of its pavement
Untouched by sinful feet.

It is true that land is peopled
By those that dwelt below;
But there they walk in remnants
As stainless as the snow;
Their souls' transparent beauty
Undimmed by thought of sin,
They outwardly are lovely,
And glorious within.

On earth even little children
Are sinful and defiled,
But yonder both are sinless
The angel and the child.
O say, can we attain to
This beautiful estate?

Who'll lead us to that kingdom,
And turn the mighty gate?

O there is one to lead us,
One who was crucified;
Whose living word is speaking
To tell us why he died.
His precious blood can cleanse us
And make us fit to stand
With all his shining angels
Within the Golden Land.

The Golden Land is shining
Beyond the azure sky,
Its pearly gates are massive
Its jasper walls are high;
But all its angels call us,
And stretch a loving hand.
For Christ has bid them help us
To reach the Golden Land.

CHARLES CLARK

Mr. Clark is chiefly known as an eloquent preacher and lecturer. He was born in London, April 19, 1838, studied at the General Baptist College near Nottingham, and, in 1862, began his ministry at Halifax, Yorkshire. He was subsequently pastor at Mazepond, London, and of the ancient and important Baptist church in Broadmead, Bristol. In 1869, he accepted an invitation to take charge of the Baptist church in Albert Street, Melbourne, Australia. He returned from Australia in 1879, and after an interval of two years, employed chiefly in lecturing, became the first minister of a beautiful chapel, newly erected, at healing, a suburb of London, where, through his labors, a numerous congregation had been gathered. Mr. Clark has not attempted much as a hymn writer, but in the "School Hymnal," a Baptist collection of hymns for the young, he is represented by the following:

Jesus, holy Savior,
Shepherd of the sheep,
In this world of danger
Me in safety keep.
While through life I journey,
Deign to be my guide;
Let me never wander
From thy sheltering side.

Tender flowers are blooming
By the sunlit way;
Birds and bees make music
Through the summer day;
All the joys of childhood
Now my spirit greet;
But that thou art near me
Makes my life most sweet.

If through gloomy valleys
Life's rough path shall lie,
Let thy staff of comfort
Evermore be nigh.
Then no threatening evil
Shall my heart affright,
While I feel my Shepherd
Near me in the night.

When in thy good pleasure

Earthly life shall cease,

May thy gentle presence

Fill my heart with peace.

May thy holy angels

Bear my soul above,

There to rest forever

In my Savior's love.

THOMAS V. TYMNS

It is well that in the church of Christ there should always be some men fitted by intellect and culture to grapple with the deeper questions of theology and philosophy. Such a man is Rev. Thomas Vincent Tymns. He was born in Westminster, London, January 5, 1842. After receiving an education for the ministry at the Baptist College in Regent's Park, he became, in 1865, pastor at Berwick-on-Tweed. Thence, in 1868, he removed to Accrington, and, in 1869, to London, where he now ministers to an intelligent and influential congregation in the Downs Chapel, Clapton.

In 1885, Mr. Tymns published a very able book entitled "The Mystery of God, a Consideration of some Intellectual Hindrances to Faith" (London, Elliot Stock). The public appreciation of it was shown in the fact that before the end of 1886, a second edition was called for. But the study of very grave questions has not prevented Mr. Tymns from employing his pen occasionally in sacred song. He has written several hymns, of which the following has been introduced into several hymn books:

Another Sabbath ended,

Its peaceful hours all flown,

We come to close its worship,

O Lord, before thy throne.

We bless thee for this earnest
Of better rest above;
This token of thy kindness.
This pledge of boundless love.

We would prolong its moments,
And linger yet a while
Amid its closing shadows,
Illumined by thy smile.
Our souls shall know no darkness
While we may look to thee;
Our eyes shall ne'er grow weary
While we thy face can see.

O Jesus! our dear Savior,
To thee our songs we raise;
Our hearts, by care untroubled,
Uplift themselves in praise.
For to God's truce with labor
More glory thou hast given;
And Sabbaths now are sweeter.
Since Christ the Lord has risen.

WILLIAM H. PARKER

William Henry Parker is an interesting example of what can be accomplished by an English workingman in the way of self-culture. He was born March 4, 1845, at New Basford, a manufacturing suburb of the town of Nottingham. At the age of thirteen he became an apprentice in the machine construction department of a large lace manufactory in his native place, and still continues in the employ of the same firm. Early in life he began to write verses, and having united with a General Baptist church, and become interested in Sunday-schools, was led to compose hymns for use on anniversary occasions. Every year he produces one or two for this purpose. Three of these hymns were introduced by his pastor, Rev. W. R. Stevenson, into the "School Hymnal" (1880), and soon found their way into other collections of hymns for the young.

In 1882, Mr. Parker published a small volume entitled "The Princess Alice, and Other Poems." In the poets' corner of the local newspapers his compositions not unfrequently have a place. The following are the first lines of the hymns to which reference above is made:

"Children know but little,"
"Jesus, I so often need thee,"
"Holy Spirit, hear us."

All these are characterized by a simplicity of language which renders them peculiarly adapted to the use of children. Owing probably to the fact that there are but few hymns addressed to the Holy Spirit, which are found in collections for children, the third of these hymns has been introduced into a number of modern Sunday-school hymn books. As found in the "School Hymnal" this hymn is as follows:

Holy Spirit, hear us;
Help us while we sing;
Breathe into the music
Of the praise we bring.

Holy Spirit, prompt us
When we kneel to pray;
Nearer come, and teach us
What we ought to say.

Holy Spirit, shine thou
On the Book we read;

138

Gild its holy pages
With the light we need.

Holy Spirit, give us
Each a lowly mind;
Make us more like Jesus,
Gentle, pure and kind.

Holy Spirit, brighten
Little deeds of toil;
And our playful pastimes
Let no folly spoil.

Holy Spirit, keep us
Safe from sins which lie
Hidden by some pleasure
From our youthful eye.

Holy Spirit, help us
Daily by thy might.
What is wrong to conquer,
And to choose the right.

JAMES T. ROBERTS

James Thomas Roberts was born at Suton, Bedfordshire, December 22, 1850. He was educated for the ministry at the Baptist College, Chilwell, near Nottingham, and, in 1874, became pastor of the Baptist church at Retford, Nottinghamshire. Subsequently he labored at Grimsley, and at Westvale, near Halifax, Yorkshire. Among the Baptist churches of Yorkshire the Sunday-school anniversary is the great festival of the year, and during Mr. Roberts' residence at Westvale he composed several hymns for use on these occasions,

"O Jesus, blessed Jesus,"

"Onward, children, onward,"

"Toil on, teachers,"

"Again unto Jesus our Savior,"

and others. These hymns were sung at various places in the district, but only one has found its way into the hymn books. Mr. Roberts is now again residing at Suton, his native place, engaged in business, but preaching on most Lord's-days in the villages adjacent. The following is from the "School Hymnal" (141):

O Jesus, blessed Jesus

Who art the children's Friend,

Hear thou our grateful praises,

"While at thy feet we bend;

As thou hast deigned to welcome —

As thou hast deigned to bless

The little ones who love thee, —

Around thee now we press.

Bless even us, dear Jesus!

For O, we long to know

The peace, the joy and gladness,

Thou only canst bestow.

To know thee, and to love thee.

Be this our early choice,

That all along life's journey

In thee we may rejoice.

We love thy name, dear Jesus.

No other name is given

That is to us so precious.

That is so dear to heaven;
It tells us of a Savior,
It tells us of a Friend
Who will with loving favor
To all our wants attend.

O guide us, blessed Jesus!
Amid the snares of youth,
For well we know our proneness
To leave the paths of truth.
May thy kind arms enfold us
So near thy loving heart,
That sheltered and defended,
We nevermore may part.

We look to thee, dear Jesus!
Our hope is stayed on thee;
O make us now, and keep us
Thine own eternally.
And, when no more thy children
Shall sing thy praises here,
May parents, teachers, scholars,
Meet in yon heavenly sphere.

WALTER J. MATHAMS

Walter John Mathams is pastor of the Baptist church at Folkirk, Scotland. He was born in London, October 30, 1853. In early life he went to sea, and had an eventful experience, being at one time shipwrecked, and at another imprisoned as a forced recruit for the Brazilian army during a war with Paraguay. On his return home he began to study for the ministry, and entered Regent's Park College in 1874. His first pastoral charge was at Preston, in Lancashire, but health failing he went for a time to Australia. Again returning to Great Britain, in 1883, he became pastor of the church to which he now ministers.

Whilst a student at Regent's Park, Mr. Mathams published a small collection of hymns and poems, entitled "At Jesus' Feet" (1876). He has since written a number of small religious books of a popular character, such as "Fireside Parables," "Sunday Parables," and "Bristles for Brooms."

Several of Mr. Mathams' hymns are to be found in the English "Baptist Hymnal," "Psalms and Hymns," and "Psalms and Hymns for School and Home." The following is 318 in the "Baptist Hymnal":

My heart, O God, be wholly thine,
I would not keep it back from thee;
Nor wish to shun the grace divine
Which asks this humble gift of me.

O take it now, and let thy love
For ever more within me dwell;
And may thy spirit from above
Teach me to serve my Master well.

Afar be every thought of sin,
Afar be every wish to stray;
Let truth and holiness begin
To lead me up the heavenward way.

Make this my only aim and care.
To seek thy praise in all I do;
To consecrate each act with prayer,
As I my daily work pursue.

More like to thee, my blessed Lord,

I would be, as my days pass by,

With patience, love, and wisdom stored,

Ready to live, and fit to die.

AMERICAN BAPTIST HYMN WRITERS AND THEIR HYMNS

BENJAMIN CLEAVLAND 1735-1811

In many American hymn books, from the beginning of the century, place has been given to a hymn commencing

Oh, could I find from day to day.

In the "Psalmist," it is credited to "Church Psalmody,'* and in "Church Psalmody," to "Methodist Coll." In the "Plymouth Collection," it is credited to the "Hartford Selection." In some other collections it is marked "Anon." It has at length been ascertained —and the discovery is due to Rev. S. Dryden Phelps, d.d., of Hartford, Conn.,—that this well known hymn was written by Benjamin Cleavland. In a communication in the Watchman and Reflector, December 22, 1870, Dr. Phelps announced his discovery. "A little, old leather-bound book" had fallen into his hands, containing some hymns by Benjamin Cleavland, and among them was this hymn. "It is the only hymn by the author," says Dr. Phelps, "that any compiler would now think of inserting in a book of psalmody." This old leather-bound hymn book is the property of Hon. J. H. Trumbull, L.L.D., of Hartford, Conn., and its title in full is as follows: "Hymns on Different Spiritual Subjects. In two Parts. Part I. Containing xxiv Hymns, on various subjects, suitable for Christian Worship. By Benjamin Cleavland. Fourth Edition. Part II. Containing xxxii Hymns by Anna Beeman, of Warren in Connecticut, and xxiv Hymns by Amos Wells. To which is added a number of Hymns, by different Authors. Particularly Adapted to the Baptist Worship. Norwich: Connecticut. Printed by John Trumbull, mdccxcii. With the Privilege of Copy Right." Dr.

Trumbull's copy of this hymn book, printed by his grandfather, is an imperfect one, ending with p. 112. The date of publication is uncertain. Dr. Trumbull says, "The margin of the page, at this point, is worn, and I am not sure of the date, which may have been mdccxciii."

As printed in this collection, Mr. Cleavland's hymn contains six stanzas, and is as follows:

O could I find from day to day
A nearness to my God;
Then should my hours glide sweet away
And lean upon thy Word.

Lord, I desire with thee to live,
Anew from day to day,
In joys the world can never give
Nor never take away.

O Jesus, come and rule my heart
And I'll be wholly thine.
And never, never more depart,
For thou art wholly mine.

Thus, till my last expiring breath,
Thy goodness I'll adore;
And when my flesh dissolves in death
My soul shall love thee more.

Through boundless grace I then shall spend
An everlasting day
In the embraces of my friend,
Who took my guilt away.

That worthy name shall have the praise

To whom all praise is due;

While angels and archangels gaze

On scenes forever new.

THOMAS BALDWIN 1753-1826

Rev. Thomas Baldwin, d.d., the only son of Thomas and Mary Baldwin, was born in Bozrah, Conn., December 23, 1753. His father, who died while his son was a youth, rose to distinction in the colonial military service. His mother, a woman of vigorous intellect and elevated piety, remarried when her son was about sixteen years of age, and the family removed to Canaan, N. H. Here Thomas was married, September 22, 1775. While yet a young man, he was elected to represent the town of Canaan in the legislature, and so satisfactorily did he discharge his duties that he was repeatedly elected to this office. The bar seemed now to open to him a field for distinction, and he commenced a course of study, with the profession of law in view. But God's plan was otherwise. In the autumn of 1777, his first-born child died, and by this affliction his thoughts were directed to sacred things. It was not until the year 1780, however, that, in connection with the labors of two Baptist ministers who visited Canaan, and held religious services, that he was led to yield his heart to the Savior. In the latter part of 1781, he was baptized by Rev. Elisha Rawson.

Such were his convictions of duty that he soon concluded to abandon his legal studies and devote himself to the work of the Christian ministry. He commenced to preach in August, 1782, and June 11, 1783, he was ordained as an evangelist at Canaan. Here, for no stipulated salary, he labored seven years, performing much evangelistic service in destitute places.

In the early part of 1790, Mr. Baldwin received an invitation to visit the Baptist church in Sturbridge, Mass., and also that in Hampton, Conn. At the opening of the summer he left his home to respond to these invitations. On the journey he received an added invitation from the Second Baptist church in Boston. The churches in Sturbridge and Hampton desired to secure his services as pastor. Proceeding to Boston, he preached in the Second Churchy July 4, 1790, and a few following Sabbaths. Here, also, he received a call to the pastorate. Many considerations seemed to indicate the path of duty, and the call to Boston was accepted. Mr. Baldwin's installation followed, November 11. Dr. Stillman preached the sermon. Dr. Smith, of Haverhill, gave the charge, Rev. Thomas Green, of Cambridge, presented the hand of fellowship, and Rev. Joseph Grafton, of Newton, offered the concluding prayer. His ministry was greatly blessed. Revival followed revival, and, in 1797, it became necessary, on account of the increase in the congregation, to enlarge the house. Repeatedly he was chosen chaplain of the General Court of Massachusetts, and, in 1802, he was appointed to deliver the annual sermon on the day of the General Election. Beside the sermons already referred to, Dr. Baldwin published "Open Communion Examined" (1789); "A Friendly Letter," addressed to Rev. Noah Webster (1794), both republished in 1806; A Series of Letters, in which the Distinguishing Sentiments of the Baptists are Explained and Vindicated, in Answer to a Late Publication by the Rev. Samuel Worcester, A. M., Addressed to the Author, Entitled 'Serious and Candid Letters' (1810); and "An Essay on the Baptism of John" (1820). He also prepared a Catechism, which had passed through six editions in 1826. By appointment of the Baptist Missionary Society of Massachusetts, he commenced, in 1803, the publication of the "American Baptist Magazine," then under the title of the "Massachusetts Baptist Missionary Magazine." From its commencement, until 1817, he was its sore editor; and from that time until his death he was its senior editor. He received the degree of Master of Arts from Brown University in 1794, and the degree of Doctor of Divinity from Union College in 1803.

Dr. Baldwin's death occurred August 29, 1826, at Waterville, Maine, whither he had gone to attend the annual commencement of Waterville College, of which he was a trustee. He retired to rest, on the evening of the day of his arrival, apparently as well as usual. After sleeping about an hour, he awoke, suddenly groaned, and "was not, for God took him." At his funeral in Boston, September 5, the sermon was preached by Rev. Daniel Sharp, from the words, "He was a good man," Acts xi. 24.

The following well known hymn was composed by Dr. Baldwin during a night journey from Newport, N. H., to Canaan. There had been alienation in the church at Newport, and Dr. Baldwin's visit had resulted in a union of its members.

From whence doth this union arise,
That hatred is conquered by love;
That fastens our souls in such ties,
As nature and time can't remove?
It cannot in Eden be found,
Nor yet in a Paradise lost;
It grows on Immanuel's ground,
And Jesus' rich blood it did cost.

My friends are so dear unto me,
Our hearts all united in love;
Where Jesus is gone we shall be,
In yonder blest mansions above.

O, why then so loath for to part,
Since we shall ere long meet again?
Engraved on Immanuel's heart,
At distance we cannot remain.

Though called to resign up this breath,
And quit these frail bodies of clay,
When freed from corruption and death,
We'll unite in the regions of day.

With Jesus we ever shall reign,

And all his bright glories shall see;

We'll sing Alleluia, Amen I

Amen! even so let it be.

JOHN LELAND 1754-1841

Elder John Leland, as he was generally known, was born in Grafton, Mass., May 14, 1754. When twenty years of age he was baptized at Northbridge by Rev. Noah Alden, of Bellingham. Shortly afterward he decided, in accordance with his conviction of duty, to devote himself to the work of the Christian ministry, and, in the autumn of 1774, he united with the Bellingham Baptist church, from which he received a license to preach. In October, 1775, he went to Virginia, where he was ordained. He labored in various parts of that State, and under his pungent preaching of the truth hundreds were brought to Christ. He remained in Virginia about fifteen years, and during this time he preached three thousand and nine sermons, and baptized seven hundred converts. Returning to his native state, he took up his residence in Cheshire, where he spent the remainder of his life. His evangelistic labors were continued, and the number of the persons he had baptized, down to 1821, he gave as one thousand three hundred and fifty-two. His last sermon was preached at North Adams, Mass., January 8, 1841. Taken severely ill that night, he lingered until the evening of the fourteenth, when he gently entered into rest.

Mr. Leland was a prolific writer. His occasional sermons and addresses and essays, on a great variety of subjects, moral, religious and political, were published, after his death, in a large octavo volume, with notice of his life by Miss L. F. Greene, of Lanesborough, Mass. Many of his hymns are included in this collection. The best of these is the following, found in most of the hymn books of the present day:

The day is past and gone;

The evening shades appear;

Oh, may I ever keep in mind,

The night of death draws near!

I lay my garments by,
Upon my bed to rest;
So death shall soon disrobe his all
And leave my soul undressed.

Lord keep me safe this night,
Secure from all my fears;
May angels guard me while I sleep,
Till morning light appears.
And when I early rise,
To view the unwearied sun,
May I set out to win the prize,
And after glory run.

And when my days are past,
And I from time remove,
Oh, may I in thy bosom rest,
The bosom of thy love.

Of this hymn the late Rev. S. W. Duffield ("English Hymns," p. 515) says: "There is an Ambrosian simplicity about this hymn which suggests at once a pure and unaffected piety, like that of the early church. The piece is really classic in its unpretending beauty." And he cites from the "Century Magazine," September, 1885, the following incident, in which there is a reference to this hymn. It is from a lady's record in a diary kept during the siege of Vicksburg (June 5, 1863), when the house where she lived was struck by a shell.

RICHARD FURMAN 1755-1825

Rev. Richard Fueman, d.d., was born in Esopus, N. Y., in 1755. His father, who was a surveyor, not long after removed to South Carolina, where he settled at the High Hills of Santee. The son received a good education in the classics as well as in the English branches. When sixteen years of age he united with the High Hills Baptist church, and two years later he commenced to preach to the church of which he was a member. Gradually he extended his labors, and through his instrumentality many churches were organized in regions hitherto destitute of gospel privileges.

During the Revolution he was greatly interested in the cause represented by the colonists, and especially in the establishment of religious freedom. For awhile he was obliged to leave South Carolina on account of the progress of the British arms, and he made his way into North Carolina, and later into Virginia. While in Virginia, he had Patrick Henry in his Sabbath congregations, and was honored by his friendship. When it was safe for him to return to South Carolina, he remained awhile at High Hills, his former residence, and, in 1787, he accepted a call to the pastorate of the First Baptist church in Charleston. Here he had a long and eminently useful ministry, and he was greatly beloved, not only by his own people, but by the whole community. He was one of the members of the convention that framed the constitution of South Carolina. In 1814, in Philadelphia, he presided over the first general convention of the Baptists of the United States. For several years he was president of the South Carolina Baptist Convention. He died August 25, 1825. His last sermon was from the text, "And Enoch walked with God, and was not, for God took him." Dr. W. B. Johnson says: "It was a noble effort, worthy of one who was standing at the portals of heaven." Referring to Dr. Furman as a preacher, Dr. Johnson says: "I remember hearing him, more than forty years ago, preach from the text, 'I am set for the defense of the gospel.' It was truly a masterly effort. Never shall I forget his solemn, impressive countenance, his dignified manner, his clear statements of the gospel doctrine and precepts, his unanswerable arguments in support of the gospel's claim to a divine origin, the lofty sentiments that he poured forth, the immovable firmness with which he maintained his position, and the commanding eloquence with which he enforced the whole argument."

Dr. Furman was the author of "Pleasures of Piety, and Other Poems." The following hymn, written by him, was included by Andrew Broaddus in his "Virginia Selection" (1842), from which it was transferred to the "Baptist Psalmody" (1850):

Sovereign of all the worlds above,
Thy glory with unclouded rays,
Shines through the realms of light and love,
Inspiring angels with thy praise.

Thy power we own, thy grace adore;
Thou deign to visit men below!
Shines through the realms of light and love,
Inspiring angels with thy praise.

Thy power we own, thy grace adore;
Thou deign to visit men below!
And in affliction's darkest hour,
The humble shall thy mercy know.

These western States, at thy command,
Rose from dependence and distress;
Prosperity now crowns the land,
And millions join thy name to bless.

Praise is thy due, eternal King!
We'll speak the wonders of thy love,
With grateful hearts our tribute bring,
And emulate the hosts above.

O! be thou still our guardian God;
Preserve these States from every foe;
Prom party rage, from scenes of blood,
From sin, and every pause of woe.

Here may the great Redeemer reign,

Display his grace and saving power!

Here liberty and truth maintain,

Till empires fall to rise no more.

MATTHEW BOLLES1769-1838

With the Baptists of Connecticut Bolles is an honored name. Rev. Matthew Bolles, a son of Rev. David Bolles, was born in Ashford, Conn., April 21, 1769. Until middle life he engaged in business, when a conviction that he ought to preach led him to withdraw from secular pursuits, and devote himself to the work of the Christian ministry. He began to preach in 1812, in Pleasant Valley, Lyme, Conn., and there, in June, 1813, he was ordained as pastor of the Baptist church. Here his ministry was greatly blessed, and he remained until 1817. From 1817, to 1838, he was pastor at Fairfield, Conn., Milford, N. H., Marblehead and West Bridgewater, Mass. He was an able and eloquent preacher, and full of the Holy Ghost. He died at Hartford, Conn., greatly lamented, September 26, 1838, in the seventieth year of his age.

In "Select Hymns," compiled by James H. Linsley and Gustavus F. Davis, and published at Hartford, Conn., in 1841, by Robins and Folger, is the following hymn (505), by Mr. Bolles, entitled "Pastor's Prayer in the Study":

Here, Lord, retired, I bow in prayer.

Refresh my soul — my heart prepare

To preach thy word with power. divine;

If it succeed, the praise be thine.

Without this grace, I strive in vain,

O God, revive thy saints again;

Convince poor sinners of their case,

Cause them to seek thy pardoning grace.

Draw thousands to thy mercy seat;

Their hearts renew — their sins remit;

Fill them with joy of faith and love

To serve on earth, to praise above.

In tears I sow the precious seed;

Cause it to spring — my work succeed.

With souls reward my work of love;

Then take me to thyself above.

JESSE MERCER 1769-1841

Rev. Jesse Mercer, d.d., was born in Halifax County, N. C, December 16, 1769, the eldest of eight children. He was a bright boy, but his early opportunities for securing an education were exceedingly limited. In his fourteenth year his father removed to Georgia, which was thenceforward his home. Four years later he was baptized by his father, and united with the Phillips' Mill's Baptist church. Soon after he began to preach. A few months later he was married to Sabrina Chivers, who was a valued helpmeet to him nearly forty years. His ordination followed, November 7, 1789. The churches which he successfully served were those of Hutton's Fork, Indian Creek, Sardis, Phillips' Mill, Powelton, Whatley's Mill, Eatonton, and Washington. Dr. Mallary says: "The field occupied by Dr. Mercer between the years 1796, and 1827, was one of the most important in the State of Georgia,—the churches which he served being in the midst of a dense population, and embracing a considerable amount of intelligence and refinement. His connection with these several churches was the means of quickening them to a higher sense of Christian obligation, of building them up in faith and holiness, and, in nearly every case, of adding largely to their numbers." Says Dr. Basil Manly, senior: "In his happy moments of preaching he would arouse and enchain the attention of reflecting men beyond any minister I have ever heard. At such times his views were vast, profound, original, striking and absorbing in the highest degree, while his language, though simple, was so terse and pithy, so pruned, consolidated, and suited to become the vehicle of the dense mass of his thoughts, that it required no ordinary effort of a well-trained mind to take in all he said."

For several years Dr. Mercer was editor of "The Index," He was also active in missionary operations. For eighteen successive years he was elected president of the Georgia Baptist Convention. He was also deeply interested in the civil affairs of the country, and in the cause of education. His gifts to Mercer University amounted to more than forty thousand dollars.

He also compiled "The Cluster of Spiritual Songs, Divine Hymns and Sacred Poems." The first edition was published in Augusta, Ga., in pamphlet form, and three editions were issued before 1817. For many years Mercer's "Cluster" was in use in the Baptist churches in that part of the country. Several of its hymns without doubt were written by Dr. Mercer himself. Hymn 233, in the later editions, is entitled "The Experience of J. M." The first of its fourteen stanzas is as follows:

<blockquote>
In sin's howling waste my poor soul was forlorn,
And load the distance full well,
When grace, on the wings of the dove to me borne,
Did snatch me, the fire-brand of hell.
</blockquote>

WILLIAM STAUGHTON 1770-1829

Rev. William Staughton, d.d., was born in Coventry, Warwickshire, England, January 4, 1770. When fourteen years of age, he was placed in the family of a pious man in Birmingham, with the design that he should learn the silversmith's trade. It was here that he was converted, and when seventeen years of age united with the Baptist church. Not long after, with the Christian ministry in view, he entered upon a course of study in Bristol College. Several churches, among them the Baptist church at Northampton, wished to secure his services on the completion of his studies, but he had set his face toward the new world, and leaving England in 1793, he made his way to the United States, and became pastor of the Baptist church in Georgetown, South Carolina. Here he remained until the close of 1795, when, finding the climate unfavorable, he removed with his family to New York. Not long after, he accepted an invitation to take charge of an academy in Bordentown, N. J. During his residence in Bordentown he frequently preached. Toward the close of 1798, he removed to Burlington, N. J., where he had a large and flourishing school. He also supplied two churches on the Sabbath, and the Baptist church in Burlington came into existence in connection with his labors. In 1805, he accepted a call to the pastorate of the First Baptist church in Philadelphia, and by his labors the interests of the denomination in that city were greatly advanced. In 1811, a colony from the First Church founded the Sansom Street church, and Dr. Staughton was induced to identify himself with the new enterprise. Here he reached the height of his influence as a preacher. As tutor of the Baptist Education Society of the Middle States of America, Dr. Staughton received into his family young men, whose studies he directed in their preparation for the work of the Gospel ministry. He was also the first corresponding secretary of the Baptist Board of Foreign Missions. As another has said, he became to the Baptist mission cause in this country what Andrew Fuller was among his brethren in England. Dr. Staughton remained in Philadelphia until 1821, when he removed to Washington, and became President of the newly established Columbian College. Resigning this position in 1829, he returned to Philadelphia, and in August of the same year accepted the presidency of a new college at Georgetown, Ky. But he never reached the scene of his proposed labors. On his way thither he was taken ill at Washington, D.C, and there he died December 12, 1829, in the sixtieth year of his age. Princeton College conferred upon him the degree of Doctor of Divinity when he was twenty-eight years of age.

At the age of twelve he evinced poetical gifts, and poems written by him at that early period were published at the request of his friends. When seventeen years old he published a volume of "Juvenile Poems." The following is the first stanza of a hymn on "Pardoning Love" included in this collection

> Involved in guilt and near despair,
> Depressed with shame, overwhelmed with tears,
> To God I raise my humble prayer;

He scattered all my groundless fears.

ANDREW BROADDUS 1770-1848

Rev. Andrew Broaddus was born in Caroline County, Va., November 4, 1770. In early life he evinced an eager thirst for knowledge, and it was the purpose of his father, who was a devout Episcopalian, that he should enter the ministry of the Episcopal church. But he came at length under Baptist influences, and May 28, 1789, he was baptized and united with the Baptist church of Upper King and Queen. Soon after he yielded to the conviction that it was his duty to engage in the work of the Christian ministry. His first sermon was preached December 24, 1789, in a private house in Caroline County, His hearers were impressed by his earnest, devout spirit, and by his graceful oratory. He used his gifts as opportunity offered, and October 16, 1791, he was ordained in the meeting-house of the church to which he belonged. His first pastorate was that of the Burrus church. Subsequently he served the Bethel, Salem, Upper King and Queen, Beulah, Mangohic, Upper Zion, and some other churches. His fame as a preacher at length extended beyond the limits of his native state, and, in 1811, he received invitations to the pastorate from the First Baptist church in Boston, and the First Baptist church in Philadelphia; in 1819, from the First Baptist church in Baltimore, and the New Market Square Baptist church in Philadelphia ; in 1824, from the Sanson Street Baptist church in Philadelphia; and in 1832, from the First Baptist church in New York. A constitutional timidity, however, restrained him from yielding to these solicitations from abroad, except in 1821, when he accepted a call as an assistant to Rev. John Courtney, pastor of the First Baptist church in Richmond, Va.

ROBERT T. DANIEL 1773-1840

Rev. Robert T. Daniel was the author of the very familiar baptismal hymn, commencing

Lord, in humble, sweet submission.

He was born in Middlesex County, Virginia, June 10, 1773. His parents subsequently removed to Chatham County, North Carolina. His religious life did not begin until 1802, when he was baptized by Rev. Isaac Hicks, and united with the Holly Springs Baptist church, in Wake County. Here he was ordained in 1803. Many parts of the country were at that time destitute of religious privileges, and Mr. Daniel devoted himself extensively to missionary work. He was the first missionary, or, at least, one of the first missionaries, of the North Carolina Baptist Benevolent Society, and in its service he visited Raleigh, where, in 1812, he organized the First Baptist church in that place. Of this church he was twice pastor. But he loved missionary work. As one has said, "His was a missionary heart, a missionary tongue, and a missionary hand." In 1833, he wrote: "During the thirty years of my ministry I have traveled about sixty thousand miles, preached about five thousand sermons, and baptized more than fifteen hundred people. Of that number many now are ministers, twelve of whom are men of distinguished talents and usefulness." His labors extended into Virginia, Mississippi and Tennessee. His ability as a preacher and his evangelistic zeal attracted to him large audiences, and his declaration of God's Word was in demonstration of the Spirit and with power. He died in Paris, Tennessee, September 14, 1840.

His baptismal hymn, above referred to, first appeared in the "Dover Selection" (1828). It was included in "Winchell's Watts " (1832), with the last two stanzas omitted. In the "Service of Song" (1871) the fifth stanza is omitted. In Dossey's "Choice" (1833) there is a hymn of two stanzas, written by Mr. Daniel, commencing

This morning let my praise arise,

and also the following hymn

The time will surely come,
When all the ransomed race.
With angels shall go shouting home,
To meet their Savior's face.

The church of God on earth,
As well as those above,
Are sheltered from the storms of wrath,
In robes of dying love.

No trials that they meet

Shall rob them of their rest;

For Jesus makes them all complete

In his own righteousness.

All hail, thou conquering King!

Come quickly from above,

And all thy chosen race shall sing

Thy free, redeeming love.

JOSEPH B. COOK 1775-1833

In the third edition of Dossey's "Choice" — published in 1830, and the earliest edition I have seen—are ten hymns by Mr. Cook, of which the first lines are as follows:

"Bought with the Savior's precious blood,"

"With reverence we would now appear,"

"Repent, repent, the Baptist cries,"

"Jesus, we own thy sovereign sway,"

"Filled with distress, the fruit of sin,"

"Hail, joyful morn, which ushered in,"

"Thou sacred Spirit, heavenly Dove,"

"Up to thy throne, O God of love,"

"O help thy servant. Lord,"

"The year has past away."

Rev. Joseph B. Cook, a son of Rev. Joseph Cook, was born September, 1775, probably at Dorchester, about eighteen miles from Charleston, S. C. January 6, 1793, he was baptized by Rev. Mr. Botsford, and united with the Welsh Neck Baptist church. In 1794, he entered Brown University, where he was graduated September 6, 1797. Soon after his graduation he became a member of the Baptist church in Charleston, S. C, and by this church he was licensed to preach

March 3, 1799, while employed as a tutor in a private family. Not long after he received a call to the pastorate of the Euhaw Baptist church, of which his father was once pastor; and January 9, 1800, he was ordained in Beaufort, where he preached half of the time. Mr. Cook was clerk of the Charleston Association in 1801, 1802, 1806, and 1820. He was moderator from 1825, to 1832. He was secretary of the South Carolina Baptist Convention in 1822, vice-president from 1826, to 1832. In 1826, he preached the introductory sermon at Greenville, and performed the same service at Robertville, in 1830. For thirty years he was a member of the Charleston Association, and beside the Euhaw and Beaufort churches, he served as pastor of the Camden, Mt. Pisgah, Bethel, and Sumterville churches. Dr. James C. Furman, of Greenville, S. C, who knew Mr. Cook, says:

"Throughout his whole course Mr. Cook bore himself as a good minister of Jesus Christ. His conduct was eminently discreet and blameless. Wherever he went, public opinion extended to him the deference paid to unquestioned piety. Of a gentle spirit, unambitious, constitutionally and by breeding urbane, he silently evoked the virtues of which his life was an exemplification. In his sermons no novel illustrations and no surprising combinations of familiar conceptions gave brilliancy to his presentations of the truth. He seemed to speak in the same spirit in which John wrote: "I have not written unto you because ye know not the truth, but because ye know it.' His spirit and manner were deeply reverential, and in his feelings toward his hearers there was a mellow earnestness, which often expressed itself in quiet tears. There was a smooth rhythmical flow in his speaking; the same as is apparent in his hymns."

WILLIAM DOSSEY 1780-1853

Very little now is known concerning Rev. William Dossey, the compiler of Dossey's "Choice," a hymn book published about the year 1820, and extensively used in some of the southern states. Virginia was his birthplace, and he was ordained in Halifax county, Va., in July, 1803. He lived for a time with Rev. William Creath, who was his theological teacher. Removing to North Carolina, he engaged in pastoral work, and here he married Mary E. Outlaw, of Bertie. Subsequently he removed to South Carolina. In the records of the Welsh Neck Baptist church, at

Society Hill, S. C, occurs the following entry, under date of June 3, 1813: "Rev. Wm. Dossey, of North Carolina, having occasionally visited this place, was unanimously called to the pastoral office of this church." This call was renewed in September following. Under date of February 5, 1814, there is this record: "Rev. Wm. Dossey, who had been called to the pastoral office, was with us this day, and on presenting letters of recommendation and dismission from a sister church in North Carolina for himself and Mrs. Mary Eliza Dossey, his wife, they were cordially received into the fellowship of the church." In 1817, he was clerk of the Charleston Association. In 1828, he preached the introductory sermon at the South Carolina Baptist Convention, held at Minervaville; text, Acts ii. 42. When the Welsh Neck Association was formed of churches connected with the Charleston Association, Mr. Dossey was the first moderator. He was moderator from 1832, to 1834, inclusive. For nearly twenty years Mr. Dossey served the Welsh Neck church as pastor. January 4, 1834, a letter of dismission was granted to him and his wife to join the Cheraw church. He was with this church only a short time, and then removed to Alabama, where he settled on a plantation, and preached to a few churches in the vicinity of Shiloh, Marengo County. He died in 1853, aged seventy-three years, at his home, which was known as "Laurel Hill."

Rev. John Stout, pastor of the Welsh Neck church, Society Hill, writes under date of April 5, 1887: "Concerning Elder William Dossey, our oldest people can only tell me that he came to this church from North Carolina. He was then an elderly man, of fine address, very dignified carriage, fluent in speech, very earnest and strong in preaching, full of zeal in evangelistic work, in which he had marked success. Educated preachers did not abound in this region in his day, and his sermons commanded attention. He was unquestionably the strongest and most effective preacher of his time in eastern South Carolina. He was a man of sterling character, and exercised a superior influence socially. I have learned that he was rather arbitrary, especially toward the close of his ministry here; but old people now living speak of him as a man universally honored, as a pastor beloved. Many of his hymns, all indeed that are not designated as from others, he composed himself. I am told that he had a remarkably powerful and melodious voice, and that he was very fond of singing."

More than one hundred hymns in the "Choice" were written by Mr. Dossey. Of these a few have been transferred to other collections. The following is number 260:

O sinners, to the Savior go!
Pour forth your ardent cries;
Let streams of sacred sorrow flow
From all your weeping eyes.

Your sins have made the Savior bleed,
Have pierced his wounded side;
Have crowned with thorns his sacred head;
For you he bled and died.

'T is sin that to destruction leads,
"With poison strews the path;
Now lift to Christ your guilty heads,
And conquer sin by faith.

He that in Christ the Lord believes
Shall sin and hell outdo;
Who Christ the conqueror receives
Shall be a conqueror too.

Faith in his name the dead awakes,
And makes the slothful move;
'T is faith that Satan's kingdom shakes,
The faith that works by love.

Arise I believer, from the earth,
The conquering shield put on;
Display the power of living faith,—
March on and take the crown.

JESSE L. HOLMAN 1783-1842

Hon. Jesse L. Holman was born in Mercer County, Ky., October 22, 1783. When he was sixteen years of age he united with the Clear Creek Baptist church. For his life-work he directed his attention to the profession of law, and was admitted to the bar in Newcastle. On account of his opposition to slavery, he crossed the Ohio river, and made his home in Indiana, on a bluff to which he gave the name Verdestan, and where he continued to reside during the remainder of his life. In 1814, he was elected a member of the territorial legislature, and near the close of the same year he was made presiding judge for his district. Under the state government, in 1816, he was appointed a judge of the supreme court, a position which he filled with honor fourteen years. In 1831, he was a candidate for United States senator, and was defeated by a single vote. Four years later he was appointed United States district judge for Indiana, and in this office he continued until his death, March 28, 1842.

Mr. Holman took a deep interest in missions, Sunday-schools, Bible and temperance work. In 1834, he was ordained, and on his circuits he frequently addressed large audiences upon topics connected with, these enterprises. For many years he was a vice president of the American Sunday-school Union. He was also president of the Western Baptist Publication and Sunday-school Society. For five years he was president of the Indiana Baptist Convention. He was also, from its organization, a member of the Indiana Baptist Education Society. His was an earnest, consecrated life, and he died at peace with his fellow-men and with God.

In "Hymns, Psalms, and Spiritual Songs," compiled by Rev. Absalom Graves, 2d ed., 1829 (the first edition was published in 1825), is a hymn (263) by Mr. Holman, consisting of nine stanzas. It also appears in Miller's "Psalms, Hymns and Spiritual Songs" (30th ed., 1842), Buck's "Baptist Hymn Book" (1842), and some other collections, but only six of the nine stanzas are inserted. The hymn is as follows:

> Lord, in thy presence here we meet,
>
> May we in thee be found;
>
> O, make the place divinely sweet;

O, let thy grace abound.

Today the order of thy house
We would in peace maintain;
We would renew our solemn vows,
And heavenly strength regain.

Thy Spirit, gracious Lord, impart,
Our faith and hope increase;
Display thy love in every heart,
And keep us all in peace.

Let no discordant passions rise,
To mar the work of love;
But hold us in those heavenly ties,
That bind the saints above.

With harmony and union bless,
That we may own to thee
How good, how sweet, how pleasant it is
When brethren all agree.

May Zion's good be kept in view,
And bless our feeble aim,
That all we undertake to do,
May glorify thy name.

May every heart be now prepared
To do thy high commands,
And may the pleasures of the Lord
Be prospered in our hands.

Of those who thy salvation know

Add to our feeble few;

And may that holy number grow,

Like drops of morning dew.

Work in us by thy gracious sway,

And make thy work appear,

That all may feel, and all may say,

The Lord indeed is here.

Another hymn (79) by Mr. Holman, in the same collection, consists of eight stanzas, and commences,

Ho! all ye sons of sin and woe.

ELISHA CUSHMAN 1788-1838

Rev. Elisha Cushman, a lineal descendant of Robert Cushman, one of the Pilgrim Fathers, was born in Kingston, Mass., May 2, 1788. He learned the carpenter's trade, and' continued in that employment until his conversion, in his twentieth year. After a somewhat severe struggle over the question of duty, he entered upon the work of the Christian ministry, and was licensed by the Kingston Baptist church, of which he had become a member. For a short time he studied under the direction of his pastor, Rev. Samuel Glover, and preached in neighboring villages. Then, for about a year, he supplied the Baptist church in Grafton, and, in 1811, he assisted Rev. Mr. Cornell, in Providence, R. I. In the following year he supplied the Baptist church in Hartford, Conn., and having at length been called to the pastorate of the church, he was ordained June 10, 1813. He served this church as pastor until 1825, and during this time was prominent in all matters pertaining to the interests of the denomination throughout the state. He was the first editor of "The Christian Secretary," established in 1822. In 1825, he accepted a call to the pastorate of the New Market Street Baptist church in Philadelphia. Here he remained four years, and then returned to Connecticut, and preached in Stratfield, a parish in the town of Fairfield, until 1831, when he accepted a call to the pastorate of the First Baptist church in New Haven. In 1835, he removed to Plymouth, Mass., where, in 1838, on account of increasing ill health, he closed his pastoral labors, and returned to Hartford for the purpose of resuming his position as editor of "The Christian Secretary." He was soon, however, obliged to lay aside his pen, and he died in Hartford, October 26, 1838.

Rev. Robert Turnbull, d.d., in a sketch of Mr. Cushman, says his preaching was simple, instructive, and often eloquent. His voice was highly musical, and adapted itself with the greatest ease to the varying moods of his mind and heart. Sometimes he indulged in quaint turns of thought and expression, and not unfrequently enlivened his discourses by appropriate anecdotes and figurative illustrations. He had a poetical turn, and in his preaching made great use of the more imaginative and striking phrases of Holy Writ.

Three hymns, written by Mr. Cushman, are included in "Select Hymns," published in Hartford, Conn., in 1836, viz.,

"Great Redeemer, let thy presence,"

"Hark the voice of injured Justice,"

and the following, which is the first hymn in the collection:

Great Fount of Beings! Mighty Lord
Of all this wondrous frame!
Produced by thy creating word
The world from nothing came.

Thy voice sent forth the high command—
It was instantly obeyed;
And through thy goodness all things stand,
Which by thy power were made.

Lord! for thy glory shine the whole;
They all reflect thy light;
For this in course the planets roll,
And day succeeds the night.

For this the earth its produce yields,
For this the waters flow:
And blooming plants adorn the fields,
And trees aspiring grow.

Inspired with praise, our minds pursue
This wise and noble end,
That all we think, and all we do,
Shall to thy glory tend.

ADONIRAM JUDSON 1788-1850

There is no name dearer to American Baptists than that of Adoniram Judson, the pioneer missionary. Dr. Judson was born August 9, 1788, in Maiden, Mass., where his father, Rev. Adoniram Judson, was pastor of the Congregational church. In 1804, he entered the sophomore class in Brown University, and in 1807, he was graduated with the highest honors of his class. The year following his graduation he taught a private school in Plymouth, Mass., where his father was then residing as pastor of the Third Congregational church. At the close of the year he set out on a tour through the northern states. During his college course he had accepted -views hostile to Christianity, but the sudden death of a skeptical classmate, the knowledge of which came to him under peculiar circumstances soon after he commenced his journey, changed the current of his thoughts, and abandoning his purpose to travel, he returned home, and devoted himself to a careful study of the claims of Christianity. For a short time he was engaged in teaching in Boston. He then entered Andover Theological Seminary as a special student, for the purpose of prosecuting still further his inquiries. These at length resulted in a hearty acceptance of Christ as his Savior, and he united with his father's church at Plymouth, May 28, 1809.

In the following month he received and declined an appointment as tutor in Brown University. God had other purposes concerning him. In September, by reading Buchanan's "Star in the East," he was led to consider the work of foreign missions, and in February, 1810, he resolved to consecrate himself to this work. Other young men in the seminary at Andover, who, while in Williams College, had pledged themselves to missionary service, were in sympathy with him. Judson completed his course at Andover, in September, 1810. As there was no foreign missionary society at that time in the United States, Judson wrote to the officers of the London Missionary Society, and received an invitation to visit England, and confer with them. At the meeting of the General Association of Massachusetts, in June, 1810, the subject of foreign missions was considered, and it was thought that an arrangement could be made which would render this step unnecessary. Disappointed in this, Judson sailed for England, January 11, 1811. The vessel was captured by a French privateer, and Judson was imprisoned at Bayonne, but he was soon released, and May 6, he arrived in London. Having conferred with the officers of the London Missionary Society, by whom he was favorably received, he sailed for New York. At a meeting of the American Board of Commissioners for Foreign Missions, at Worcester, Mass., September 18, 1811, Judson and his associates were advised not to place themselves under the direction of the London Missionary Society, and the Board accepted Judson, Newell, Nott and Hall as their own missionaries, and pledged themselves to undertake their support.

On his arrival he made Rangoon his home, and here he continued his missionary labors until the autumn of 1849, when disease compelled him to relinquish them. He then took a short sea-voyage in order to recruit his failing strength, but without obtaining the boon he sought he returned to Mauhnain. In April, 1850, another sea-voyage was recommended, and with a single attendant, his wife being too ill to accompany him, Dr. Judson set sail for the Isle of France. But he continued to grow weaker, and April 12, nine days after the embarkation at Mauhnain, he died, and was buried in the ocean, latitude thirteen degrees north, longitude ninety-three degrees east.

Only occasionally was Dr. Judson accustomed to give his thoughts a poetical dress. Tender lines he "Addressed to an Infant Daughter, Twenty Days Old, in the Condemned Prison at Ava." "They were composed in my mind at the time," said Dr. Judson, "and afterward written down." The following versification of the Lord's Prayer, which is found in "The Psalmist" and other collections, was composed in the same place a few weeks later. "It illustrates," says Dr. Edward Judson, in his admirable life of his father, "the nature of the subjects which occupied the thoughts of the missionary during this long protracted agony. It is comprised in fewer words than the original Greek, and contains only two more than the common translation:

Our Father, God, who art in heaven,
All hallowed be thy name;
Thy kingdom come, thy will be done
In earth and heaven the same.

Give us this day our daily bread;
And, as we those forgive
Who sin against us, so may we
Forgiving grace receive.

Into temptation lead us not;
From evil set us free;
The kingdom, power, and glory, Lord,
Ever belong to thee.

WILLIAM C. BUCK 1790-1872

Rev. William C. Buck was born in Shenandoah (now Warren) County, Virginia, August 23, 1790. His early years were spent on his father's farm. In his seventeenth year he was baptized, and united with the Water Lick Baptist church. His thoughts were early directed to the Christian ministry, and in 1812, he was ordained pastor of the church of which he was a member. In the war between the United States and Great Britain, 1812-1815, he served as a lieutenant. In 1820, he made his way to Union County, Kentucky, where for many years he was engaged in missionary work. In 1836, he accepted a call to the pastorate of the First Baptist church in Louisville. Not long after he aided in the organization of the East Baptist church. He was also editor of "The Baptist Banner and Western Pioneer." In 1851, he was elected secretary of the Bible Board of the Southern Baptist Convention. This position he held until March, 1854, when he was called to the pastorate of the Baptist church in Columbus, Miss. In May, 1857, he became pastor of the Baptist church in Greensborough, Ala. In the following year he served the Baptist church in Selma. Subsequently, until the outbreak of the civil war, he published "The Baptist Correspondent" at Marion, Ala. Then he became a missionary in the Confederate army. In 1864, he was appointed superintendent of the Orphan's Home at Lauderdale Springs, Miss. He also had the pastoral oversight of the Sharon church. In 1866, he removed to Texas, where he continued to labor for the Master, until his death at Waco, May 18, 1872.

Gen. Mason Brayman, who knew Mr. Buck during his residence at Louisville, says: "Mr. Buck was robust in constitution, of wonderful force of character, full of enterprise and hard work. He was an eloquent and impressive preacher, and the first to set on foot in Kentucky the China mission." His published works were "The Philosophy of Religion" and "The Science of Life." In 1842, with the purpose of giving to the Baptists of the south and west a better hymn book than any then in use in those parts of the country, he published "The Baptist Hymn Book." In the preface he says: "It was commenced upon my knees, and in every stage of my labors, assistance has been sought from on high." It comprised one thousand and eighty nine hymns, eight hundred and seventy eight in the first part and two hundred and eleven in the second. Of these, five were written by Mr. Buck,

"Great God, our thought of thee,"

"Gracious Lord, hast thou redeemed me?"

O shout! for the day of the Lord,"

"Alone in the world though a pilgrim I roam,'

and the following:

Behold, O Lord, at thy command.
Thy saints assembled from afar,
To send thy word to every land;
O! condescend to hear our prayer!

O fire our souls with holy zeal;
Dissolve our hearts in love to thee;
And teach us, as thyself, to feel
For fallen man, wherever he be.

From every continent and isle.
From every nation on the earth,
We hear the dying sinner's wail,
And long to send the gospel forth.

A thousand hearts to thee are bowed;
A thousand hands with thine employ;
O come and help us, blessed God,
The powers of darkness to destroy.
Gird on thy sword, victorious Prince,
Thy blood-stained banner wide display;
Haste on thy conquests, King of Peace,
And bring thy glorious latter day.

NATHANIEL COLVER 1794-1870

"A noble, great-souled, loving man " was Dr. Rollin H. Neale's testimony concerning Nathaniel Colver, D.D., who was born in Orwell, Vt., May 10, 1794. When he was between one and two years of age his father removed to Champlain, in northern New York, and later, when he was about sixteen years of age, to West Stockbridge, Mass. Subsequently he was apprenticed to a tanner and currier. His conversion occurred when he was twenty-three years of age, and he was baptized June 9, 1817, by Rev. John M. Peck, then on a visit to West Stockbridge. The proposal of his brethren that he should devote himself to the work of the ministry he met at first with a firm refusal, on account of his conviction of his personal unfitness; but he afterward yielded, and he was ordained at West Clarendon, Vt., in 1819. There he labored as pastor of the Baptist church two years. He was afterward pastor at Fort Covington, N. Y., and later, at Kingsbury, Fort Ann and Union Village. In 1834, he became pastor of the Baptist church in Holmesburgh, near Philadelphia, Penn., but a few months later he returned to Union Village, where he remained as pastor of the church until 1838. That year was spent in the service of the American Antislavery Society, and he lectured in many places in New England. It was in this way that he became acquainted with the brethren who organized what is now the Union Temple Baptist church, which, since 1843, has worshiped in Tremont Temple, Boston. Timothy Gilbert was the leading spirit of this enterprise, and he found in Nathaniel Colver a true yoke-fellow. Here Dr. Colver found a field fitted for his peculiar gifts, and here he preached with growing power. He was in sympathy with the prominent reforms of the day, and as pastor of Tremont Temple he was in the very heart of the antislavery agitation.

In 1852, he resigned his Boston pastorate, and accepted a call to the pastorate of the Baptist church at South Abington, Mass. Here he remained until April, 1853, when he accepted a call to the pastorate of the First Baptist church in Detroit, Mich. In 1856, he became pastor of the First Baptist church in Cincinnati, Ohio. Soon after, Granville College, now Denison University, conferred upon him the degree of doctor of divinity. In 1861, he removed to Chicago, to take the pastorate of the Tabernacle, now the Second Baptist church. While in Chicago he took a deep interest in the organization of what is now the Theological Seminary at Morgan Park. In 1867-70, he was president of the Freedman's Institute, at Richmond, Va., and laid the foundations of the excellent work since carried on by Dr. Corey and his assistants. On account of failing health Dr. Colver returned to Chicago, where he died, September 25, 1870.

In the " Christian Melodist," compiled by Dr. Banvard, and published in 1848, are sixteen hymns by Dr. Colver. The one (198) which is still most in use, having been transferred to other collections, is the following:

Come, Lord, in mercy come again,
With thy converting power;
The fields of Zion thirst for rain,
O send a gracious shower!

Our hearts are filled with sore distress,
While sinners all around
Are pressing on to endless death.
And no relief is found.

Dear Savior! come with quickening power,
Thy mourning people cry;
Salvation bring in mercy's hour,
Nor let the sinner die.

Once more let converts throng thy house,
And shouts of victory raise;
Then shall our griefs be turned to joy,
And sighs to songs of praise.

THOMAS B. RIPLEY 1795-1876

Rev. Thomas B. Ripley, a younger brother of Henry J. Ripley, d.d., long a professor in Newton Theological Institution, was born in Boston, Mass., November 20, 1795, and received his name, Thomas Baldwin, in honor of the well known pastor of his parents. When about fifteen years of age he united with Dr. Baldwin's church, and in the fall of that year, 1810, he entered Brown University. After his graduation, in 1814, he went to Philadelphia, where he pursued theological studies under Dr. William Staughton. Returning to Boston in 1815, he was invited in the fall of that year to supply the pulpit of the Baptist church in Portland, Maine. He was not then quite twenty years of age, but his labors were so much appreciated that after a few months he was called to the pastorate of the church and in the following year, July 24, 1816, he was ordained as pastor of the church. Dr. Baldwin preaching the sermon. A very extensive revival of religion followed, and more than seventy united with the church. He enjoyed the friendship and companionship of the sainted Payson, whose church was near his own. Here he remained twelve years, when he accepted the pastorate of the First Baptist church in Bangor. Leaving Bangor in 1834, he became for a short time the pastor of the Baptist church in Woburn, Mass., and later he supplied the pulpit of the First Baptist church in Providence, R. I. We next find him in Nashville, Tenn., where he was engaged in preaching, and giving instruction in a young ladies' seminary. He remained in Nashville until 1852, and then returned to New England.

About this time occurred the death of his only son, a young man of much promise, a graduate of Brown University, and at that time a student in Newton Theological Institution. It was an affliction hard to bear, but not a murmur passed the good man's lips. And so he came back to Portland, where not long after he was appointed city missionary. It was a service for which he had many excellent qualifications. His very presence in any place was a Christian benediction. He had a heart full of tenderest sympathy for the sick among the children of toil and want, and it was a pleasure for him to minister to them. Almost to the close of life, when bowed with age, and hardly able to leave his home on account of his infirmities, he would go forth on errands of mercy, thinking not of himself, but only of others. "When death came, May 4, 1876, he was ready to meet the summons. He had not laid up for himself earthly treasures. Indeed, his citizenship had long been in heaven.

On them thy Holy Spirit pour,
While they thy sacred footsteps trace,
Make this to them a heavenly hour;
O fill their hearts with thy rich grace.

Buried with thee, may they arise
To live a life divinely new;
To serve thee here, till in the skies
Thy unveiled presence they shall view.

And may each one of them at last

Appear before thy radiant throne,

Their golden crowns before thee cast,

And ever praise the great Three One.

Rev. F. M. Bird, the well known hymnologist, suggests that hymns 24, 113, 136 and 169, in this second edition, were a}so written by Mr. Ripley at least, they are not found elsewhere.

SAMUEL W. LYND 1796-1876

Samuel W. Lyxd, son of Samuel Lynd, a prosperous silk merchant in Philadelphia, Penn., was born in that city, December 23, 1796. He received a good classical, though not a collegiate, education. At the age of twenty-four he was converted, and was baptized by Dr. William Staughton, whose eldest daughter, Leonora, he married. He studied theology with Dr. Staughton, but the failure of his voice compelled him to delay entrance upon the work of the Christian ministry, and for several years he and Mrs. Lynd, a most efficient helper, conducted a school for young ladies in Baltimore. In January, 1824, Mr. Lynd became pastor of the Navy Yard J3aptist church, Washington, D. C. January 1, 1831, he accepted the pastorate of the Sixth Street, now the Ninth Street Baptist church in Cincinnati, Ohio, and he continued in that relation until December, 1845, when he accepted a call to the pastorate of the Second Baptist church in St. Louis, Mo. In 1848, he became president of the Western Baptist Theological Seminary, at Covington, Ky., and subsequently of Georgetown College, Ky. In 1853, he removed to a farm near Lockport, 111, but a few years afterward he became pastor of the Fourth Baptist church, Chicago, 111. Subsequently, for a while, he was pastor of the Mt. Auburn Baptist church, Cincinnati, Ohio. About 1863-4, he returned to Lockport, 111, where he died, June 17, 1876.

Dr. Lynd was a man of great personal worth, and probably did more than any other one man to build up the Baptist cause in Cincinnati and vicinity. In his own church he was a power.

He found it a little band of nineteen members, and left it with a membership of about five hundred, having vainly urged it to colonize, saying to his brethren that if they did not di vide, the devil would divide them, a task which the latter soon after undertook with considerable success. Dr. Lynd took a prominent part in the controversy growing out of the slavery question, also of Campbellism (wrestling with Alexander Campbell in the columns of "The Millennial Harbinger," conducted by the latter), and standing firmly for missions, when the Miami Association was rent by the anti-mission element. He was a member of the committee which approved and commended "The Psalmist" to the Baptist churches of the country, and he preached the sermon before the Missionary Union in Philadelphia, in 1844.

Hail, brethren, while together met,
Welcome your counsels and your prayers;
May kindred objects love beget.
And love disperse our anxious cares.

May every heart with thanks abound,
And courage take from mutual aims;
May Zion's interests dear be found
To every breast which truth inflames.

Here may the cause of Christ employ
Our willing hearts and faithful hands;
And all our powers engage with joy
To break the tempter's fatal bands.

May holy zeal our souls inspire
And self in noble deeds be lost;
Christ and his cross our bosoms fire,
Glory to God our only boast.

O Lord, thy blessing we implore;

On this alone our hope relies;

Grant us but this, we ask no more,

No richer boon beneath the skies.

JAMES D. KNOWLES 1798-1838

Prof. James Davis Knowles was born in Providence, R. I., July 6, 1798. His father having died when he was twelve years of age, he was apprenticed to a printer, and acquired a thorough acquaintance with the various departments of work in a printing-office, and also considerable facility in writing for the press. At the age of twenty-one he became a co-editor of "The Rhode Island American." In March, 1820, he was baptized by Rev. Dr. Gano, pastor of the First Baptist church, Providence, and in the autumn following, having decided to enter upon the work of the Christian ministry, he was licensed by the church, and entered the Theological Seminary in Philadelphia, of which Dr. William Staughton and Rev. Irah Chase were the professors. In January, 1822, the seminary was united with Columbian College, Washington, D. C, and Mr. Knowles followed his instructors thither, and entered the college. Here he not only pursued the studies of his class with such success that he carried off the highest honors at his graduation, in 1824, but he also edited with ability, during his college course, '^The Columbian Star," a weekly religious paper. After his graduation he was made a tutor in the college, but in the autumn of the following year, having received a call to the pastorate of the Second Baptist church in Boston, then vacant by the death of Dr. Baldwin, he removed to Boston, where he was ordained, December 28, 1825.

Here he remained seven years, and then, on account of impaired health, he resigned, and accepted the professorship of Pastoral Duties and Sacred Rhetoric in Newton Theological Institution, to which he had been previously appointed. The change proved to be a favorable one, and with restored health he devoted himself to the duties of his new position with diligence and success, and at length took upon himself the editorship of "The Christian Review."

On his return from a visit to New York, early in May, 1838, he was stricken down by an attack of confluent small-pox, and died May 9, at the age of forty years. His grave is on the Institution grounds, a little in the rear of Sturtevant Hall. In an account of his death, written by his wife, it is stated: "The day before he left home for his last fatal journey, while passing through the grounds to attend public worship, he observed the springing vegetation, and, with lifted hand, repeated with earnest emphasis these lines of Seattle's:

> Shall I be left forgotten in the dust
>
> When Fate relenting lets the flower revive?
>
> Shall Nature's voice, to man alone unjust,
>
> Bid him, though doomed to perish, hope to live?"

ROBERT W. CUSHMAN 1800-1868

Rev. Robert W. Cushman, d.d., a distinguished preacher and a well known educator, was born in Woolwich, Maine, April 10, 1800. In the death of his parents, in his early years, he met with an irreparable loss. He received a careful training, however, and when sixteen years of age he accepted Christ as his personal Savior. Having in view the work of the Christian ministry, he entered Columbian College, Washington, D. C, where he was graduated in 1825. In August, 1826, he was ordained as pastor of the Baptist church in Poughkeepsie, N. Y. Here he remained three years. Then he removed to Philadelphia, where he established the "Cushman Collegiate Institute," for the education of young ladies. In 1841, he accepted the pastorate of the Bowdoin Square Baptist church, Boston, a position which he retained six years, attracting large congregations. He then removed to Washington, D. C, where he established a school for young ladies similar to that with which he was connected in Philadelphia. After a few years he returned to Boston, and became principal of the Mount Vernon Ladies' School. At the same time he supplied the pulpit of the Baptist church in Charlestown. For awhile, also, he gave instruction in sacred rhetoric at Newton Theological Institution. Subsequently he retired to Wakefield, Mass., where he spent the closing years of his life. He died April 7, 1868.

Prof. George H. Whittemore, who listened to Dr. Cushman during his pastorate at Bowdoin Square, and greatly admired him, says: "There was a dignity, impressiveness and elegance about his person, bearing, and diction, which I can never forget, though I cannot recall the matter as well as the manner of his efforts. I remember to have heard very high praise bestowed upon his production 'A Pure Christianity the World's only Hope.' He was an exceedingly sensitive person, and some asperity of temper and speech has at times been ascribed to him, I believe; but this shadow is dashed into the sketch of one whose memory I love and venerate to moderate the ideal and exaggerated glow of his image as I always recall it."

Lo! on a mount that Burma rears
To greet the morn in eastern skies,
A sable son of Shem appears,
And westward turns his longing eyes.

No sacrifice the man prepares
For gods of stone, or gods of gold;
But, near his heart he fondly bears
A book, in many a careful fold.

That book contains the words of prayer,
And tells of Christ for sinners slain;
But he has no interpreter
To make its mystic pages plain.
But he has heard of holy men
Who yet should come and pour a ray
Upon the soul of the Karen,
And turn his darkness into day.

The tidings spread, "They're come, they're come
They stand on western shores afar!"
With bounding joy he leaves his horn,

And hastes the word of life to share.

Before him lies the lengthening plain;
Before him rolls the swelling flood;
And on him falls the ceaseless rain;
And near him tigers thirst for blood.

But tigers' howls affright him not;
The wilderness, the swelling flood,
And falling storms are all forgot;
He hastes to seek the unknown God.

And shall he, with no Bible given
To cheer his path, go home again?
Forbid it, loved forbid it, heaven!
We'll haste to bless the dark Karen.

To this hymn is appended the following note: "When the deputation from the Karens in the interior of Burma came to the missionaries to inquire if they had, and could give to them, ' the word of the eternal God,' they had in their possession, as an object of religious adoration, a book, which the missionaries, on unfolding, found to be an English Prayer Book."

The first of the three hymns by Dr. Cushman, found in the "Baptist Harmony," was included in Dr. S. S. Cutting's "Hymns for the Vestry" (1841), and Dr. A. D. Gillette's "Hymns for Social Meetings" (1843).

CHARLES THURBER 1803-1886

Hon. Charles Thurber was born January 2, 1803, in Brookfield, Mass., where his father, Bev. Laban Thurber, was pastor of the Baptist church. When twenty years of age he entered the freshman class in Brown University, and was graduated in 1827, having as classmates Hon. John H. Clifford, Judge Mellen Chamberlain, Ebenezer Thresher, and other men distinguished in public life. His commencement part was a poem entitled "The Fall of Mexico." For four years after his graduation, he was preceptor of Milford Academy. Then, for eight years, he was master of the Latin Grammar School at Worcester, Mass. He now directed his attention to mercantile pursuits, and after twelve years devoted to business in Worcester he retired with a comfortable fortune. During his residence in Worcester he served as County Commissioner four years, and also as a member of the Massachusetts Senate. Upon retiring from business he spent six years in Europe. After his return to this country he made his home in Brooklyn, N. Y. In 1853, he was made a trustee of Brown University. He was a Baptist church member fifty-five years, and closed his life at Nashua, N. H., November 7, 1886, at the ripe age of eighty-four years, honored and beloved by a very wide circle of friends.

Mr. Thurber was a man of literary tastes and acquirements. Frequently he gave expression to his thoughts in verse, and he was a favorite poet on commencement occasions, viz.: at Union College, Denison University, the University of Lewisburg (now Bucknell University), Middletown University, the University of Rochester, Madison University twice, Colby University three times. Brown University many times, and other literary institutions. He also wrote a large number of songs and hymns for festal occasions and religious gatherings. The following Home Missionary Hymn, written by Mr. Thurber, is from the "Baptist Praise Book" (1872):

> From yonder Rocky Mountains,
> With summits white and cold;
> From California's fountains,
> That pour down virgin gold;

> From every western prairie,
> From every mystic mound,

They call on us to carry
The gospel's joyful sound.

Oh! shall we close our bosoms,
While every breath 's a cry?
While brothers drop like blossoms,
And there forever die?

Oh! Christian, rest not, sleep not,
But pray and toil and fight,
Till those who're weeping, weep not,
And darkness turns to light.

Then, when enthroned in glory
With Jesus' ransomed fold.
We tell Love's wondrous story.
Upon our harps of gold

Each effort that we're making
Will sweeten heaven's employ,
And every cross we're taking.
Add rapture to its joy.

JOHN NEWTON BROWN 1803-1868

Rev. John Newton Brown, d.d., is now best known in connection with the New Hampshire Declaration of Faith, which has been very extensively adopted by Baptist churches in different parts of the country. Dr. Brown was chairman of the committee which presented the

Declaration, and performed valuable service in its preparation. He was born in New London, Conn., June 29, 1803. When fourteen years of age he was baptized at Hudson, N. Y. Having had his thoughts turned toward the work of the ministry, he entered Hamilton Theological Seminary, and was graduated in 1823. He was ordained at Buffalo, in 1828. A year later he removed to Providence, R. I., to assist Rev. Dr. Gano, pastor of the First Baptist church. In 1827, he became pastor of the Baptist church in Maiden, Mass. In 1829, he removed to Exeter, N. H., where he had accepted the pastorate of the Baptist church. In 1838, he became associate professor of theology and pastoral relations in the New Hampton Literary and Theological Institution, at New Hampton, N. H., and discharged the duties of this position until 1845, when he became pastor of the Baptist church in Lexington, Va. On account of ill health he was compelled to withdraw from the pastorate in 1849, and he then became connected with the American Baptist Publication Society as editorial secretary. He was also editor of "The Christian Chronicle" and "The National Baptist." During his residence at Exeter he edited his "Encyclopedia of Religious Knowledge," which was published in Brattleborough, in 1835, and republished in England.

There are also three hymns by Dr. Brown in Phineas Stowe's "Ocean Melodies":
"Come sinner! at our Lord's command,"
"And wilt thou stoop. Great God, so low,"
"O Thou! the high and lofty One."

The following hymn by Dr. Brown is found in "The Psalmist" and other collections:
Go, spirit of the sainted dead.
Go to thy longed-for, happy home
The tears of man are o'er thee shed;
The voice of angels bids thee come.
If life be not in length of days,
In silvered locks and furrowed brow,
But living to the Savior's praise,
How few have lived so long as thou!

Though earth may boast one gem the less,

May not even heaven the richer be?

And myriads on thy footsteps press,

To share thy blest eternity

SARAH B. JUDSON 1803-1845

In Urwick's Selection, Dublin, 1829, appeared a fine hymn of four stanzas, without the author's name, commencing

Proclaim the lofty praise

Of him who once was slain,

But now is risen, through endless days

To live and reign.

He lives and reigns on high,

Who bought us with his blood,

Enthroned above the farthest sky,

Our Savior, God.

This hymn was transferred to "The Psalmist" (1843), ascribed to Urwick's Collection. By Dr. Hatfield, the well known hymnologist, this hymn is ascribed to Mrs. Sarah B. Judson, but on what grounds I am not informed.

Sarah Boardman Judson, the second wife of Adoniram Judson, and the eldest daughter of Ralph and Abiah Hall, was born in Alstead, N. H., November 4, 1803. Her parents subsequently removed to Danvers, Mass., and then to Salem, Mass., wdiere, in her seventeenth year, she became a member of the First Baptist church, of which Dr. Lucius Bolles was pastor. The work of Christian missions was prominent in the thoughts of the members of that church. Dr. Bolles, as early as 1812, had organized in Salem a society to aid Dr. Carey in translating and publishing the Scriptures, and the young convert was impressed with a desire to follow Judson and his associates, who, a few years before, had sailed from Salem to engage in missionary work on heathen shores. The way was at length opened; and as the wife of George Dana Boardman, to whom she was married July 4, 1825, she embarked July 19, following, for Calcutta, where they arrived December 13. Here, on account of the Burmese war, they were obliged to remain until March, 1827. They then proceeded to Amherst, shortly after to Maulmain, and later to Tavoy. Meanwhile three children were born to them, of whom only one, George Dana, survived the perils of infancy. Mr. Boardman died at Tavoy, February 11, 1831. "When I first stood by the grave of my husband," wrote Mrs. Boardman, "I thought I must go home with George. But these poor, inquiring and Christian Karens, and the school boys, and the Burmese Christians, would then be left without any one to instruct them; and the poor, stupid Tavoyans would go on in the road to death, with no one to warn them of their danger. How then, oh, how can I go? We shall not be separated long. A few more years, and we shall all meet in yonder blissful world, whither those we love have gone before us."

Mrs. Judson early evinced skill in poetical composition. Among other productions written when she was thirteen years of age is a "Versification of David's Lament over Saul and Jonathan," commencing

> The beauty of Israel forever is fled,
> And low lie the noble and strong;
> Ye daughters of music encircle the dead,
> And chant the funeral sons;

These early lines were amended by the cultivated taste of later years, and in their altered dress appear in Mrs. Judson's "Life." A later poem, entitled "Come Over and Help Us," and written after she had become interested in Christian missions, voices a plea from the heathen world, of which the following is the first stanza,

> Ye, on whom the glorious Gospel
> Shines with beams serenely bright,
> Pity the deluded nations
> Wrapped in shades of dismal night;
> Ye, whose bosoms glow with rapture

At the precious hopes they bear;

Ye, who know a Savior's mercy.

Listen to our earnest prayer!

LEVI KNEELAND 1803-1834

Rev. Levi Kneeland was a native of Masonville, N. Y., and was born November 7, 1803. Converted at the age of fifteen, he united with the Baptist church in Masonville, and when twenty years of age he was licensed to preach. In 1824, he entered Hamilton Literary and Theological Institution, where he remained four years. Having been called to the pastorate of the Baptist church in Packerville. Conn., he was ordained in that place, October 8, 1828. Earnest, devout, wholly consecrated to his work, he labored for the salvation of souls, and during the six years of his ministry, he baptized more than three hundred converts. Greatly lamented, he died at Packerville, August 23, 1834, aged thirty-one years.

In "Select Hymns" (Hartford, 1836) is the following hymn by Mr. Kneeland:

Christian worship — how inviting

Is the social praying band!

Happy concert thrice delighting,

Bound to Canaan's holy land.

See how joyful they assemble

At the consecrated hourly

How they heaven's host resemble

While they God Most High adore!

See them in sweet concert moving,

Each their humble part fulfil!

Bound to love, each other loving,

Thus they do the Savior's will.

Now they bow in adoration

Low before Jehovah's throne,

Giving honor and salvation

To the High and Holy One.

GEORGE B. IDE 1804-1872

Rev. George Ide, d.d., was born in Coventry, Vt., February 17, 1804. His father, Rev. John Ide, was a well known Baptist minister, who early discovered the promise of his son, and aided him in securing a good academic and collegiate education. He was converted in 1824. In 1827, he entered Middlebury College with advanced standing, and was graduated in 1830. During his college course he received a license to preach, and supplied churches in Cornwall, Cambridge, Newport, etc. For awhile after his graduation, he labored as an evangelist in northern Vermont, especially in Derby, Newport, and Passumpsic. In November, 1832, he became pastor of the Baptist church in Brandon, Vt. September 1, 1834, he accepted a call to the pastorate of the First Baptist church in Albany, N. Y. Here he remained a little more than a year only, and then resigned to become pastor of the Federal Street Baptist church (now Clarendon Street), Boston. After a pastorate of a little more than two years, he accepted, in April, 1838, a call to the pastorate of the First Baptist church, Philadelphia, where he remained nearly fifteen years. December 5, 1852, he was called to Springfield, Mass., where he was the beloved pastor of the First Baptist church, until his death. During this period of nearly twenty years, he received calls to other prominent pulpits, but these were declined; and such was his influence in Springfield, and throughout western Massachusetts, that it is doubtful if elsewhere he could have occupied so commanding a position. He died in Springfield, of heart disease, April 16, 1872.

THOMAS U. WALTER 1804-1887

Dr. Thomas U. Walter, an eminent American architect, was born in Philadelphia, Penn., September 4, 1804. His taste for architecture was early evinced, and he pursued an elaborate course of instruction, in order thoroughly to fit himself for the profession in which he achieved so much distinction. He entered upon his life work in his native city. In 1831, his plans for the Philadelphia county buildings were accepted, and two years later, his design for Girard College. This substantial structure, which was fourteen years in building, is not only a monument to the generous founder of the college, but also to the architectural skill of Dr. Walter. The latter' s greatest work, however, was in connection with the extension of the Capitol at Washington. In 1851, he submitted plans for the new structure, with its magnificent dome. The plans, were accepted, and Dr. Walter was appointed by President Fillmore to take charge of the work. He also designed the east and west wing of the Patent Office, the extension of the building occupied by the Post-office Department, the new Treasury Building, and several government buildings in other places. He was also the architect of the old Chapel at Waterville College, now Colby University. In 1849, Madison University conferred upon Mr. Walter the honorary degree of master of arts. In 1855, Bucknell University conferred upon him the degree of doctor of philosophy, and in 1857, Harvard University conferred upon him the degree of doctor of laws.

In the "Baptist Harp," published by the American Baptist Publication Society, in 1849, is the following hymn (414) by Dr. Walter, entitled "Go to Jesus."

Desponding soul, O cease thy we;
Dry lip thy tears, to Jesus go,
In faith's appointed way.
Let not thy unbelieving fears
Still hold thee back —thy Savior hears —
From him no longer stay.

No works of thine can ever impart
A balm to heal thy wounded heart,
Or solid comfort give;
Turn, then, to him who freely gave
His precious blood thy soul to save;

Even now he bids thee live.

Helpless and lost, to Jesus fly!
His power and love are ever nigh
To those who seek his face;
Thy deepest guilt on him was laid,
He bore thy sins, thy ransom paid;
O haste to share his grace.

Dr. Walter died in Philadelphia, October 30, 1887. At the time of his death he was president of the American Institute of Architects.

CAROLINE T. DAYTON 1806-1879

Mrs. Dayton, a daughter of John and Lydia Erving, was born in Concord, Mass., August 5, 1806. Her father removed to Hartford, Conn., when she was but a child, and with the exception of a brief residence in Worcester, Mass., Hartford continued to be her home until her death. For many years her membership was with the First Baptist church in Hartford, but subsequently she became a member of the South Baptist church. She was an earnest, sincere Christian, and her life was one of sacrifice, toil and devotion. Almost her last words were, "I trust in my Savior." She died in Hartford, May 30, 1879, after a long and painful illness.

Two hymns, written by Mrs. Dayton before her marriage,

"Send, O send, the glorious Gospel,"

"This is thine earthly temple, Lord,"

are found in "Select Hymns" (Hartford, 1836). She was also a frequent contributor to the Christian Secretary, Watchman and Reflector, New York Recorder, and other religious journals. The following hymn, written by Mrs. Dayton in 1840, and entitled "Faint, yet Pursuing," was first published in the Christian Secretary:

Look above —the skies are clearing

Higher up the Christian way,

And the promised land is nearer,

And the peace of heavenly day.

Darkest clouds may gather o'er thee,

Angry waves and billows roll.

Still a light will shine before thee,

To illume thy trusting soul.

Look away from earthly pleasures,

To those streams that never dry,

Look above to heavenly treasures,

Up to mansions in the sky.

Earth's false treasures will deceive you,

All her tempting charms decay,

Her polluted streams will grieve you,

And her friendship flee away.

Look above, when snares beset thee.

And when dangers thick abound,

There is one who'll never forget thee.

Who the friend of sinners found.

Higher up, the fields are vernal,

Blooming on in heavenly love,

Joys immortal and eternal

Near the paradise above.

Look above when sorrows pain thee,

In affliction's darkest way,

There is one who can sustain thee.

Give thee strength unto thy day.
Higher up, the clouds are parted,
And the joyous sun appears,
Balm to heal the broken-hearted.
And a hand to wipe thy tears.

When some silken cord is broken,
When thy dearest comforts die,
Look above, some cheering token
Beams upon thee from on high;
Higher up, the way of glory.
Up the steep of Zion's hill
Bethlehem's star will go before thee,
And thy soul shall fear no ill.

Christian, faint not, ne'er grow weary,
Still pursue the narrow way;
Though it oft be rugged — dreary.
It will end in blessed day.
Look above, to crowns of brightness,
Heavenly mansions for the blest,
Spotless robes of pearly whiteness,
To the faithful pilgrim's rest.

JOHN BOWLING 1807-1878

Pavensey, Sussex, England, was the early home of Dr. Dowling, and here he was born. May 12, 1807. Having removed to London, he united with the Eagle Street Baptist church, when he was seventeen years of age. From childhood, he had evinced a great fondness for books, and so rapid was his advancement in his studies, that, when nineteen years old he received an appointment as tutor in the Latin language and literature at a classical institute in London. Two years later he became instructor in Hebrew, Greek, Latin and French in the Buckinghamshire Classical Institute. At length, in 1829, he established a classical boarding-school in Oxfordshire, near Oxford, which he continued until 1832, when, with his family, he turned his face toward the new world. It was his purpose in coming to the United States to engage in the work of the Christian ministry, and November 14, 1832, he was ordained pastor of the Baptist church in Catskill, N. Y. In 1834, he became pastor of the Second Baptist church in Newport, R. I. Two years later, he accepted a call to the pastorate of a church worshiping in Gothic Masonic Hall, New York. He was also for several years pastor of the Broadway church in Hope Chapel. Then he went to Providence, R. L, where he was pastor of the Pine Street Baptist church. In 1844, he became pastor of the Berean Baptist church, Bedford Street, New York. In 1852, he accepted a call to Philadelphia, but returned to the Berean church in 1856. His second pastorate with this church continued twelve years. He subsequently was pastor of the South Baptist church in Newark, N. J., and the South Baptist church in New York city. He received the degree of doctor of divinity from Transylvania University in 1846. His death occurred at Middletown, N. Y., July 4, 1878.

Children of Zion! what harp-notes are stealing
So soft o'er our senses, so soothingly sweet?
'T is the music of angels, their raptures revealing,
That you have been brought to the Holy One's feet.
Children of Zion! we join in their welcome,
'T is sweet to lie low at that blessed retreat.

Children of Zion! no longer in sadness
Refrain from the feast that your Savior hath given;
Come, taste of the cup of salvation with gladness,
And think of the banquet still sweeter in heaven.
Children of Zion! our hearts bid you welcome
To the church of the ransomed, the kingdom of heaven.

Children of Zion! we joyfully hail you

Who've entered the sheepfold through Jesus, the door;

While pilgrims on earth, though the foe may assail you,

Press forward, and soon will the conflict be o'er.

Children of Zion! O, welcome, thrice welcome!

Till we meet, the foe shall oppress you no more.

ABRAM D. GILLETTE 1807-1882

Rev. Abeam D. Gillette, d.d., was born in Cambridge, Washington County, N. Y., September 8, 1807. His father died when he was eleven years of age, and a few months after he entered the service of Major Calvin Jillson, a tanner in Hartford, who subsequently removed to West Granville. While living here, the tanner's clerk, thirsting for an education, availed himself of the advantages of a very flourishing academy. In early life he had become interested in the religion of Christ, and when fourteen years of age it was his purpose, God helping him, to preach the Gospel. It was not until May, 1827, however, that he was baptized, and united with the Baptist church. Soon after he was appointed teacher of a village school, and in the following year his gifts having been recognized by the church he received a license to preach. His desire for a collegiate education led him to Madison University, Hamilton, N. Y., where for a while he supported himself by teaching. But ere long he was compelled to relinquish his studies on account of a disease of the eyes. He then accepted a position as Bible colporteur. Subsequently he was invited to supply the Baptist church in Schenectady. Receiving a call to the pastorate of this little flock, he was ordained September 29, 1831. During the first year of his labors the membership of the church was doubled. Later it became necessary to enlarge the house of worship, and when he left the church at the close of 1834, the sixty members had increased to six hundred.

He now became pastor of the Fifth Baptist church in Philadelphia. With this church he remained until 1838. Shortly after he was called to the pastorate of the newly organized Eleventh Baptist church in the same city. As heretofore, large accessions were the result of his earnest labors. With this church Dr. Gillette remained until 1852, baptizing four hundred and eighty-eight, and receiving by letter five hundred and seventy-two. It was at Dr. Gillette's house in Philadelphia that Dr. Judson, during his visit to that city in 1851, met Miss Emily Chubbuck (Fanny Forester), who afterward became his wife.

During his residence in Philadelphia, Dr. Gillette arranged and edited the minutes of the Philadelphia Baptist Association from its organization in 1707, to 1807,—a most valuable contribution to American Baptist history. In 1843, he published a small hymn book entitled "Hymns for Social Meetings." Of its two hundred and one hymns, twelve were written by Dr. Gillette. One of these is the following missionary hymn:

> Far off beyond the sea, I love
> To see the Gospel heralds go,
> Bearing the news from heaven above.
> Which Jesus brought to earth below.

> May skies above them shine serene,
> May earth beneath them fruitful be.
> May plants of Eden, fresh and green,
> Bloom and regale their pious way.

> Him may they preach, who wont to stray,
> By power oppressed, and mocked by pride,
> A pilgrim on the world's highway,—
> My Lord, the Lamb, the Crucified.

> On heralds, on, and as of old
> The Baptist cleared his Master's way,
> May you demolish sin's stronghold,
> And turn its darkness into day.

May you in preaching wake the strain

Of triumph over sin and death;

Say: Lord the Savior comes to reign;

O, preach him in your dying breath.

WILLIAM HAGUE 1808-1887

For many years Rev. William Hague, d.d., was a prominent figure in the American Baptist pulpit. He was born in Pelham, Westchester County, New York, January 4, 1808. In an interesting sketch of Old Pelham and New Rochelle, in the Magazine of American History, August, 1882, and reprinted in his "'Life Notes," Dr. Hague refers to a visit he had recently made to the home of his childhood. Turning toward the church burial-ground, he sought the grave of his grandparents. "Long shimmering memories were awakened, roused first of all by the sight of the marble that marked the grave of my grandmother, — Sarah Pell, widow of Captain William Bayley,—whose funeral service, ministered in the churchyard by her aged relative, the rector. Rev. Theodosius Bartow, I had attended, with a large family gathering, in the month of March, 1819, being then eleven years of age. The form of the venerable clergyman, in his official robes, at the grave, his bald head uncovered, despite the chill of a heavy snowfall, is vividly remembered now as if it had figured in a scene of yesterday." Here, at Old Pelham, Dr. Hague remained until 1814, when the family removed to New York city. There his school-life commenced, including the preparation for Columbia College. In this way eight years were passed. Afterward he spent a year on a farm, followed by a four months' visit to England. He then entered Hamilton College, and was admitted to the third term of the sophomore year, for which he had made the needful preparation. Here he was graduated in 1826. He then entered Newton Theological Institution, which had recently been established at Newton Center, Mass.

Dr. Hague was graduated at Newton Theological Institution in 1829, and October 20, he was ordained pastor of the Second Baptist church in Utica, N. Y. Here he remained a little more than a year, when he accepted a call to the pastorate of the First Baptist church in Boston. The installation occurred February 3, 1831, Dr. Wayland preaching the sermon. He closed his labors with this church in June, 1837, and July 12, following, he was installed as pastor of the First Baptist church in Providence, R. I. At the second centennial of this church, which occurred November 7, 1839, Dr. Hague preached a memorial discourse, which was published. August 20, 1840, he resigned, and returned to Boston as the pastor of the Federal Street Baptist church. Dr. Hague's subsequent pastorates were at Jamaica Plain, Mass., Newark, N. J., Albany, New York city, N. Y., Chicago, Orange, N. J., and Wollaston, Mass. From the active pastorate of the Wollaston church he retired several years before his death, which occurred suddenly in front of Tremont Temple, Boston, August 1, 1887. Impressive funeral services were held in Tremont Temple on the following Thursday, and were attended by a large concourse of people.

In Dr. S. S. Cutting's "Hymns for the Vestry and the Fireside" is a hymn written by Dr. Hague. It is the only hymn he ever published, and probably the only hymn he ever wrote. The title is "Divine Pleadings":

Hark! sinner, hark! God speaks to thee:
How shall I let thee go?
How shall I thy destruction see,
And all thine anguish know?

Sinner, how shall I give thee up?
I've loved thee as a child;
Yet of thy sins, thou fill'st the cup,
As if with passion wild.

Sinner, how shall I let thee go?
My heart doth yearn for thee.
Yet thou dost love transgression so,
Thou wilt not turn to me.

O sinner, stop! pause in thy path,—

196

Pause! ere it he too late;

And now, while I hold back my wrath.

Escape thy threatening fate.

But if thou wilt not, then I must

Forever let thee go;

And that I am both kind and just.

The universe shall know.

SAMUEL F. SMITH

In the front rank of American hymn writers Rev. Samuel Francis Smith, d.d., has long had a place. He was born in Boston, October 21, 1808, and received his classical training at the Boston Latin School. In 1825, he entered Harvard College, where he was a classmate of Oliver Wendell Holmes. Having completed his collegiate studies with the class of 1829, he entered upon a course of theological study at Andover Theological Seminary, and was graduated in 1832. For a year and a half subsequent to his graduation he was employed as editor of the Baptist Missionary Magazine. Having accepted a call to the pastorate of the Baptist church in Waterville, Me., he was ordained February 12, 1834, and for eight years he was the beloved pastor of this people. During this time he also performed the duties of the professorship of modern languages in Waterville College, now Colby University. In 1842, having received a call to the pastorate of the First Baptist church in Newton, Mass., he removed to Newton Center, which has since been his home. In 1854, he resigned his pastorate in order to devote himself to the editorship of the publications of the American Baptist Missionary Union, and to other literary work.

From 1842, to 1848, Dr. Smith edited the Christian Review. With the assistance of Dr. Baron Stow he compiled "The Psalmist," a hymn book of great excellence, published in 1843, and long in use in Baptist churches. This was followed in 1844, with a book for conference meetings and family worship, entitled "The Social Psalmist." In the same year he published a volume entitled "Lyric Gems." In 1848, appeared his "Life of Rev. Joseph Grafton." He also edited several volumes for D. Lothrop & Co., among them "Rock of Ages" (1866). In recent years lie has published "Missionary Sketches" (1879), "History of Newton, Mass." (1880), and "Rambles in Mission Fields" (1884), the last being an account of a visit in 1880, to various mission fields in Asia and Europe. In 1853, Colby University, then Waterville College, conferred upon him the honorary degree of doctor of divinity.

Dr. Smith's well known hymn,

My country , it is of thee,

also grew out of his intimacy with Lowell Mason. While Dr. Smith was a student at Andover, Mr. William C. Woodbridge returned from Germany, bringing with him a large number of German hymn books, with music, which he put into the hands of Mr. Mason. Mr. Mason brought them to Mr. Smith, saying, "You can read these books, but I cannot tell what is in them." The music of one of the hymns pleased Dr. Smith, and he dashed off the words of this man, without any expectation that it would ever become a favorite with anybody, much less a national hymn. He gave the hymn to Mr. Mason, and it was first sung at a Fourth of July Sunday-school celebration in Park Street church, Boston, in 1832. It soon became popular in children's celebrations, patriotic meetings, thanksgivings, and having come into general use in this country, it has traveled round the globe, and is everywhere known as the American national hymn. In May, 1887, Dr. Smith visited the Board of Trade in Chicago, and while sitting in the gallery he was pointed out to some of the members, and soon became the center of considerable notice. All at once the trading on the floor ceased, and from the wheat pit came the familiar words

My country, 't is of thee.

After two stanzas had been sung, Dr. Smith rose and bowed. Then a rousing cheer was given by those on the floor, to which Dr. Smith was now escorted by the secretary of the Board. The members flocked around him and grasped his hand. Then they opened a passage through the crowd, and led him into the wheat pit, where they took off their hats, and sung the rest of the hymn.

LEONARD MARSHALL

This veteran in musical circles in Boston was born in Hudson, N. H., May 3, 1809. In early life, he evinced great fondness for music, and availed himself of every opportunity to obtain musical instruction. Having obtained a violincello, he was wont to continue his practice until two and three o'clock in the morning, evoking not unfrequently from his mother the inquiry, "Are you not going to bed tonight, my son?" In 1835, he made his way to Boston, where he became a pupil of Prof. John Paddon, of London, who pronounced his voice a superior tenor, and with whom he remained for a long time. He was also a pupil of Charles Zeuner, who was considered the best and most original harmonist in the United States. About the year 1844, he was appointed the first tenor soloist of the Handel and Haydn Society, and for six years he sung for the society the principal tenor solos. For twenty-one years, commencing in 1836, he had charge of the music, and sang the tenor in the quartette at the Twelfth Congregational church, Boston. Afterward, for ten years, he was engaged at Tremont Temple, as conductor of the chorus choir. Still later, he furnished the music at the Bowdoin Square Baptist church three years, Charles Street Baptist church five years. Harvard Street Baptist church five years, and for a lesser period at other churches in Boston. For many years he conducted musical conventions and associations, and sang in concerts in all of the New England states. Much of his time during his residence in Boston has been devoted to teaching. He is the author of many popular songs, including "Don't Give up the Ship," and "The Mountaineer." He has also edited thirteen church music books. The words of an Easter hymn, commencing

Jesus Christ, our precious Savior,

were written by Mr. Marshall; also the following hymn:

Ever gracious, loving Savior,
Come and bless us from on high;
Give to us thy living water,

199

May we drink and never die.

Blessed Savior,

To thy presence we would fly.

We no refuge have but Jesus,

Who the soul from death can save;

He from every danger frees us,

And redeems us from the grave;

Blessed Jesus,

Life and peace in thee we have.

Vain are all our human labors

Until thou thine aid bestow;

But thou waitest to be gracious,

All our weakness thou dost know;

Blessed Jesus,

Help and mercy to us show.

ROBERT TURNBULL 1809-1877

The Baptists of Connecticut will long have occasion to remember Rev. Robert Turnbull, d.d. He was born in Whiteburn, Linlithgowshire, Scotland, September 10, 1809. His home training he received at the University of Glasgow. Subsequently he attended the theological lectures of Dr. Chalmers, at Edinburgh. It was while he was pursuing his theological studies that he became a Baptist. For a year and a half, on the completion of his course, he preached in Westmancotte, Worcestershire, England. In 1833, when he was twenty-four years of age, he came to the United States, and accepted the pastorate of the Second Baptist church in Danbury, Conn. Two years later he became pastor of the First Baptist church in Detroit, Mich. Here he remained two years, and then returned to Connecticut, where he settled as pastor of the South

Baptist church in Hartford. In 1839, he accepted a call to the pastorate of the Boylston Street, now Harvard Street Baptist church, Boston. In July, 1845, he returned to Hartford, Conn., and took the pastorate of the First Baptist church, a position which he held until 1869. His ministry throughout was blest with revivals. He was an eloquent preacher, an easy, graceful writer, a friend of missions and of every good work.

After leaving the pastorate, he continued to preach, and was useful in promoting church work in different places. In 1872, he was elected corresponding secretary of the Connecticut Baptist Convention, and up to the time of his last illness, he devoted himself to the interest of the smaller churches in the state. He died at his home in Hartford, November 20, 1877, aged sixty-eight years.

Dr. Turnbull was also a writer of hymns. The following hymn first appeared in Dr. Cutting's "Hymns for Vestry and Fireside" (1841), from which it was transferred to other collections. It was sung at Dr. Turnbull's funeral. Originally in the first line "waveless" had the place of "sacred."

There is a place of sacred rest,
Far, far beyond the skies,
Where beauty smiles eternally,
And pleasure never dies;
My Father's house, my heavenly home,
Where "many mansions" stand.
Prepared by hands divine for all
Who seek the better land.

When tossed upon the waves of life,
With fear on every side,
When fiercely howls the gathering storm.
And foams the angry tide.
Beyond the storm, beyond the gloom,
Breaks forth the light of morn,

Bright beaming from my Father's house,

To cheer the soul forlorn.

Yes, even at that fearful hour,

When death shall seize its prey.

And from the place that knows us now

Shall hurry us away,

The vision of that heavenly home

Shall cheer the parting soul.

And over it, mounting to the skies,

A tide of rapture roll.

In that pure home of tearless joy.

Earth's parted friends shall meet.

With smiles of love that never fade,

And blessedness complete;

There, there adieus are sounds unknown,

Death frowns not on that scene

But life, and glorious beauty shine,

Untroubled and serene.

ABRAM M. POINDEXTER 1809-1872

In any reference to their pulpit orators and denominational leaders, the Baptists of the south give d prominent place to Abram Maer Poindexter. He was of Huguenot ancestry, and was born in Bertie County, North Carolina, September 22, 1809. His father, Richard Jones Poindexter, was a Baptist minister, and he gave his son such educational advantages as he could command. In July, 1831, having yielded his heart to Christ, he united with the Cashie Baptist church. He soon decided to enter the Christian ministry, and received a license to preach in

February, 1832. For a while he studied with Rev. A. W. Clopton, in Charlotte County, Va,, and February 12, 1833, he entered Columbian College, in Washington, D. C. On account of ill-health he remained in Washington less than a year. A short time he then spent in North Carolina, and there, in June, 1834, he was ordained. As soon as he felt well enough to preach he attended a protracted meeting at Catawba church, Halifax County, Va., and in July, 1835, he accepted a call to the pastorate of this church and of the church in Clarksville, in Mecklenburg County. Luther Rice said of him at that time that he was the most prominent young preacher whom he knew. His engagements were numerous, and wherever he went crowds of delighted hearers attended upon his ministry. In 1843, Columbian College conferred upon him the degree of doctor of divinity. In 1845, he became an agent for Columbian College. In August, 1848, he was elected corresponding secretary of the Southern Baptist Publication Society. From June, 1851, to June, 1854, he was agent for Richmond College. In June, 1854, he became assistant secretary of the Foreign Mission Board of the Southern Baptist Convention, and he removed his residence from Halifax to Richmond, where he remained until the early part of the war, and then returned to Halifax.

For the "Baptist Psalmody," compiled by Basil Manly and Basil Manly, Jr., Dr. Poindexter contributed seven hymns, and spent several weeks in Charleston in aiding in the final revision of the work. The first lines of his own hymns are as follows:

"Eternal God! Almighty Power,"
"Faith is of endless life the spring,"
"While through this wilderness below,"
"lest Sabbath! day of holy rest,"
"O our Redeemer, God,"
"His sacred head the Holy One,"
"Head of the church! to thee we bow."

The fifth of these hymns was suggested by Isaiah lxiii. 17:

O our Redeemer, God,
On thee thy people wait;
We faint beneath thy chastening rod,

Thy house is desolate.

Yet are we not thine own,
Though now in deep distress?
Then be to us thy mercy shown,
Thy mourning people bless.
Spirit of God, return,
Thy cheering light impart;
O, may thy love within us burn.
And warm each languid heart.

Over all assembled here
Assert thy gracious power;
And to our friends and kindred dear
Be this salvation's hour.

O Lord, our God, descend
Our fainting hearts revive:
On thee alone our hopes depend,
For thou canst make us live

MARY ANN COLLIER 1810-1866

In "The Psalmist" (1843) is the following hymn (948) by M. A. Collier, entitled "Welcoming a Pastor":

The sun, that lights yon broad, blue sky,
May see his radiance dim;
The stars that circle bright and high,
May hush their joyous hymn;

The spring may breathe her balmy airs,

Yet earth no verdure show;

The purest love a mother bears

May lose its wonted glow

But still within the Savior's breast

There dwells a quenchless flame;

The earth may sink, the hills depart—

It lives, it burns the same.

O ransomed church, the Son of God

Still loves thy children well;

For thee the paths of death he trod;

'T is thine his grace to tell.

Savior, thy messenger we greet

Within this hallowed spot;

O, may we here thy presence meet;

Our God, forsake us not.

Miss Collier, the author of this hymn, was a daughter of Rev. William Collier, who was born in Scituate, Mass., October 11, 1771, and after pastorates in Newport, R. I., and New York city, became pastor of the First Baptist church in Charlestown, Mass. Here he remained, honored and beloved, sixteen years. In 1812, during his pastorate at Charlestown, he published "A New Selection of Hymns," compiled by himself. The first hymn in this collection,

What favor, Lord, that I should meet,

was doubtless written by Mr. Collier, and probably others. Mr. Collier's daughter, Mary Ann Collier, was born in Charlestown, December 23, 1810. She died in Alexandria, Va., December 25, 1866.

WILLIAM L. DENNIS 1811-1874

In "The Baptist Harp" (1849), a collection of hymns published in Philadelphia by the American Baptist Publication Society, there are two hymns (113, 379) by W. L. Dennis. The writer of these hymns. Rev. William L. Dennis, was born in Newport, R. I., in 1811. His father, Robert Dennis, was a baker in that place, and, later in life, keeper of the Dutch Island lighthouse, Narragansett Bay. William was educated in the Newport schools, and at the academy in East Greenwich, R. I. Without pursuing his studies further, he entered upon the work of the Christian ministry. He was a pastor in New York State, and later of the New Market Street Baptist church, in Philadelphia. Subsequently he withdrew from the ministry, and was admitted to the bar in Philadelphia, April 11, 1853. He was a brilliant speaker, and achieved considerable reputation at the bar, as he had already done in the pulpit. In his later years it was his custom to spend his summers in his native place. He came to Newport, July 4, 1874.

PHINEAS STOWE 1812-1868

Rev. Phineas Stowe was born in Milford, Conn., March 30, 1812. When fifteen years of age he obtained a clerkship in New Haven, Conn., and there, July 2, 1831, having been baptized by Rev. Elisha Cushman, he united with the First Baptist church. When Dr. R. H. Neale became pastor of this church, he made the acquaintance of young Stowe. He was attracted to him by the sweetness of his voice in Christian song, his fervency in prayer and his readiness to engage in every good work. Not long after, at Dr. Neale's earnest solicitation, young Stowe left a lucrative business, and entered upon a course of theological study at the Literary and Theological Institution at New Hampton, N. H. Here he remained four or five years. He then accepted the pastorate of the Baptist church at South Danvers, Mass. In 1837, Dr. Neale became pastor of the First Baptist church in Boston, and discovering a field for which Mr. Stowe, as he believed, had peculiar qualifications, he persuaded him to come to Boston as a preacher to seamen. Mr. Stowe entered upon his work with an enthusiasm that was contagious, and for more than twenty years he prosecuted it with the most blessed results. He loved the work, and lie did it with all his might. Dr. Neale says:

"There was no end to his conversations with individuals in the streets, on the wharves, and at his own house. He would take the sailor to his parlor, and talk, and pray, and weep with him there. He would follow him with his influence when he went to sea, telling; him to write to him, or if he could not send letters, to keep a journal, and bring it home if he should ever return."

His power with men is well illustrated by an incident recorded in the Atlantic Monthly after Mr. Stowe's death. He was visiting a coal mine in Pennsylvania:

"When he found himself in the heart of the mountain, surrounded by this immense body of coal, which he was told extended for miles on every side, he looked about him for some moments in speechless awe and wonder, then reverently took off his hat; theology bowed before geology; and he called out to the miners, in a sudden, loud voice, that echoed portentously through the long, dim-lighted cavern, 'Praise the Lord! Get down on your knees, every one of you, and praise the Lord for his wonderful providence!' This summons he delivered with such prophetic power of lungs and spirit, that all the miners except one threw down their tools, and knelt with him on the spot. 'I thought at first I wouldn't kneel,' said the exception; 'I never had knelt for any man, and I didn't believe I ever should. But he began to pray, and I tell you if my knees didn't begin to give way under me; he put in, and my legs crooked and crooked, till I could stand it no longer. By George, he prayed me down!'"

He found it difficult, however, to find in collections in use the hymns which he needed, and he not only solicited hymns adapted to the purpose he had in view, but wrote a large number of hymns himself. Says one of his intimate friends: "He did not pretend to be a poet, but it was to him a great joy to rhyme, and he did this with so much genuine kindness that his rhymes were felt to be acceptable, even when the muse halted in her stately tread." Twenty-eight of Mr. Stowe's hymns are included in "Ocean Melodies," among them the following hymn, entitled "The True Friend":

> There is a Friend, who's always nigh
> To those who on his word rely;
> When storms arise, and billows roll,

He will protect the humble soul.

When dangers in their pathway lie,
And howling tempests rage and sigh,
He then will keep with watchful care
All those who seek his face by prayer.

When sickness rends their mortal frame,
And human aid appears in vain,
He'll prove a Friend in time of need
To all who will his promise plead.

Come, then, bold seaman, seek this Friend!
He'll constant prove till time shall end;
And when the voyage of life is over
He'll land you safe on Canaan's shore.

The first edition of "Ocean Melodies" was prepared by Dr. J. H. Hanaford. To aid him in his temperance work, Mr. Stowe compiled another hymn book, entitled "Temperance Melodies."

LORENZO B. ALLEN 1812-1872

Rev. Lorenzo B. Allen, d.d., the eldest son of Rev. William Allen, was born in Jefferson, Me., June 4, 1812. When twelve years of age he left home to enter upon a course of study preparatory to entering college, first at Waterville, and afterward at China. In 1831, he entered Waterville College, now Colby University. After his graduation in 1835, he took charge of the Academy in Richmond, Me. In the following year he was licensed to preach, and supplied the Baptist church in Bowdoinhain. He then became connected with the theological seminary at Thomaston, Me., both as an instructor and a student. May 27, 1840, he was ordained as pastor of the First Baptist church in Thomaston, afterward South Thomaston. In January, 1844, he accepted a call to the pastorate of the Second Baptist church in Thomaston, where he remained until July, 1849. As secretary of the Maine Baptist Missionary Society, he now, for a short time, devoted himself wholly to work in behalf of the mission churches. November 3, 1849, he became pastor of the Baptist church in Yarmouth, Me, From this position, November 2, 1856, he asked to be relieved, in the hope that a change of climate would be beneficial to his health ; and in the following April he removed to Burlington, Iowa, where he became connected with Burlington University, as professor of the ancient languages. Subsequently he became president of the institution. Here he remained until 1865, when he accepted a call from the First Baptist church in Minneapolis. In 1868, he removed to Wasioja, and took charge of Groveland Seminary. Here, as at Burlington, he gathered around him a class of theological students. He was also associated with Rev. V. B. Conklin in the pastorate of the church. But his labors were too arduous, and he was soon obliged to relinquish them. He died August 20, 1872, and is remembered as a man of eminent piety, sound judgment, and a faithful, devoted servant of Jesus Christ.

In "The Iris," a collection of hymns with music, compiled by H. H. Hawley, and published in 1881 (Chicago, C. Swift & Co.), is a hymn by Dr. Allen, with music by Mr. Hawley:

> How sweet is the Sabbath! how hallowed its hours,
> To the sorrowing soul that is panting for heaven;
> How it wakes the dull spirit, enlivens its powers,
> When to heavenly worship its moments are given.

> How soft the repose that it sheds o'er the earth,
> In the hush of its tumult, the calm of its strife,
> Like the quiet of heaven, it is God gives it birth,
> And the heart beats responsive to an angelic life.

> Then hail, blessed Sabbath, in rich mercy given
> To revive us, and cheer all along the way down,
> Even through the dark valley till Ave pass into heaven.

Where the Savior will give us the harp and the crown.

SEWALL S. CUTTING 1813-1882

Rev. Sewall Sylvester Cutting, d.d., was born in Windsor, Vt., January 19, 1813. In his boyhood his parents removed to Westport, N. Y., and there, when fourteen years of age, he was baptized, and united with the Baptist church. Two years later he commenced the study of Law, but in the following year his purposes were changed, and he decided to enter the Christian ministry. His collegiate preparatory studies he completed at South Reading, Mass., and in 1831, he entered Waterville College, at Waterville, Maine. Here he remained two years. He finished his course at the University of Vermont, where he was graduated with the highest honors of his class, in 1835. Without receiving a theological training, he accepted the pastorate of the Baptist church in West Boylston, Mass., where he was ordained March 31, 1836. In the following year he accepted a call to the pastorate of the Baptist church in Southbridge, Mass., where he remained eight years. He then, in 1845, accepted the editorship of the Baptist Advocate, a New York religious journal, and changed its name to the New York Recorder. For five years he held this position with honor to himself and usefulness to the denomination. In 1850, he was elected corresponding secretary of the American and Foreign Bible Society, and accepting the office provisionally, he participated in the discussion between the friends of that society and the friends of the American Bible Union. In 1851, he became one of the editorial staff of the Watchman and Reflector. He was the editor of the Christian Review, from 1849, to 1852. In 1853, he renewed his connection with the New York Recorder. In 1855, the Recorder was consolidated with the Baptist Register, and the new paper received the name of the Examiner. Dr. Cutting then accepted an appointment as professor of Rhetoric and History in the University at Rochester. This position he resigned in 1868, in order to accept the secretaryship of the American Baptist Educational Commission. Perhaps he performed no more important service for the denomination to which he belonged than in awakening among Baptists, especially in the northern states, a deeper interest in their educational institutions. In 1876, he was elected corresponding secretary of the American Baptist Home Mission Society, a position which he held three years.

Subsequently, by appointment of the board, he was engaged in special matters pertaining to the society's investments. He then went to Europe for needed rest, and remained abroad more than a year. January 16, 1882, in Brooklyn, N. Y., he was stricken down with paralysis, and February 7, following, he died. He was a clear thinker, a vigorous writer, and possessed administrative abilities of a high order. At all times and in all places he was true to his convictions, and nothing could swerve him from what he regarded as the path of duty.

A beautiful hymn by Dr. Cutting is included in the "Calvary Selection of Spiritual Songs," commencing,

O Savior, I am blind

But the best known of his hymns is the following:

God of the world, near and afar
Thy glories shine in earth and star;
We see thy love in opening flower.
In distant orb thy wondrous power.

God of our lives, the throbbing heart
Doth at thy beck its action start,
Throbs on, obedient to thy will,
Or ceases at thy fatal chill.

God of the harvest, sun and shower
Own the high mandate of thy power;
Plenty her rich profusion strews
When thou dost bid, or Want her woes.

God of eternal life, thy love
Doth every stain of sin remove;
To thine exalted Son shall come
Earth's wandering tribes to find their home.

211

God of all goodness, to the skies
Our hearts in grateful anthems rise;
And to thy service shall be given
The rest of life, the whole of heaven.

ALBERT G. PALMER

Rev. Albert G. Palmer, d.d., was born in North Stonington, Conn., May 11, 1813. His early life was spent on his father's farm. When nine years of age he experienced religion, and this shaped his entire life. In 1829, he united with the Baptist church in his native town, and soon after he began to preach. He also entered upon a course of classical and theological study at Kingston and Pawtucket, R. I., and Andover, Mass. He was ordained at North Stonington in 1834. His first pastorate was at Western, R. I., beginning in 1837, and closing in 1843, a period of successful labor, during which the membership of the church was increased from thirty to three hundred. In 1843, he accepted the pastorate of the Baptist church in Stonington. Here he remained nine years, when he accepted a call to become pastor of the First Baptist church in Syracuse, N. Y. In 1855, he received and accepted a call to Bridgeport, Conn. He labored there three years, and then accepted the pastorate of the Baptist church in Wakefield, R. I. In 1861, he removed to Stonington, Conn., in response to an earnest call from the church of which he had already been pastor, and here he still remains, exerting a wide influence, and held in deserved honor for his own and for his works' sake. Madison University conferred upon him the degree of doctor of divinity in 1880.

Dr. Palmer has been a frequent contributor to the Christian Secretary, and other religious journals. He has also published "The Early Baptists of Connecticut" (1844), and a "Historical

Discourse" (1872), preached before the Stonington Union Association. He is also the author of many fine poems and memorial sonnets. A volume of selections from his poetical writings, edited by his daughter, Miss Sara A. Palmer, and entitled "Psalms of Faith and Songs of Life," was published in 1884. The poet John G. Whittier says of this volume: "The religious pieces are especially valuable.

The following hymn, "The Dying Christian to his Soul," is a translation by Dr. Palmer from the Latin of Musculus:

How sinks my heart in death's cold, deadly strife!
Nothing of earth's sweet light to me remains,
Yet Christ, my everlasting life and light,
My fearing, trembling, sinking soul sustains.

But why, my soul! O wherefore should thou fear
To rise to the bright mansions of the blest?
Behold, thy angel guide himself is near
To lead thee to yon seats of peace and rest.

O leave this wretched, moldering house of clay,
Shattered and crumbling down to earth and dust;
God's faithful hand will, at the appointed day,
A glorious form, restore the sacred trust.

Ah! thou hast sinned! alas! thou hast, I know;
But Christ hast purged, by his own precious blood,
The sins of all believers, white as snow,
In blood-washed robes, presenting them to God!

But death is terrible! It is, I own;
But when thy immortality is nigh.
And when thy Savior calls thee from his throne,

Wilt thou, O trembling soul, still fear to die?

Since Christ for thee has triumphed over death.

And sin and Satan put beneath thy feet,

Tear not to yield to him thy parting breath,

But spread thy joyful wings thy Lord to meet.

HENRY S. WASHBURN

Hon. Henry S. Washburn was born in Providence, R. I., June 10, 1813. His boyhood was passed at Kingston, Mass., the home of his paternal ancestors. After receiving a common school education he was placed at the age of thirteen years in a bookstore in Boston. Here, with opportunities to gratify his taste for reading, the desire for a liberal education influenced him, and he went to Worcester to prepare for college at the Worcester Academy. In 1836, he entered Brown University, but on account of ill health he was obliged to leave college. For seven years he had charge of the publishing department of the New England Sabbath School Union. Subsequently he was engaged in manufacturing pursuits in Worcester and Boston, and afterward he became president of the Un ion Mutual Life Insurance Company. Meanwhile many positions of trust and power came to him. He was a member of the city government of Worcester. For four years he was president of the Worcester County Manufacturers and Mechanics Association. For nine years he was a member of the Boston School Board. He was a member of the Massachusetts House of Representatives in 1871, and 1872, and of the Senate in 1873. He resigned the presidency of the Union Mutual Life Insurance Company in 1876 and went abroad in its behalf. During his absence he investigated the life insurance companies in Great Britain, France, and Germany. He returned to the United States in 1879. He has now retired mostly from active business pursuits.

The following hymn (Psalmist, 1843) was written for the dedication of the Harvard Street Baptist church, Boston, in 1841.

Almighty God, thy constant care
Hath been our sure support and stay,
And hither gladly we repair,
Our early sacrifice to pay.

Accept our vows; in humble trust
This house we consecrate to thee;
O may thy promise to the just
Forever, Lord, our portion be.

And may that stream which maketh glad
The city of our God below,
Revive the drooping, cheer the sad,
As still its healing waters flow.

So let thy people here enjoy
The blessings which thy grace hath given,
That they may hail, with purer joy,
The usual perfect bliss of heaven.

ARCHIBALD KENYON.

Rev. Archibald Kenyon was born in Athol, Warren County, N. Y., July 31, 1813. His early school advantages were very limited, and he was compelled to make up the lack by personal efforts. In November, 1831, he became interested in the subject of religion, and July 8, 1832, he was baptized, and united with the Wait's Corner, or White Creek Baptist church. In the winter of 1833, he removed his membership to the Hague Baptist church, by which he was licensed to preach March 18. At this time he received much encouragement and advice from Rev. Nathaniel Colver. For awhile he studied at Woodworth Academy, Sandy Hill, and then at the Academy at East Bennington. April 15, 1835, he was ordained at Adamsville, N. Y., where he was preaching half of the time, alternating with Lakeville. Subsequently he was pastor at South Salem. The year 1838, he spent in evangelistic work in Vermont and elsewhere. He then accepted a call to the pastorate of the West Baptist church in Providence, R. I. In 1843, he removed to Vernon, Oneida County, N. Y. After a year he went to Clinton, near Utica, where he remained three years and a half. At Cleveland, Ohio, he organized an anti-slavery Baptist church. Five years he spent in preaching on the Reserve. He became connected with the Free Mission movement, and edited the Free Mission Visitor. In 1852, he accepted a call to the pastorate of the Tabernacle Baptist church, Chicago. In 1857, he organized and became pastor of the Bureau Baptist church. From Chicago he removed to Iowa City, Iowa. Subsequently returning to Illinois, he had pastorates at New Rutland, Union, Wis., Peoria, Chatsworth, East Lynn and Hooperton, and Thompsonville, Wis.

Mr. Kenyon is the author of a large number of hymns, some of which have been set to music by Rev. Robert Lowry, d.d., and are found in the "Royal Diadem," "Pure Gold," "River of Life," "Songs of Love," "Our Glad Hosanna," "Glad Refrain," etc. He has also written many Christian ballads and temperance songs. The following hymn by Mr. Kenyon is from "Our Glad Hosanna":

Jesus, hear me when I pray,
Keep and help me all the day;
Save from fear and care and sin,
Make me pure and strong within.

Weak I am, and weak must be,
Lost unless I'm saved by thee;
Jesus, now thy grace impart,

Keep my trembling, wandering heart.

Power and grace are thine, I know,
Richest love thou canst bestow;
Save my soul from Satan's wiles.
Cheer my pathway with thy smiles.

Only now a pilgrim, I,
Look for mansions in the sky.
There to dwell with angels bright,
Clothed in robes of heavenly light.

JOHN B. HAGUE

In the "Psalmist" (1843) is the following hymn, founded on the passage "The harvest is past, the summer is ended":

Hark, sinner, while God from on high doth entreat thee,
And warnings, with accents of mercy doth blend;
Give ear to his voice, lest in judgment he meet thee:
"The harvest is passing, the summer will end."

How oft of thy danger and guilt he hath told thee I
How oft still the message of mercy doth send
Haste, haste, while he waits in his arms to enfold thee;
"The harvest is passing, the summer will end."

Despised, rejected, at length he may leave thee;
What anguish and horror thy bosom will rend!
Then haste thee, O sinner, while he will receive thee;
"The harvest is passing, the summer will end."

Ere long, and Jehovah will come in his power;
Our God will arise with his foes to contend;
Haste, haste thee, O sinner, prepare for that hour;
"The harvest is passing, the summer will end."

The Savior will call thee in judgment before him;
O, bow to his scepter, and make him thy Friend;
Now yield him thy heart; make haste to adore him;
Thy harvest is passing, thy summer will end.

Mr. Hague was born in New Rochelle, N. Y., in 1813. He was graduated at Hamilton College in 1832. His theological course he took at Newton Theological Institution, where he was graduated in 1835. Having received a call to the pastorate of the Baptist church in Eastport, Me., he was ordained at Eastport, September 20, 1835. Here he remained ten years. Since 1845, he has devoted himself to teaching, and has had young ladies' schools at Jamaica Plain, and Newton Center, Mass., Hudson, N. Y., and Hackensack, N. J. For some time Mr. Hague has been a lay member of the Protestant Episcopal Church.

SIDNEY DYER

The name of Rev. Sidney Dyer is a familiar one in very many Baptist households. Dr. Dyer was born at White Creek, Washington County, N. Y., February 11, 1814. When seventeen years of age he entered the military service, and participated in the Black Hawk war. At twenty-two he commenced a course of study for the Christian ministry, under the direction of Rev.

Charles G. Sommers, d.d., pastor of the South Baptist church. New York. In 1842, he was ordained, and preached awhile at Brownsville. Later he was employed as a missionary among the Choctaw Indians. In 1852, he accepted a call to the pastorate of the First Baptist church in Indianapolis, Ind. In 1859, he received an appointment as district secretary of the American Baptist Publication Society, at Philadelphia, and continued in this position until November 30, 1885. He now resides in DeLand, Fla. The honorary degree of a.m. he received from the Indiana State University, and that of PH.D. from Bucknell University, at Lewisburgh, Penn.

The following is one of Dr. Dyer's many hymns:

When, faint and weary, toiling.
The sweat-drops on my brow,
I long to cease from labor,
To drop the burden now,
There comes a gentle chiding
To quell each murmuring sigh,
Work while the day is shining,
There's resting by-and-by.

'T is not to hear thy groaning,
Thy task is heavy made,
Nor adding to thy sorrow,
That succor is delayed;
When, bending beneath the burden,
You toil, and sweat, and cry,
"Be patient," is the answer,
"There's resting by-and-by."

The way is rough and thorny,
The way is dark and drear,
My step is growing weary,
The night is drawing near;

219

Behold this verdant wayside,
How cool the shadows lie I
"Nay, pause not in thy journey,
There's resting by-and-by."

Ah! when the crown is waiting,
And room enough in heaven,
Why urge a further warfare
When dreadful wounds are given?
O, give me now the trophy I
Why not, my Savior, why?
"Still bear the cross a season.
There's resting by-and-by."

This life to toil is given.
And he improves it best
Who seeks by cheerful labor
To enter into rest.
Then, pilgrim, worn and weary,
Press on, the goal is nigh;
The prize is straight before thee,
There's resting by-and-by.

Nor ask, when overburdened,
You long for friendly aid,
"Why idle stands my brother,
No yoke upon him laid?"
The Master bids him tarry,
And dare you ask him why?
"Go labor in my vineyard.
There's resting by-and-by."

Wan reaper in the harvest,

Let this thy strength sustain.

Each sheaf that fills the garner

Brings you eternal gain!

Then bear the cross with patience,

To fields of labor lie,

'T is sweet to work for Jesus,

There's resting by-and-by.

JACOB R. SCOTT 1815-1861

Rev. Jacob Richardson Scott was born in Boston, Mass., March 1, 1815. In early life he showed a fondness for study, and having prepared for college at South Reading, Mass., he entered Brown University in 1832, and was graduated in 1836. Several years were spent in teaching, and having decided to study for the ministry, he entered Newton Theological Institution in 1839, and was graduated in 1842. In September following he was ordained pastor of the Market Street Baptist church in Petersburgh, Va., where he remained until 1844. From 1844, to 1847, he was pastor of the Baptist church in Hampton, Va. During this pastorate he was twice elected chaplain of the University of Virginia, His health having become injured he returned to the North and took a somewhat prolonged rest. In October 1849, he became pastor of the First Baptist church in Portland, Me. When he resigned in April, 1853, he was under appointment of the American Baptist Missionary Union to go as a missionary to France, but providential circumstances detained him in this country. In 1853, he became pastor of the First Baptist church in Fall River, Mass. In 1854, he accepted a call to the pastorate of the First Baptist church in Rochester, N. Y. Here he remained until 1857. His last settlement, 1858-1860, was at Yonkers, N. Y. His health, which for some time had been exceedingly precarious, no longer warranted his continuance in the pastoral office, and reluctantly he resigned. Having removed to Maiden, Mass., he accepted the office of superintendent of schools, but his work was done. He died December 10, 1861. Rev. W. H. Shailer, d.d., bears this testimony concerning Mr. Scott:

Mr. Scott, whose graduating exercise at Brown University was a poem entitled "Paul at Athens," may have continued the exercise of his poetical gifts, but he is represented in our hymn books by the following dedication hymn only ("Psalmist," 944):

To thee this temple we devote,
Our Father and our God;
Accept it thine, and seal it now
Thy Spirit's blest abode.

Here may the prayer of faith ascend,
The voice of praise arise;
Of may each lowly service prove
Accepted sacrifice.

Here may the sinner learn his guilt,
And weep before his Lord;
Here, pardoned, sing a Savior's love,
And here his vows record.

Here may affliction dry the tear,
And learn to trust in God,
Convinced it is a Father smites,
And love that guides the rod.

Peace be within these sacred walls;
Prosperity be here;
Long smile upon thy people, Lord,
And ever more be near.

J. M. D. GATES 1815-1887

Rev. J. M. D. Gates was born in Orange County, N. C., June 5, 1815. His ancestors came to Virginia from England in the early settlement of the colonies. In the nineteenth year of his age he left his native place for Tennessee, locating first at Maryville, and nearly four years later at McMinnville. Here, March 11, 1838, he was baptized by Rev. Noah Gates, and united with the Baptist church. Near the close of this year he was married to Miss Ann P. Lyon. With her he engaged in school teaching in Alabama and Mississippi until the death of Mrs. Gates, which occurred October 16, 1841. He then returned to McMinnville, where in 1842, he was licensed to preach by the McMinnville church. February 4, 1844, he was appointed a missionary by the executive board of Liberty Association. His ordination followed, October 13. In 1846, he located at Marion, now Cateston, Gannon Gounty, and early in 1847, he was elected pastor of the Marion church. Here he was married in September, 1848, to Miss M. J. Taylor, and this continued to be his home until his death, August 1, 1887.

For many years Mr. Gates was active in literary labors, writing frequently for religious papers, and from 1874, to 1881, he was the editor and publisher of the Baptist Messenger. He also wrote and published several books, viz.: "Marriage and the Married Life," "The Voice of Truth," "Reply to Ariel." He also compiled three hymn books which were published, viz.: "The Companion" (1846), "The Baptist Companion" (1857), and "The Sacred Harp" (1867). In the latter Mr. Cates included twelve hymns written by himself. Of these the following is number 137:

> The sacred day of rest
> Has sweetly passed away;
> In love and peace, in prayer and praise,
> We've kept the holy day.
>
> How pure, and how divine,
> The streams of joy that flow
> From Zion's sacred hills, to bless

With life and peace below.

How precious to the soul,
Such bliss to feel, and know
'T is but a taste of rest above,
Where joys celestial flow.

O may our thoughts still dwell
On scenes of pure delight;
May angels guard us while we sleep,
And bring the morning light.

And when life's fleeting sun
Shall set and cease to be;
O may our souls with Jesus rest,
Through all eternity.

JESSE CLEMENT 1815-1883

Jesse Clement was born June 12, 1815, in Dracut, near Lowell, Mass. He was educated at the Academy in New Hampton, N. H., and after completing his course of study, he taught there two years. In 1842, he went to Buffalo, N. Y., where for fourteen years he was editor of the Western Literary Messenger, and connected with the Commercial Advertiser. He also wrote a great deal, both prose and poetry, for secular and religious papers and magazines, and published "Noble Deeds of American Women," and "Life of Adoniram Judson." He next removed to

Dubuque, Iowa, and founded the Daily Times. In 1868, he went to Chicago, and soon became connected with the Inter-Ocean, and afterward edited several volumes of the "United States Biographical Dictionary." He was an ardent Baptist, and served as deacon of churches in Buffalo, Dubuque and Chicago. He was also an earnest worker in all Christian organizations. He died very suddenly, Christmas morning, 1883, at Butler, Missouri.

Mr. Clement was frequently called upon to write odes and hymns, not only for secular and educational gatherings, but also for Sunday-school, church, and Y. M. C. A. dedicatory and anniversary services. In "Songs of Delight" (1875) there are seven hymns by Mr. Clement. The following hymn was written by him for the dedication, in 1871, of the University Place church, Chicago, of which he was a constituent member and a deacon for fifteen years:

Thou whose dwelling-place so lofty
Ne'er was seen by mortal eye:
Like a breeze from heaven, softly,
God, our Father! draw thou nigh;
Let thy presence
This new temple glorify.

Thou whose blood was shed for mortals
Freely as the waters flow.
Enter thou these sacred portals,
And thy love on all bestow;
Bleeding Savior,
Here thy wounds to sinners show.

Shining One, this altar brighten
With thy radiance all divine;
Every burdened spirit lighten.
In its darkest chambers shine;
Dove, white pinioned,
Hover near with smiles benign.

Triune God! we come before thee,

That our hearts, from sin set free,

Here may worship, here adore thee.

And our eyes thy glory see;

May we ever

In this temple meet with thee.

EDMUND TURNEY 1816-1872

Rev. Edmund Turney, d.d., was born in Easton, Conn., May 6, 1816. He was graduated at Madison University, Hamilton, N. Y., in 1838, and at the theological seminary at Hamilton, in 1840. In the spring of 1841, he was ordained as pastor of the South Baptist church, Hartford, Conn. Two years later he accepted a call to the pastorate of the Baptist church in Granville, Ohio. Here he remained five years, exerting a wide influence in the community and the state. He then became pastor of the Broad Street Baptist church in Utica, N. Y. In 1850, he was appointed professor of biblical criticism in Hamilton Theological Seminary. From 1853, to 1858, he was a professor in Fairmount Theological Seminary, Cincinnati, Ohio. Subsequently he had charge of a charitable institution in New York. In 1865, in Washington, D. C, he began the first organized effort for the education of colored teachers and preachers. He believed that God had prepared him for this work, and notwithstanding many hindrances he prosecuted it with untiring energy and fidelity, until he received the summons that called him from his work to his reward. He died in Washington, September 28, 1872.

Dr. Turney was a conscientious, devout scholar, and possessed the martyr-spirit. Professor Huntington, of Columbian College, Washington, D. C, says of him: "Turning aside from 'positions more pleasant, and, in the world's estimation, more honorable,—positions which by his talents and his learning he was fitted to adorn—he consented to toil in a hard and obscure field, where he well knew that no dignified repose was to be enjoyed, and no worldly laurels were to be gathered."

In 1862, Dr. Turney published "Baptismal Harmonies; or Baptismal Hymns, with Appropriate Original Music." The collection comprised thirty-one hymns, all written by Dr. Turney, and all but three designed for use at baptismal services. One of these three is the following, for use at the Lord's Supper:

Oh, love divine! oh, matchless grace
Which in this sacred rite
Shines forth so full, so free, in rays
Of purest living light.

Oh, wondrous death! oh, precious blood
For us so freely spilt,
To cleanse our sin-polluted souls
From every stain of guilt.

Oh, covenant of life and peace,
By blood and suffering sealed!
All the rich gifts of Gospel grace
Are here to faith revealed.

Jesus, we bow our souls to thee.
Our Life, our Hope, our All,
While we, with thankful, contrite hearts,
Thy dying love recall.

Oh may thy pure and perfect laws
Be written on our minds;
Nor earth, nor self, nor sin obscure
The ever radiant lines.

GEORGE W. ANDERSON

Rev. George W. Anderson, d.d., was born in Philadelphia, May 15, 1816. When a child he entered upon a religious life, and March 20, 1826, he was baptized by Rev. T. T. Woolsey, and united with the Central Baptist church in his native city. Having completed his preparatory studies he entered Madison University, from which he was graduated in 1814. In the autumn of that year he entered Hamilton Theological Seminary, and was graduated in 1846. He then assumed the editorial management of a Baptist paper, the Christian Chronicle, published in the interest of the newly established university at Lewisburgh, Penn. Three years later he was elected professor of the Latin language and literature in the same university. In 1854, he was ordained, and became pastor of the Northeast Baptist church, Dutchess County, N. Y. Four years later he accepted the pastorate of the Lower Merion Baptist church, Montgomery County, Penn. In 1864, he was appointed literary editor of the American Baptist Publication Society, a position which he still holds, and in which he has rendered valuable service to American Baptists, For many years he has been a diligent student of our denominational history both in this country and in Europe. He also takes a deep interest in our educational and denominational work. In 1869, the University at Lewisburgh, now Bucknell University, conferred upon him the degree of doctor of divinity.

Dr. Anderson has been a frequent contributor to the National Baptist and other papers. He is also the author of "The Way to Christ and the Walk in Christ" (1853); "A Plea for Principles; or the Baptists and the Ordinances" (1859); "First Scripture Question Book" (1862); "The Good News" (1863); "The Baptists in the United States" (1875); "The Missionary Outlook" (1884); and "Footprints of Baptism in Europe" (1885). The following hymn (502), written by Dr. Anderson, appeared in "The Baptist Harp" (1849), and is included in several later collections:

> Onward, herald of the gospel,
> Bear thy tidings through the land;
> Preach the word, as heaven's apostle,
> Sent by Christ's divine command.

Jesus, once the gospel preaching.

Through his native Judah went,

Salem's sons in mercy teaching,

Calling Israel to repent.

Israel, all his deep love slighting,

Spurning all his tenderness,

Still he followed, still inviting,

Weeping where he could not bless.

Follow then, thy Lord's example;

Toil in hope, nor faint, nor fear,

For thy needs his grace is ample,

At thy side he's ever near.

Work, until the day is ended,

Till thy sun sinks in the west;

Then, with joy and triumph blended,

Christ shall bring thee to his rest.

JAMES SPENCER

Rev. James Spencer has three hymns in the "Canadian Baptist Hymnal" (1888). Two of these were written for seamen's services. The following hymn was written in 1869, on the occasion of the departure of Rev. William George to enter upon missionary service in Burma:

Constrained by love, go and proclaim
To distant heathen, veiled in night,
The potency of that blessed name,
Which turned our darkness into light.

Go, then, and seek that wandering flock
Whose laud no living waters give;
And point to that once smitten Rock,
And bid them drink thereof, and live.

Go to that parched and arid field,
And with good seed implant the ground;
The dreary desert fruit shall yield,
And with the reaper's song redound.

Go, take to them the living bread,
Which God to us has freely given;
So shall their hungry souls be fed
With manna that came down from heaven.

Go, bid the lame with gladness bound,
And teach their silent tongues to sing;
And let the distant vales resound
With praise to Zion's glorious King.

Mr. Spencer was born October 13, 1816, at Mire River, twelve miles from the old city of Louisburg, Island of Cape Breton, Nova Scotia. During the early part of his life he was engaged in mercantile pursuits. When thirty years of age he became acquainted with experimental Christianity, and as a result of his study of the Scriptures, he became a Baptist. Soon afterward he was impressed with the duty of preaching to others the gospel he had received. In 1853, he was ordained at Chester, N. S., and there he remained, engaged in pastoral work, two years. Then he was pastor seven years of the Baptist church in Lower Granville, during which time ninety persons were baptized. Four years he was pastor of the Baptist church in Digby, and preached also to other small churches in the vicinity. Since 1864, he has efficiently labored in St. John, N. B., as seamen's chaplain, preaching to those who go down to the sea in ships, as well as others, the truth as it is in Jesus.

EDWIN BURNHAM 1817-1887

Rev. Edwin Burnham was born in Essex, Mass., May 10, 1817. He had only a common school education, and beyond that was entirely a self-educated man. When nineteen years of age he was ordained at Springfield, N. H., as a minister of the Christian Baptist denomination. His first charge was at Kennebunk, Me., where he was settled the year following his ordination. Subsequently he was pastor of a Christian Baptist church in Boston, and later in Exeter, N. H., and Newburyport, Mass. In 1865, he united with the Second Baptist church in Holyoke, Mass., where he was re-ordained December 22. For about a year he served this church as pastor. In 1869, he entered upon evangelistic work, to which he gave the remainder of his life, and in which he was greatly blessed. He had a commanding presence, a fine voice, and his words in presenting the claims of the gospel could not fail to arouse the hearts and consciences of his hearers. He died at his home in Newburyport, Mass., January 29, 1887.

Mr. Burnham, in 1867, published "Revival Hymns, Original and Selected." The following hymn, written by Mr. Burnham in 1848, is number 435 in Rev.:

Thine oath, and promise, mighty God,

Recorded in thy word,

Become our hope's foundation broad,

And confidence afford.

Like Abraham, the friend of God,

Thy faithfulness we prove;

We tread in paths the fathers trod,
Blest with thy light and love.

Largely our consolation flows,
While we expect the day
That ends our griefs and pains and woes,
And drives our fears away.

Let floods of mighty vengeance roll,
And compass earth around;
Let thunders sound from pole to pole,
And earthquakes vast astound;

Let nature all convulse and shake,
And angry nations rage;
Thy name our hiding-place we make;
To save thou dost engage.

EMILY C. JUDSON 1817-1854

In Dyer's "Psalmist" there is a hymn by Emily E. Chubbuck, commencing

Mother, has the dove that nestled.

Miss Chubbuck, also known by her nom, de jilume "Fanny Forester," was born in Eaton, a small town in Central New York, August 22, 1817. Her parents were poor, and at an early age she assisted in supporting the family by her work in a woolen factory. Afterward she taught the village school, and when she was twenty years of age she was a welcome contributor to the poetical column of the village newspaper. Having attracted the attention of the Misses Sheldon, who kept a well known young ladies' school in Utica, she was made welcome to advantages of which she gladly availed herself. In the hope of continuing the assistance she had rendered her parents, she commenced to write the stories for children which, later, were published under the title of " Alderbrook." Then N. P. Willis made her welcome to the columns of the Evening Mirror, and so, after a long struggle with poverty and other adverse circumstances, she had made her way to a position of honor and influence in the literary world.

Converted when eight years of age, she early had a conviction that at some time she would be a missionary. In January, 1846, she met Dr. Adoniram Judson at the home of Rev. A. D. Gillette, d.d., in Philadelphia, and they were married June 2, of that year. In a few weeks they embarked for Burma. Off St. Helena Mrs. Judson wrote the following beautiful tribute to the memory of Sarah Boardman Judson:

> Blow softly, gales! a tender sigh
> Is flung upon your wing;
> Lose not the treasure, as ye fly,
> Bear it where love and beauty lie,
>
> Silent and withering.
> Flow gently, waves! a tear is laid
> Upon your heaving breast;
> Leave it within yon dark rock's shade,
>
> Or weave it in an iris braid,
> To crown the Christian's rest.
> Bloom, ocean isle! lone ocean isle!
> Thou keep'st a jewel rare;
>
> Let rugged rock and dark defile
> Above the slumbering stranger smile,
> And deck her couch with care.
> Weep, ye bereaved! a dearer head
>
> Never left the pillowing breast;

The good, the pure, the lovely fled

When, mingling with the shadowy dead,

She meekly went to rest.

Mourn, Burma, mourn! a bow, which spanned

Thy cloud, has passed away;

A flower has withered on thy sand,

A pitying spirit left thy strand,

A saint has ceased to pray.

Dr. and Mrs. Judson arrived at Maulmain, November 30, 1846, and Dr. Judson re-entered upon his missionary labors. He found in Mrs. Judson an efficient helper. She devoted herself at first to the work of learning the language, and of preparing a biography of Sarah Boardman Judson.

The following are the first lines of a poem which was addressed by Mrs. Judson to a missionary friend in Burma, on the death of an infant:

A mound is in the graveyard,

A short and narrow bed,

'No grass is growing on it.

And no marble at its head;

Ye may go and weep beside it,

Ye may kneel and kiss the sod,

But ye'll find no balm for sorrow.

In the cold and silent clod.

WILLIAM C. RICHARDS

Rev. William C. Richards, Ph.D., was born in London, England, November 24, 1818. His father removed to the United States in 1831, and accepted the pastorate of the Baptist church in Hudson, N. Y. The son united with his father's church in 1833; and in the following year he entered Hamilton Literary and Theological Institution, where he was graduated in 1840. For about ten years he was engaged in literary and educational work in the south. In 1852, he returned to the north, purposing to enter the ministry. He was ordained in July, 1855, and for awhile was associate pastor of the First Baptist church in Providence, R. I. A new interest was soon started, afterward known as the Brown Street Baptist church. Of this church Mr. Richards accepted the pastorate, and with it he remained until 1862, when on account of failing health he resigned, and not long after began to give, for the most part under the auspices of the Y. M. C. A., popular lectures on physical science, which he has continued to the present time, with the exception of three years, from 1865, to the close of 1868, when he was pastor of the Baptist church in Pittsfield, Mass., and professor of chemistry for two years in the Berkshire Medical College. Since 1876, his residence has been in Chicago, Ill.

O happy service that invites
My willing feet to go
Up to the temple of delights
Where heaven begins below.

From palaces of earthly kings,
Where daintiest feasts are spread,
Fain would I fly on love's swift wings,
To feed on heavenly bread.

No Eschol clusters, large and fine,
Could turn my steps aside,
From that dear feast where holy wine
Is Calvary's mystic tide.
For bread and wine the Christ reveal
To my believing eyes;

In their clear sighs the power I feel
Of his great sacrifice.

O happy service that invites
My joyful feet to go
Up to the temple of delights
Where heaven is felt below.

J. H. HANAFORD

J. H. Hanaford, M.D., was born in New Hampton, N. H., January 27, 1819. His education he received at the well known academy in his native town. For awhile he devoted himself to teaching, but his health at length becoming impaired, he decided to study medicine, and went to New York for this purpose. After graduation, he commenced the practice of medicine in Nantucket, Mass., where he remained six years. The climate not proving favorable, he removed to Beverly, Mass., and subsequently to Reading, Mass., where he still resides.

Dr. Hanaford has given much attention to literary work. He is the author of a number of books, "Mother and Child," etc., and is now (1887) assisting in the preparation of a history of his native town. In 1848, he published a collection of hymns for seamen, entitled "Ocean Melodies," and furnished for it nineteen hymns of his own composition. The second edition of this collection, with additions, was brought out by Rev. Phineas Stowe. The following hymn by Dr. Hanaford is from "Ocean Melodies":

Great God, at thy command,
We launch upon the deep;
O guide us in our devious way,
Our souls in safety keep.

When dangers round us crowd,

And toils our course attend,

Be thou our help, our sure defense,

Our everlasting Friend.

Should stormy winds arise,

And tempests madly beat,

O grant us grace to trust in thee,

And near the mercy-seat.

And though in distant climes,

Over Imaging seas we ride,

We trust in thee, thou gracious God,

Our Savior and our Guide.

And should our fragile bark

To ocean's depths be hurled,

O may we reach a sheltering port,

A fairer, brighter world.

MARIA FRANCES ANDERSON

Mrs. Maria Frances Anderson, a daughter of Thomas F. Hill, of Exeter, England, was born in Paris, France, January 30, 1819. In 1845, she was baptized at Pittsburgh, Penn., by Rev. William Shadrach, d.d., and united with the Grant Street Baptist church, of which Dr. Shadrach was at that time pastor. In April, 1847, she was married to Rev. George W. Anderson, D.D., of Philadelphia.

Mrs. Anderson is the author of a Sunday-school book "Jessie Carey" (1853), and "The Baptists in Sweden" (1861). A home mission hymn, written by Mrs. Anderson in 1849, is in many of our best collections. Dr. George B. Ide, then pastor of the First Baptist church in Philadelphia, had seen some of Mrs. Anderson's poetical productions in the Christian Chronicle, and as he wished to have a home mission hymn in the "Baptist Harp" which he was then compiling, he asked her if she would write one in the same measure as Bishop Heber's

From Greenland's icy mountains.

Mrs. Anderson acceded to his request, and her hymn was sung for the first time at a home mission meeting in the First Baptist church, Philadelphia. Dr. B. M. Hill, corresponding secretary of the American Baptist Home Mission Society, who was present, and read the hymn, introduced it with the remark, "We will now sing a home mission hymn written by a lady of this city, and just published in the 'Baptist Harp." The hymn, as it appeared in this collection, is as follows:

Our country's voice is pleading,

Ye men of God, arise!

His providence is leading,

The land before you lies.

Day gleams are o'er it brightening

And promise clothes the soil;

Wide fields for harvests whitening,

Invite the readers' toil.

Go where the waves are breaking

On California's shore,

Christ's precious gospel taking,

More rich than golden ore;

On Alleghany's mountains,

Through all the western vale,

Beside Missouri's fountains,

Rehearse the wonderous tale.

Where prairie flowers are blooming,

Plant Sharon's fairer rose;

The farthest wilds illuming,

With light that ever glows;

To each lone forest ranger.

The Word of Life unseal;

To every exile stranger,

It's saving truths reveal.

The love of Christ unfolding,

Speed on from east to west.

Till all, his cross beholding.

In him are fully blest.

Great Author of salvation.

Haste, haste the glorious day.

When a ransomed nation.

Thy scepter shall obey.

In the "Calvary Selection " (892) and the "Baptist Hymnal" (594) this hymn has three stanzas, the third given above being omitted. In the "Baptist Harp" Mrs. Anderson has another hymn (112) commencing,

Yes, she is gone, yet do not thou

The goodness of the Lord distrust.

FREDERIC DENISON

Rev. Frederic Denison is a native of Stonington, Conn., where he was born September 28, 1819. He was graduated at Brown University in 1847, and was ordained in the same year as pastor of the Baptist church in Westerly, R. I. This church he served in two pastorates fifteen years. He was afterward pastor of the Central Baptist church in Norwich, Conn., and of the Baptist church in Central Falls, R. I. During the civil war he was chaplain of the First Rhode Island Cavalry, and the Third Rhode Island Heavy Artillery, serving three years. After the war, he had pastorates in Westerly, R. I., New Haven, Conn., Woonsocket, and Providence, R. I. In recent years he has devoted himself to literary work. Among the writings he has published are the following: "The Sabbath Institution" (1855); "Notes of the Baptists and their Principles, in Norwich, Conn." (1857); "The Supper Institution" (1860); "The Evangelist, or Life and Labors of Rev. Jabez S. Swan" (1873); "Sabers and Spurs, or History of the First Rhode Island Cavalry" (1876); "Westerly, and its Witnesses for Two Hundred and Fifty Years" (1878); and "Shot and Shell, or History of the Third Rhode Island Heavy Artillery" (1879). He has also published several sermons, orations, and memorial addresses, and has been a frequent contributor to the secular and religious press.

Mr. Denison is also the author of an ode, on the unveiling, in 1885, of the painting of the arrival of Roger Williams with the first charter of Rhode Island; an ode on the centennial of the capture of General Prescott; an ode at the French Memorial in 1882; an ode at the unveiling of the soldiers' and sailors' monument, in South Kingston, R. I., in 1886; an ode at the dedication of the memorial of Col. John S. Slocum, in Providence, R. I., in 1886; a poem on the Baptist pioneers of Groton, Conn., in 1887; also many other occasional poems.

He has also hymns in "Welcome Tidings" and "Glorious Tidings," and among them the following:

Bethesda is open, the angel has come,
The Spirit is calling for thee;
The waters are troubled, behold, there is room;
Salvation through Jesus is free.

Come, press to the waters while mercy is here.
Accept of a cleansing complete;
O hear the entreaty, —dismissing your fear,
Lo! judgment and mercy now meet.

The house of Bethesda for sinners was built,
The pool is a fountain of love;

The waters are troubled for cancelling guilt,
And still for our healing they move.

Then come to the fountain, ye needy and lost,
Come now while the Savior is nigh;
This grace has been purchased at infinite cost;
And they that reject it must die.

JAMES TUPPER 1819-1868

Mr. Tupper was born in Charleston, S. C, December 9, 1819. In early life he received permanent religious impressions, and when sixteen years of age he united with the First Baptist church in his native city. A few years later he received a license to preach, but as it was his purpose to engage in the profession of law he was not ordained. When twenty one years of age he was admitted to the bar. His progress in his profession was rapid. He was early elected a member of the state legislature, from which he received an appointment as master in equity, and held the position through life. For a while also, he was auditor of the state, filling the office alike with honor to himself and to those whom he served. In all his trusts he was faithful, and in everything he adorned his religion. Prominent in Sunday-school work, he was never so happy as in leading the young along the paths of wisdom and virtue. His life was one of earnest, consecrated effort, and having served his generation with all fidelity he fell asleep at Summerville, S. C, August 28, 1868.

Mr. Tupper was the author of hymn 155 in "The Baptist Psalmody," from which it has been transferred to other collections. The hymn is as follows:

Dark was the hour, when Jesus bore
The sorrows of Gethsemane;
Strong was the grief, which caused to flow
His bloody sweat of agony.

He came with fallen man to dwell,
And suffer in his guilty stead;
He came, and now God's anger fell
Unmixed upon his sinless head.
O, hear the fainting Sufferer pray,
As all the powers of nature sink,—
"O, Father, take this cup away,
The bitter cup, alone, I drink."

"Yet not my will," he humbly cries
"Thine, Father, be as ever done."
Amazing wonder! heaven denies
The prayer of its own Holy One.

It could not pass, for he alone
Was strong to suffer and to save;
By him, in blood, our sins were borne,
And death he conquered in the grave.

KAZLITT ARVINE 1819-1851

Rev. Kazlitt Arvine is well known as the author of a "Cyclopasdia of Moral and Religious Anecdotes," and a "Cyclopaedia of Anecdotes of Literature and the Fine Arts." He was born in Centreville, Allegany County, N. Y., December 18, 1819. Having pursued preparatory studies, he entered Wesleyan University, at Middletown, Conn., where he was graduated in 1841. In 1842, he entered Newton Theological Institution. In the catalogue for 1842-3, his name appears as Silas W. Palmer. While he was at Newton his name was changed to Kazlitt Arvine by an act of the Massachusetts legislature. Mr. Arvine was a very zealous abolitionist, and during his theological course he became secretary of the "Provisional Committee," which afterward gave way to the Free Mission Society. He was very popular as a preacher, and supplied the pulpit of the First Baptist church, Boston, in the summer of 1843, while pastor Neale was in Europe. He was graduated . at Newton in 1845, and November 6, 1845, he was ordained as pastor of the Baptist church in Woonsocket, R. I. Rev. N. Colver, of Boston, preached the sermon, and John G. Whittier wrote for the occasion a hymn of seven stanzas, commencing

> A strength thy service cannot tire,
> A faith which doubt can never dim,
> A heart of love, a lip of fire,
> O Freedom's God! be thou to him.

Mr. Arvine remained in Woonsocket two years. He then became pastor of what was known as the Providence church in New York. A tendency to consumption had already developed, and on account of failing strength he was obliged to resign in a few months. His health having been in part restored, he accepted a call to the pastorate of the Baptist church in West Boylston, Mass. But he soon again began to decline, and he died at East Brookfield, Mass., July 15, 1851, greatly beloved by the people whom he served.

Mr. Arvine in early life achieved some reputation as a poet, and later he published a volume of poems. The following hymn, written by him, was sung at his ordination:

> Tar and wide, in mercy great,
> Lord, make known thy Word, which flings
> O'er our sad and darkened state,
> Joy and sunshine from its wings;
> Grace for guilt, it bids us crave,
> Hope for fear, and peace for strife;
> And, through Jesus' trusting grace,
> Opens up our way to life.
>
> Lord, increase and bless, we pray,
> Those who teach thy gospel's plan;

Oh, vouchsafe them, day by day,

Power with God, and power with man;

"While they 're echoing thy will,

'Mid the wrecks of sin and death.

Spirit, come, the slain to fill

With thy resurrection breath.

Round her leaders, bring thy church

All to conflict, armed with prayer;

Then ere long, shall victory perch

On the banner-cross they bear;

Then shall Zion's light go forth

Brighter than the noonday sun;

Christ shall come and reign on earth,

Making all its kingdoms one.

LUCY S. (HILL) DOUGHERTY 1822-1847

When floating on life's troubled sea,

By storms and tempests driven,

Hope, with her radiant finger, points

To brighter scenes in heaven.

She bids the storms of life to cease.

The troubled breast be calm;

And in the wounded heart she pours

Religion's healing balm.

Her hallowed influence cheers life's hours

Of sadness and of gloom;

She guides us through this vale of tears
To joys beyond the tomb.

And when our fleeting days are o'er,
And life's last hour draws near,
With still unwearied wing she hastes
To wipe the falling tear.
She bids the anguished heart rejoice;
Though earthly ties are riven.
We still may hope to meet again
In yonder peaceful heaven.

This hymn was published anonymously in the Christian Watchman, October 31, 1839. Rev. S. F. Smith, D.D., subsequently included it in "The Psalmist" (1843), of which he was one of the compilers. In the first edition it was marked "anon," but the authorship of the hymn was afterward made known to Dr. Baron Stow, Dr. Smith's associate in the preparation of the "Psalmist," and the pastor of the writer of the hymn, and in all subsequent editions the name L. S. Hill has been added. The hymn has been transferred to many later collections.

Lucy Simonds Hill was born in Boston, Mass., June 17, 1822. From a child she was thoughtful and conscientious, obedient to her parents, kind-hearted, truthful and studious. In 1839, having been led to accept Christ as her Savior, she was baptized by Rev. Baron Stow, and united with the Baldwin Place Baptist church in Boston. In her religious life she received counsel and assistance from her mother and elder sister, Abby S. Another sister, Harriet E., who was two years younger, should also be mentioned, for a sketch of one could hardly be written without a reference to the other. Both were detained from entering the grammar school till beyond the usual age for admission. But these years of home service were not passed unimproved, the elder sister, a diligent scholar, directing their studies, though with meagre facilities in the way of books. The two sisters at length entered the Bowdoin school, and from it they were graduated at the same age as their more favored classmates, Harriet having the valedictory, a poem which was published in the Advertiser by the school committee. After leaving school, Lucy added to her acquirements a knowledge of Latin and French, pursuing these studies at home without a tutor. She also took lessons in vocal and instrumental music, and continued the study of English composition and mathematics, with the purpose of becoming a teacher of these branches.

DANIEL C. EDDY

Rev. Daniel C. Eddy, d.d., was born in Salem, Mass., May 21, 1823, and when nineteen years of age he united with the First Baptist church in that city. On the completion of his literary and theological studies, he accepted a call to the pastorate of the First Baptist church in Lowell, Mass., and was ordained in January, 1846. He remained in Lowell ten years, and during this time he baptized six hundred and thirty-seven converts, and one thousand and five new members were added to the church. In 1854, he was elected a member of the legislature of Massachusetts, and at the organization of the house of representatives he was chosen speaker. This honorable position he filled so acceptably that at the close of the session he received a unanimous vote of thanks for his promptness, ability, and urbanity. In 1856, he accepted a call to the pastorate of the Harvard Street Baptist church, Boston, and here, as in Lowell, large audiences were attracted by his preaching, and large additions were made to the membership of the church. In 1862, he became pastor of the Tabernacle Baptist church, in Philadelphia, and after two years of service he returned to Boston, as pastor of the Baldwin Place Baptist church, which subsequently gave up its old place of worship, and erected a new church edifice on Warren Avenue. From Boston, in 1871, Dr. Eddy was called to the pastorate of the First Baptist church in Fall River, Mass. In 1873, he again returned to Boston, and was engaged in the erection of a new church at the south end; but the enterprise, for various reasons, was at length abandoned, and in 1877, Dr. Eddy became pastor of the Baptist church in Hyde Park, Mass. In 1881, he accepted a call to the pastorate of the First Baptist church, east district, Brooklyn, N. Y.., where he still (1888) remains. The church has erected a new house of worship, and is prospering under Dr. Eddy's leadership.

The degree of master of arts was conferred upon Dr. Eddy by Harvard College in 1855. Madison University, in 1856, conferred upon him the degree of doctor of divinity.

The following dedication hymn by Dr. Eddy has a place in the "Baptist Praise Book" (1874):

Maker of land and rolling sea,
We dedicate this house to thee;
And what our willing hands have done,
We give to God and to the Son.

Come fill this house with heavenly grace,
While sinners throng the heavenly place,
And saints below with saints above,
Unite to sing redeeming love.

Here let the cross be lifted high
Before a world condemned to die:
Here flow the blood of sacrifice,
To hush the Law's avenging cries.

Here let the mourning soul find rest
Upon the Savior's loving breast;
And with the sense of sins forgiven,
Each heart aspire to God and heaven.

Long may this sacred temple be
A monument of praise to thee;
And when to this no more we come,
Be heaven our high, eternal home.

Dr. Eddy has nearly ready for publication a hymn book entitled "The Memorial Hymnal."

J. WHEATON SMITH

Rev. J. Wheaton Smith, d.d., was born in Providence, R. I., June 26, 1823. When he was ten years of age his parents removed to Calais, Me., and there, two years later, he was baptized by Rev. James Huckins, and united with the Calais Baptist church, of which his father was a deacon. In 1844, he entered Brown University, and was graduated in 1848, receiving the Jackson premium for the best essay on moral philosophy. Entering Newton Theological Institution, he was graduated in 1851. March 30, of that year, and while a student at Newton, he was ordained pastor of the Worthen Street Baptist church, Lowell, Mass. In 1853, he became pastor of the Spruce Street Baptist church, Philadelphia. Here he remained until 1870, when with a colony from that church he organized the Beth Eden Baptist church, corner of Broad and Spruce Streets. Here he remained as pastor until 1880, when impaired health induced him to tender his resignation. Since that time, while making Philadelphia his home, he has supplied churches in Montreal and elsewhere, and has continued his usefulness in the management of important secular and religious trusts. He received, in 1862, the degree of doctor of divinity from the University of Lewisburgh, now Bucknell University.

Dr. Smith has been a frequent contributor to the religious press. He is also the author of the "Life of John P. Crozer" (1868). In "The Devotional Hymn and Tune Book" he has the following hymn:

This sweet in the trials of conflict and sin,
Temptation without and temptation within,
To know through the journey of life as I roam,
I am bound for the mansions of glory at home.

It is sweet in the gloom of earth's sorrow or fears,

My eyes overflowing with penitent tears,
To know, though the billows around me may foam,
I am bound for the mansions of glory at home.

I ask not to hasten from duty or care,
The troubles of life let me patiently bear,
If only I know as I look through the gloom,
I am bound for the mansions of glory at home.

When all earthly conflicts and trials are o'er,
When sin and temptation beset me no more,
Still trusting in Jesus, I'll welcome the tomb,
For I'm bound for the mansions of glory at home.

EDWIN T. WINKLER 1823-1883

Rev. Edwin Theodore Winkler, d.d., was born in Savannah, Ga., November 13, 1823. Having pursued preparatory studies in Chatham Academy, Savannah, he entered Brown University, Providence, R. I., where he was graduated in 1843, It was his purpose to engage in the work of the Christian ministry, and he commenced a course of theological study in Newton Theological Institution. He remained at Newton two years, and then returned to the south, where he became assistant editor of the Christian Index, and supplied the pulpit of the Baptist church in Columbia, Ga., for six months. In 1846, he was ordained as pastor of the Baptist church in Gillisonville, S. C, where he remained three years. In 1852, he removed to Charleston, S. C, and became editor of the Southern Baptist, and corresponding secretary of the Southern Baptist Publication Society. In 1854, he accepted a call to the pastorate of the First Baptist church in Charleston, and with the exception of service as chaplain in the confederate army during the civil war, he remained in this position until 1872, when he became pastor of the Baptist church in Marion, Ala. In 1874, in addition to his pastorate, he assumed the editorship of the Alabama

Baptist, and these two positions he held until his death, which occurred at Marion, November 10, 1883.

Dr. Winkler was a man of broad and generous culture. He was also an accomplished speaker, and was often invited to preach on special occasions, and to address literary societies. In 1871, he preached a memorable sermon on the education of the colored ministry before the American Baptist Home Mission Society, and in 1876, he delivered a centennial discourse at Newton Theological Institution. In 1858, Furman University conferred upon him the degree of doctor of divinity.

Some of these hymns have been transferred to other collections. They are not all of equal excellence. Perhaps the best hymn is the following:

O sinner, idly dreaming

The hours of life away,

While fainter grows the beaming

Of mercy's precious day.

Soon — spent their little number—

The night of death may break.

And thou bewail thy slumber;

O spell-bound sinner, wake.

As the fleet eagle, darting

With all his might of wing,

As the swift arrow, starting

From the resounding string,

So moments of probation

Their quick departure take;

If thou wouldst win salvation,

O spell-bound sinner, wake.

Time flies to reach the ending

Of all thy hopeful years,

To meet the Judge, descending

Along the darkened spheres;

O, if that dreadful morrow

Thy dream of life shall break,

Vain, vain will be thy sorrow;

Then, spell-bound sinner, wake.

Today the soft sky o'er thee

Still shines with gracious blue,

Today the work before thee

Thou mayst with ardor do;

Thou mayst receive God's Spirit,

And for thy Savior's sake.

Eternal life inherit;

O spell-bound sinner, wake!

RICHARD S. JAMES

Rev. Richard S. James, d.d., was born in Philadelphia, Penn., June 18, 1824. He was educated at Brown University and Columbian College, and began to preach when he was eighteen years of age. In 1859, he was ordained, and for nine years he was pastor at Camden and Marlton, N. J. Subsequently he was pastor of the Baptist church at West Newton, Mass., and of the Market Street Baptist church in Zanesville, Ohio. He then accepted a professorship in Hillsdale College, Mich. Afterward he was principal of Oak Grove Academy, at Mcdina, Mich. In 1880, he became president of Judson University, at Judsonia, Ark. On account of a burdensome debt the university was at length closed, and Dr. James accepted the presidency of Buckner College, at Witcherville, Sebastian County, Ark., an institution established by the Baptists of western Arkansas and Indian Territory, and named in honor of Dr. Buckner, who for thirty five years was a devoted missionary of the Southern Board to the Indians.

The following hymn by Dr. James is from "The Devotional Hymn and Tune Book" (1864).

Hastening on to death's dark river,
Daily nearer to the shore,
When, our warfare ceased forever,
We shall meet the foe no more.

Soon we'll see that blissful region,
Where the Prince of Peace doth reign.
Blessed thought! no hostile legion
Enters there with grief or pain.

Clothed with bodies pure and glorious,
God's free grace we there shall own,
In the Savior's strength victorious,
Cast before him every crown.

NATHANIEL BUTLER

Rev. Nathaniel Butler, d.d., son of Rev. John Butler, a well known preacher and revivalist, was born in Waterville, Me., October 19, 1824. He was fitted for college at the academy in Yarmouth. The first three years of his collegiate course he spent at Georgetown College, Ky., but he was graduated at Waterville College, now Colby University, in 1842. October 28, 1845, he was ordained pastor of the Baptist church in Turner, Maine. Here he remained until 1850, when he accepted an appointment as agent for the American Baptist Missionary Union for Maine and eastern Massachusetts. A few months later he accepted a call to the pastorate of the Baptist church in Eastport, Maine. Here he remained nine years. His subsequent pastorates were as follows: From 1860, to 1863, at Auburn, Me.; from 1864, to 1869, at Camden, Me.; from 1869, to 1872, at Albion, 111; from 1872, to 1873, at Leavenworth, Kan.; from 1873, to 1876, at Bangor, Me. ; from 1876, to 1877, at Dexter, Me.; 1877, to 1878, at North Vassalborough, Me.; and from 1880, to 1881, at Hallowell, Me. Then for several years, he was connected with the monumental department of the Bodwell Granite Company. In 1887, he went west, and engaged in evangelistic labor.

Dr. Butler was private secretary of Vice-president Hamlin from 1861, to 1865. He represented Vassalborough and Windsor in the Maine legislature of 1880. In 1856, he was elected a trustee of Colby University, and in 1873, he received from that institution the degree of doctor of divinity.

In 1877, he published a "Memorial of Nathaniel Milton Wood, with Sermons." He has also written not a little in prose and verse for the religious and secular press. The following hymn, written in 1849, is from the "Christian Melodist" (254):

How sweet, when worn with cares of life,
From all its busy scenes to flee;
To leave awhile its toil and strife,
And hold communion, Lord, with thee.

When the tired spirit seeks its rest,
'Tis there a sure repose I meet;
'T is there my weary soul is blest.
Kneeling before thy mercy-seat.

When sin overcasts with clouds my sky.
And Jesus hides his face from me,
Then to thy mercy-seat I fly,
And bow in humble prayer to thee.

There all the clouds of earth depart.

And heaven itself I almost see;

The Savior whispers to my heart

And shows his smiling face to me.

There Jesus' voice of love I hear;

There glory sheds its light around,

Eye never looked on things so fair;

Earth never heard so sweet a sound

Thou Lamb of God! O, let me dwell

Forever at thy sacred feet,

To hear the voice I love so well,

And ne'er forsake the mercy-seat.

JOHN M. EVANS

John M. Evans was born November 30, 1825, in Hilltown, Bucks County, Penn. In November, 1841, he was baptized in Philadelphia by Rev. J. H. Kennard, d.d., and united with the Tenth Baptist church, of which Dr. Kennard was pastor. He at once became identified with the music in both the church and Sunday-school, In 1854, on the opening of the new edifice of the Tenth church, he assumed the charge of the music, and was appointed superintendent of the Sunday-school. This was the first Sunday-school in Philadelphia to make music a prominent feature in its exercises. In 1864, Mr. Evans connected himself with the Tabernacle Baptist church, and for fourteen years had the entire charge of the music in the church and Sunday-school. In 1883, he became a member of the Memorial Baptist church, and at the organization of the Temple Baptist church at Tioga, in 1885, he identified himself with that new interest.

Mr. Evans is the author of several hymns, and also of several well known tunes. The following hymn is number 303 in the "Devotional Hymn and Tune Book" (1864), and was written by Mr. Evans about the year 1860:

Amid the joyous scenes of earth,
When hope's bright visions round us play,
There still remains an hour most dear:
The merry of that happy day,
Happy day, happy day,
When Jesus washed my sins away, etc.

Should all the joys of earth grow dim,
And melt like fancy's dreams away,
There linger deep within the heart
Fond memories of that happy day,
Happy day, etc.

When sorrow's clouds around us lower,
Amid the gloom a cheering ray
Comes gently stealing o'er the soul;
It is the memory of that day,
Happy day, etc.

When death's dark shadows gather round,
When nature's noblest powers decay,
A spirit's whispering voice recalls
The blessed memories of that day,
Happy day, etc.

ROBERT LOWRY

The author of

Shall we gather at the river

was born in Philadelphia, Penn., March 12, 1826. At the age of seventeen years he became a disciple of Christ, and although his parents were members of the Associate Presbyterian church, his study of the Scriptures led him to cast in his lot with the Baptists, and having been baptized by Rev. Geo. B. Ide, d.d., he united with the First Baptist church in Philadelphia. At once he devoted himself to Christian work, especially in connection with Sunday-schools. The desire to consecrate his life to Christ's cause, gradually took possession of him, and at length his pastor drew from him the confession that his thoughts had been directed to the work of the Christian ministry. Encouraged by Dr. Ide to prepare himself for this work, he entered Lewisburgh, now Bucknell University, where he was graduated with valedictory honors in 1854. The same year he was ordained and became pastor of the First Baptist church in West Chester, Penn., where he remained for five years. In 1858, he accepted a call to the pastorate of the Bloomingdale Baptist church, New York. In 1861, he became pastor of the Hanson Place Baptist church, Brooklyn. Here he remained until 1869, when he accepted the professorship of belles-lettres in his alma mater, together with the pastorate of the Lewisburgh Baptist church. This double service he performed six years, and then removed to Plainfield, N. J. Here a new church was organized, and Dr. Lowry—the honorary degree of doctor of divinity having been conferred upon him by Lewisburgh University—was called to the pastorate of what has since been known as the Park Avenue Baptist church. In 1880, Dr. Lowry took a rest of four years, and visited Europe. In 1885, he felt that he must have a longer respite, and after nine years of labor with a people to whom he was tenderly attached, he resigned. An effort was made to have him reconsider his action, and continue his ministry in Plainfield; but he was firm in the conviction that in taking this step he was in the path of duty, and for a time he traveled in the south and west, and subsequently in Mexico. At length, re-invigorated in health, he returned to Plainfield, where he still resides, devoting himself to the work which he loves so well, and in which he has achieved abundant success.

For, successful as Dr. Lowry has been as a pastor and preacher, multitudes know him better as a writer of hymns and composer of sacred music. On the death of William B. Bradbury, the music publishing business which he had built up in New York was continued by Biglow & Main. The new firm made a proposal to Dr. Lowry to prepare a book for use in Sunday-schools. At first Dr. Lowry shrank from the undertaking, fearing that it would interfere with his ministerial duties. He was at length, however, induced to enter upon the preparation of the proposed book. The work then begun has been continued to the present time.

A meeting not long ago was held in the Mission Hall in Salmon's Lane, Limehouse, London, to greet Lady Colin Campbell, who has shown in various ways her sympathy with the poor of the East End. The exercises consisted of cheers of welcome, prayer, singing and remarks by Walter Austin, the founder of the mission.

Working will not save me.
Purest deeds that I can do,
Holiest thoughts and feelings too,
Cannot form my soul anew;
Working will not save me.

Waiting will not save me.
Helpless, guilty, lost, I lie,
In my ear is mercy's cry;
If I wait I can but die;
Waiting will not save me.

Faith in Christ will save me.
Let me trust thy weeping Son,
Trust the work that he has done,
To his arms, Lord, help me run;
Faith in Christ will save me.

WILLIAM F. SHERWIN 1826-1888

Although remembered chiefly as a musical composer and conductor, William Fisk Sherwin has also a place among hymn writers. He was born in Buckland, Mass., March 14, 1826. On account of the long-continued illness of his parents, the family was reduced to extreme poverty, so that, although he early manifested decided musical abilities, it was impossible for him in his boyhood to obtain other instruction in music than that furnished by the old-fashioned singing; school. Of this he made the most, and so rapid was his progress that at the age of fifteen he was the leader of a large chorus choir. When eighteen years old he went west, and taught a district school. After his return he again devoted himself to music, and by his classes he aided in the support of the family. Accordingly he visited Boston in order to receive instruction from such masters as Lowell Mason and George J. Webb. At twenty-five years of age, he was well known in New England musical conventions. For a while he was a choir leader and conductor of a musical society in North Adams, Mass. Afterward he was professor of music in a female seminary in Hudson, N. Y. About the year 18-54, he was invited to take charge of the music in the Pearl Street Baptist church in Albany, N. Y., then under the pastoral charge of Rev. William Hague, d.d. He was also called to a professorship in the Albany Female Academy. Both positions he retained ten years, when, on account of failing health, he resigned, and removed to New York.

Brought up as a Congregationalist, he had always believed that immersion was New Testament baptism, and it is not strange that during his residence in Albany, under the preaching of Dr. Hague, he became a staunch Baptist.

Many of his anniversary and Christmas hymns have had a wide circulation in this country and in England. In 1884, out of one hundred hymns written for the semi-centennial of the American Baptist Home Mission Society, a committee selected a hymn by Professor Sherwin as one of the three best; and in 1885, a committee of the Methodist General Conference awarded him the first prize for "the best hymn and tune together, both original." The following stanzas by Professor Sherwin, form the introduction to a volume of scripture selections designed as a helper "in time of need":

"In time of need" —
So dost thou come with helpfulness, O Lord,

To those who trust thee and believe thy word;
With grace so like a mother's tenderness.
Enfolding all with thy great lovingness
In time of need.

In time of need,
No stinted measure doth the Father give
To those who daily strive near him to live;
"According to his riches" doth he succor bring,
And "of his fullness" giveth like a king,
In time of need.

Our time of need
Is day by day, and even hour by hour;
Each heart's pulsation tells us of his power
Who counts our moments, orders every breath,
And guards each footstep, lest it lead to death.
How great our need!
'T is time of need
When blessings countless as the stars at night
Flood all our pathway with a heavenly light;
Lest we grow vain —too self-reliant be —
And, in our selfishness, forget to see
And feel our need.

Oh! time of need
When anxious cares overwhelm the sinking heart,
And storm-clouds darkly lower, and joys depart!
When friends forsake us, or the loved ones go
Beyond where death's dark, chilling waters flow,
How sore our need!

No time of need

Can come to any soul with power so great,

No sorrow leave the heart so desolate.

But earnest prayer may bring, from realms above,

The strength and comfort of eternal love

To meet the need.

God knows our need!

Look up, O storm-tossed soul, look up!

Even though thy lips press sorrow's bitter cup

Receive the promise in the holy word,

And cast thine every burden on the Lord

In time of need.

J. N. FOLWELL

Rev. J. N. Folwell was born in Philadelphia, Penn., June 1, 1827, of Quaker parents. In his fourteenth year he was graduated from one of the district schools in his native city, and entering a mercantile establishment in Philadelphia, by a peculiar providence he was made the junior salesman two weeks later. In his nineteenth year he met with a change of heart through the renewing of the Holy Spirit, and March, 1847, he was baptized by Rev. J. fi. Kennard, d.d., and united with the Tenth Baptist church. Ten months later, through the influence of his pastor, and by the agency of Rev. Eugenio Kincaid, D.D., he was led to withdraw from a business life, and to enter upon a course of study preparatory for the Christian ministry. He was one of the first students in the institution now known as Bucknell University, but on account of illness was obliged to leave the institution in his junior year. From Madison University, at Hamilton, N. Y., he received the honorary degree of master of arts.

Mr. Folwell is the author of several hymns, some of which have appeared in the Watchman, and other religious journals. Two of these have found their way into Dr. Lowry's hymn books. One, entitled "The Child's Prayer," has a place in "Bright Jewels," and the other is included in "Our Glad Hosanna" more recent hymn written by Mr. Folwell is entitled "Prayer for the Holy Spirit."

Holy Spirit, at this hour
Let us feel thy quickening power;
Come upon us as we meet
At the heavenly mercy-seat.

Shed abroad thy love divine,
From all sin our hearts refine,
Make our lives from day to day
Jesus' love to men display.

Give us zeal the lost to seek,
And the gospel to them speak;
Make the fruits of grace abound
In our life the year around.

Fix our eye on Christ alone,
To our souls his joy make known.
All thy work in us complete,
For his presence make us meet.

Seal us for the life above,
O thou blest, eternal Dove I
Clothed in white, cause us to be,
And in peace God's face to see.

CARLOS SWIFT

Rev. Carlos Swift was born in Fabius, Onondaga County, N. Y., January 12, 1829. He was educated at Pompey Academy, Union College and Madison University. November 6, 1851, in Trenton, near Utica, he was ordained to the work of the Christian ministry. His principal pastorates have been at Clinton four years, Waterville four years, and Madison five years, all in New York; Mount Carroll three years. Normal two years, and Aurora one year, all in Illinois; Comanche, Iowa, two years; and in Chicago, seven years. He still resides in Chicago, but since 1864, ill health has greatly interfered with his ministerial labors.

Two hymns written by Mr. Swift are included in "The Iris, Songs of Jesus for Sunday Schools and Devotional Meetings," compiled by H. H. Hawley. One of these is a Christmas hymn. The other is entitled "Rejoicing in Hope," and is as follows:

In that far distant land where the angels of light

Are resplendent with glory no mortal hath known,

Where the praise of the Lord is their holy delight,

As with melodies sweet they encircle the throne;

I've a Savior whose glory outshines all beside.

From whose bosom the fullness of love overflows,

Who once visited earth, and in bitterness died

To redeem my dark soul from its sin and its woes.

In that far distant home where the angels of peace

Are united in love, and where harmony reigns,

Where the Father of all in his infinite grace

Sweetly smiles on the children his bounty sustains;

I've a mansion of bliss which my Savior has given,

Who with blood sealed my pardon and made me his own,

To partake of his fullness of glory in heaven,

And to sit at his side on his beautiful throne.

J. BYINGTON SMITH

Rev. J. Byington Smith, d.d., was born in Schroon, N. Y., May 1, 1830. When sixteen years of age he united with the Baptist church in Elbridge, N. Y. His collegiate studies he pursued at the University of Rochester, where he was graduated in 1852. From the Rochester Theological Seminary he was graduated in 1854. November 23, 1854, he was ordained at Dunkirk, and here he labored a few months. In the following year he accepted the pastorate of the Baptist church in Fayetteville, N. Y., where his ministry was signally blessed, many being added to the membership of the church. In 1860, he became pastor of the Baptist church in Farmersville, N. Y. During the six years which he spent with this church a new house of worship was erected. From 1865, to 1869, he was chaplain of the state prison at Sing Sing. Then he accepted a call to the pastorate of the Baptist church in Geneva, N. Y, Here he remained seven years. The year following his resignation he spent in Europe, and on his return he became pastor of the Baptist church in Peekskill, N. Y. He now resides in Saratoga, N. Y.

During his chaplaincy at Sing Sing Dr. Smith compiled a "Prison Hymn Book," which included some of the compiler's own hymns. Several hymns, written by Dr. Smith, are found in "Songs of Gladness" (1875). The following is entitled "The Hand that Lifts Me":

> When the mountain of sin rose above me,
> And I could not scale its bleak height,
> Its dark shadows were falling upon me,
> And gathering the blackness of night;
> Then a hand took me over the mountain
> To my home which was far out of sight.
>
> When I sank in the horrible dungeon,
> That horrible pit where I lay,

When the terrors of death were upon me.

And nothing my fears could allay,

Then a hand underneath me up bore me

To the brightness and gladness of day.

When I'm sinking in death's gloomy river.

And down in the surges I lie.

Then this hand is extended to rescue.

And lift to my home in the sky;

'T is the hand of my Savior that takes me,

And will lift me to dwell upon high.

Unto him who thus graciously saves me

From sorrow and sadness and sin,

I will cling till in love he shall bring me

Where never a sorrow has been;

And where he at the door will be waiting

To lift me, a poor wanderer, in.

Dr. Smith has published several sermons and addresses, lie is also the author of "Sayings and Doings of Children."

CHRISTOPHER R. BLACKALL

For many years Dr. Blackall has occupied a prominent position in Baptist Sunday-school work. He was born in Albany, N. Y., September 18, 1830. It was his purpose to enter the medical profession, and he studied medicine in New York, and later in Chicago, where he was graduated from the Rush Medical College. Daring the civil war he served about two years as a surgeon of the Thirty-Third Wisconsin Volunteer Infantry. He then resigned on account of impaired health, and returned to Chicago. Deeply interested in Sunday-school work, he accepted the secretaryship of the Chicago Sunday School Union, and in May, 1866, he became its general superintendent, succeeding Rev. J. H. Vincent, d.d. In 1867, he accepted an appointment as district Sunday-school secretary of the American Baptist Publication Society for the northwest, with headquarters in Chicago, and a year later he established the Chicago branch of the society. Here he remained until 1879, when he removed to New York to assume the management of the branch house in that city. In 1882, the enlargement of the Sunday-school periodical work made necessary the appointment of an office editor, and Dr. Blackall was transferred to Philadelphia. For ten years he had been editor of the primary class paper "Our Little Ones," and for three years editor of the "Bible Lesson Quarterly." He had also been a frequent contributor to the other publications of the society. This work he continued, and he also, in 1884, became editor of the "Baptist Superintendent." His assistance is frequently sought in Sunday-school conventions, institutes and assemblies.

Dr. Blackall is the author of the popular cantatas "Belshazzar" and "Ruth." He is also the author of a poem, "Nellie's Work for Jesus," which has reached a sale of twelve thousand copies. He has also published "Lessons on the Lord's Prayer" (1869), and "A Story of Six Decades" (1885), an interesting history of the work of the American Baptist Publication Society for sixty years.

Dr. Diane afterward wrote music for it, and inserted it in the "Glad Refrain." Dr. Blackall had been spending a couple of weeks at the Mammoth Cave, Kentucky, where for safety it was necessary to follow the guide. On the morning of his departure, recalling his experiences with the guide, the words of this hymn came to him, and were written out on the railway train immediately after.

Follow the paths of Jesus,
Walk where his footsteps lead,
Keep in his beaming presence,
Every counsel heed.

Watch, while the hours are flying,
Ready some good to do;
Quick, while his voice is calling,
Yield obedience true.

Cling to the hand of Jesus,
All through the day and night,
Dark though the way and dreary,
He will guide you right.

Live for the good of others,
Helpless, oppressed and wrong;
Lift them from depths of sorrow,
In his strength be strong.

HENRY C. GRAVES

In "Gospel Hymns" (consolidated) there is a hymn (356) by Rev. Henry C. Graves, d.d., entitled "Hear thou my Prayer." The music is by Geo. C. Stebbins, and the hymn first appeared in "Welcome Songs, No. 2," in 1879. The hymn is as follows:

All seeing, gracious Lord,
My heart before thee lies;
All sin of thought and life abhorred,
My soul to thee would rise.

Refrain. — Hear thou my prayer, O God,
Unite my heart to thee;
Beneath thy love, beneath thy rod,
From sin deliver me.

Thou knowest all my need,
My inmost thought dost see;
Ah, Lord I from all allurements freed,
Like thee transformed I 'd be.

Thou holy, blessed One,
To me, I pray, draw near;
My spirit fill, O heavenly Son,
With loving, godly fear.

Bind thou my life to thine,
To me thy life is given.
While I my all to thee resign,
Thou art my all in heaven.

Dr. Graves was born in Deerfield, Mass., September 22, 1830. When fourteen years of age he became a member of the Baptist church in North Sunderland, Mass., of which his father, Newcomb Graves, was a deacon for many years. A college education was his great desire from his childhood, and his parents, at a very great sacrifice on their part, aided him in its accomplishment. He prepared for college at Shelburne Falls and East Hampton; was graduated at Amherst College in 1856; and pursued his theological studies at Newton Theological Institution 1856-1858. He was ordained March 9, 1858, and his pastorates have been as follows: Charlestown, Mass., 1858-1863; Providence, R. I., 1863-1874; Fall River, Mass., 1874-1880; Haverhill, Mass., 1880-1886; New Bedford, Mass., 1886.

From his mother, who possessed a fine voice, and was familiar with the best music of the old masters, and also those of her own time. Dr. Graves inherited a love for sacred song. His first hymn, written when he was fifteen years old, was sung at the funeral service of a little child, by the choir of which he was a member. His hymns have been to him the expression of sympathy and religious feeling. Several of them were written as the conclusion of sermons, and they contain, in rhythmical form, the thoughts of the discourse. His occasional hymns have found a place in prominent religious and secular journals, and also in several collections of hymns for Sunday-schools, social worship, and church services. At the present time he has in preparation a volume of translations from Latin, French, and German hymn writers, some new versions of old English lyrics, and original hymns.

EDWARD G. TAYLOR 1830-1887

Rev. Edward G. Taylor, d.d., was born in Fox Chase, Philadelphia, Penn., November 25, 1830. He was graduated at the University of Lewisburgh, now Bucknell University, in 1854, and at Rochester Theological Seminary, in 1856. Having received a call to the pastorate of the Baptist church in Terre Haute, Ind., he was ordained in that place in June, 1857, and continued to serve that church as its pastor until 1860. From 1860, to 1864, he was pastor of the First Baptist church in Cincinnati, Ohio. He then removed to Chicago, where he was pastor of the Park Avenue Baptist church from 1864, to 1870. He then became pastor of the Coliseum Place Baptist church, in New Orleans, La., where he did a needed work in freeing the church from a heavy debt and in gathering a large congregation. He remained in New Orleans from 1870, to 1875, when he accepted the pastorate of the First Baptist church in Providence, R. I. Here he was especially prominent in Sunday-school work. In the large edifice of that historic church he gave each week an exposition of the Sunday-school International lessons, which was largely attended by Sunday-school teachers of different denominations. From Providence, in 1881, he went to New York as pastor of the Mount Morris Baptist church. Here he remained until September, 1882, when, on account of impaired health, he resigned, and went abroad. Upon his return, he became pastor of the First Baptist church, Newark, N. J. In the autumn of 1885, he accepted the call of the Delaware Avenue Baptist church, Buffalo, N. Y., and there he remained until his death, which occurred, after a brief illness, on Sunday, April 10, 1887.

The following hymn is a rendering into verse of an incident in the story of Mephibosheth, as related in 2 Sam. ix.:

At the King's table the kindness of God

Has made rich provision for me;
Costly the banquet —the purchase of blood —
Yet, large as its price, it is free.
Pardon and peace are the meats of his board,
And grace in abundance is there;
Glorious the feast that is spread by the Lord
For all his saved people to share.

At the King's table in gladness I sit,
Made pure from the sin that defiled;
Robed in the garments of righteousness, fit
For one whom he owns as his child;
There in his beauty the king I behold;
Ah! matchless is he in his grace,
Charms that by mortals can never be told
Adorn both his speech and his face.

At the King's table a company grand
Is gathered—once poor and unknown -
Princes are they by the touch of his hand,
And heirs to a crown and a throne.
To the King's table the kindness of God
Invites every sinner to come;
Tree its provision—the purchase of blood-
And mercy cries, "Still there is room."

CLARA B. HEATH

Mrs. Clara B. Heath, a daughter of Reuben G. and Sophia (Brown) Sawyer, was born in Manchester, N. H., July 28, 1831. She was educated in the public schools of that city, and attended a select school in a neighboring town about a year. In 1853, she was married to Robert Heath, a native of Chester, N. H., whose residence is now in Manchester. Mrs. Heath has been a contributor to the Watchman many years. Several of her hymns are included in Z. M. Parvin's "Songs of Delight," published in 1875, by A. S. Barnes & Co., New York. In 1881, she published a volume of poems, entitled "Water Lilies and Other Poems," which found a ready sale. The following lines in this collection are entitled "The Great Shepherd," 1 Cor. ii. 9:

"Eye hath not seen." O human eye!
Bewildered by the earth below,
The matchless glories of the sky.
The shining waves that ebb and flow,

The flowers with all their varied tints,
Brighter than ever monarch wore,—
Are these fair things indeed but hints
Of what our Father has in store?

"Ear hath not heard." O human ear
Charmed with the music of the sea,
Grilled with the sounds that greet thee here,
Rejoicing in their harmony.
Entranced by every word and tone
From loving lips that rise and fall.
Hast thou indeed, then, never known
The heavenly sounds that will enthrall?

"No heart conceives." Strange human heart
Proud of thine unseen depths below.
Buoyed by the hopes that from thee dart,
Is there still more for thee to know?
Capacious heart, that burns and thrills,
And throbs again with ecstasy,

When earth-born joys such caverns fill,
How deep the heavenly tide must be!

"For those who love him." Weary soul,
Drink deeply of the promised bliss.
How round and beautiful the whole
Of one great promise such as this
O wondrous ocean of God's love!
Beyond all comprehension wide.
Thy waves will bear the saints above,
Where all are more than satisfied.

WILLIAM H. DOANE

De. William Howard Doane, musical composer, was born in Preston, New London County, Conn., February 3, 1832. He received his education in the public schools of that place, and subsequently he attended the Academy at Woodstock, where he was graduated in 1848. His father was an extensive cotton manufacturer, and at an early age William was placed in an important position in his counting-room. About three years later he accepted a still higher and more responsible position in the counting-room of James S. Treat, an extensive manufacturer of cotton goods in Voluntown. After remaining there three years he was called to Norwich to take charge of the books and finances of J. A. Fay & Co., at that time extensive manufacturers of wood-working machinery. He remained with them about five years and then was transferred by the company to Chicago, Ill, and placed in charge of their western business as general agent. In 1860, he became a partner in the business, and having removed to Cincinnati, Ohio, he became president of the company, and has since had the complete control and management of the business. The sole manufacturing establishment of the company is now in Cincinnati. Dr. Doane was converted in 1847, and in 1851, he was baptized by Rev. Frederic Denison, and united with the Central Baptist church in Norwich, Conn. In 1857, he was married to Fanny M. Treat, daughter of his father's partner. Dr. Doane lives at Mount Auburn, a suburb of Cincinnati, and is a prominent member of the Mount Auburn Baptist church.

From his early boyhood Dr. Doane was interested in music. At the age of six years he sang frequently in public, and at the age of ten he sang in the church choir. At twelve he was considered an exceptionally fine flutist. At thirteen, he could play on the double bass viol, and at fifteen with equal skill he could play on the cabinet organ. About this time, he commenced musical composition. In thorough bass, etc., he was favored with good instructors, among them, Holbrook, B. F. Baker, A. N. Johnson, and the great German musician, Ranhoiser. In 1852-4, he was conductor of the Norwich Harmonic Society. In 1854, he assisted B. F, Baker in a musical convention.

Dr. Doane has composed more than six hundred Sunday-school songs, at least one hundred and fifty church and prayer-meeting hymns, and two hundred and fifty other songs and ballads, beside anthems, cantatas, etc.

CHARLES W. RAY

Rev. Charles W. Ray, d.d., was born in Burlington, Otsego County, N. Y., February 20, 1832. His early life was spent in Otselic, where he was trained to business; but at length, having made himself familiar with most branches pursued in our higher schools of learning, he turned his attention to the work of the Christian ministry, and was ordained pastor of the First Baptist church in Otselic, June 9, 1857. April 1, 1859, he entered upon his labors as pastor of the First Baptist church in North Stonington. Three years later he accepted the pastorate of the Third Baptist church in the same town. Here he remained four years, when he became pastor of the Baptist church in East Greenwich, R. I. After two years of service he accepted the pastorate of the Baptist church in Jewett City, Conn. Two years later he became pastor of the First Baptist church in Bristol, Conn, Subsequently lie was employed by the Connecticut Baptist Convention to organize a new church in Bridgeport. In recent years he has been a missionary and agent of the

American Baptist Publication Society, but is now devoting himself to evangelistic work, in which he has been greatly blessed. In 1884, he received the degree of doctor of divinity from Monongahela College, Jefferson, Penn.

Dr. Ray is the author of several books, among them a volume of poems entitled "Looking Forward, or Recognition and Reunion in Heaven." (J. B. Lippincott & Co., 1885). With the co-operation of Charles E. Pryor, he compiled a book of praise for the Sunday-school, entitled "Spicy Breezes," including a large number of Dr. Ray's own hymns.

Dr. Ray has written a large number of Christmas hymns. The following was recently published by McCalla & Co., Philadelphia:

'T is night, 't is night, and silence falls
O'er shepherd's fold and humble cot,
O'er temples, towers, and city walls,
And all is hushed and seems forgot.
But from the stable and the stall,
Upon the eager listening ear,
A baby's gentle sobbing fall.
And Christ, the new-born King, is here!

'T is night, 't is night, and from afar,
More bright than kingly diadem.
Is seen the strange prophetic star.
O'er David's city, Bethlehem;
The Prince of Life, the King Supreme,
At whose behest the worlds were made,
Who comes his people to redeem,
Is in the lowly manger laid.

'T is night, 't is night, and watchful eyes
Behold the shining angel throng.

Descending from the starry skies
With joyous shout and grateful song.
The shepherds leave their flocks to see
What wondrous things the Lord hath done,
And who the infant Prince can be I
'Tis Jesus, God's incarnate Son!

'T is night, 't is night! and yet the songs
Are heard o'er all the Bethlehem hills.
While echo sweet each note prolongs.
And every heart with rapture thrills.
What wondrous strains, what glad refrains
Of holy angels from on high,
Resounding o'er Judea's plains.
And through the blue ethereal sky

WILLIAM S. MCKENZIE

Rev. William Scott McKenzie, d.d., was born of Scotch parents, February 29, 1832, in Liverpool, Nova Scotia. When about fourteen years of age, he was converted and received as a member of a small Baptist church in his native town. Two years later he attended, at Wolfville, the academy which has been made somewhat famous by the late Professor James De Mille's series of publications known as the "B. O. W. C. Books." Here young McKenzie pursued his college preparatory studies, and was matriculated at Acadia College, Wolfville. But before his first year in college closed his health became impaired, and he went to Boston. Here, in about six months, he regained his health, but instead of returning to Wolfville, he resumed study at Worcester Academy, Worcester, Mass., where he passed a year in obtaining a more thorough preparation for college. He then entered Harvard University, from which he was graduated in 1855. The two subsequent years he spent at the Newton Theological Institution. In April, 1857, he was ordained, and supplied for awhile the Baptist church in East Abington, Mass. In 1858, he accepted a call to the pastorate of the Baptist church in Andover, Mass., where he availed himself of advantages for further theological study. While in Andover, at the suggestion of the late Dr. H. B. Hackett, he prepared for publication a series of Sunday-school question books on the Life of Christ. These books had a large sale, reaching an issue of nearly ninety thousand copies. From Andover Mr. McKenzie was called in 1860, to the pastorate of Friendship Street Baptist church, Providence, R. I. Here he remained until 1866, when he resigned on account of ill health, and spent the following year in seeking restoration in the rugged climate of Miramichi, on the Gulf of St. Lawrence. He then accepted a call to the pastorate of the Leinster Street Baptist church in St. John, N. B. Here he spent six years, when he was called by the board of the American Baptist Missionary Union to the office of district secretary for New England, in which service he is still engaged. The decree of doctor of divinity was conferred upon him by La Grange College.

The following is one of Dr. McKenzie's translations of the Dies Irse, a hymn written probably by Thomas of Celano, an Italian, who died about the year 1255:

Day of wrath and consternation!
World-wide sweeps that conflagration
Long foretold by inspiration.

Sudden fear on men is falling
For the Judge, to judgment calling,
Searcheth all with gaze appalling.

Peals the trumpet's blast of wonder;
Bursting every tomb asunder;
Citing all with voice of thunder.

Death and Nature, awestruck, quaking,
See the sleeping dead awaking
At the call the Judge is making.

God's own book of registration
Bears impartial attestation
In the great adjudication.

On his throne the Judge is dealing
With each hidden deed and feeling;
Wrath against all wrong revealing.

What for me can be expected,
By no patron's plea protected.
Where the just may be rejected?

O thou King of awful splendor—
Yet a Savior, loving, tender,
Source of love! be my defender.

Blessed Jesus! my salvation.
Brought thee down from exaltation:
Rescue me from reprobation.

Worn and wasted thou hast sought me;
With thy death-pangs thou hast bought me;
Shield the hope such anguish brought me.

Stay, just Judge, thine indignation;
Grant me pardon and salvation
Ere the judgment proclamation.

Bowed with guilt my soul is groaning;
Guilt ray crimsoned face is owning —

Spare, O God, a suppliant moaning.

Mary found in thee remission;
Thou didst heed the thief's petition:
Hope may I in my contrition.

Never can my prayers commend me;
Graciously wilt thou befriend me,
And from quenchless flames defend me.

When the sheep shall be selected,
Severed from the goats rejected.
Raise me to thy right perfected.

When thy foes in flames are wailing,
Where all cries are unavailing,
Summon me to joys unfailing.

Low before thee I am bending;
Sharp remorse my soul is rending:
Succor me when life is ending.

On that day of woe and weeping.
When from dust where he is sleeping,
Man shall wake and rise to meet thee,
Spare him! Jesus, I entreat thee.

WILLIAM C. WILKINSON

William Cleaver Wilkinson, d.d., was born in Westford, Vt., October 19, 1833. He was graduated at the University of Rochester, at Rochester, N. Y., in 1857, and at Rochester Theological Seminary in 1859. After his graduation he visited Great Britain, and on his return, in November, 1859, he became pastor of the Wooster Place Baptist church, New Haven, Conn. On account of ill health he resigned his pastorate in 1861, and again went abroad. On his return in 1863, he became professor ad interim of modern languages in the University of Rochester. Not long after he accepted the pastorate of the Mount Auburn Baptist church in Cincinnati, Ohio. Resigning this pastorate in 1866, he opened a private school at Tarrytown, N. Y. In 1872, he was elected professor of homiletics and pastoral theology in Rochester Theological Seminary, a position which he filled with marked ability until 1882, when he resigned. He has since devoted himself entirely to literary work. In 1871, he was offered the chair of the German language and literature in the University of Michigan, and that of English literature in 1873. In the same year the University of Rochester conferred upon him the honorary degree of doctor of divinity.

Dr. Wilkinson is a master of clear and vigorous English, and his writings are characterized by excellent judgment and a pleasing style. He is the author of "The Dance of Modern Society" (1868), "A Free Lance in the Field of Life and Letters" (1874), "Preparatory Greek Course in English " (1882), "Preparatory Latin Course in English" (1883), "College Greek Course in English" (1884), "College Latin Course in English" (1885), "Classic French Course in English" (1887), a volume of "Poems" (1883), and "Edwin Arnold as Poetizer and as Paganizer" (1885).

The following anniversary hymn by Dr. Wilkinson is from his volume of "Poems":

O thou with whom a thousand years
And a swift day are one,
Behold, our human hopes and fears
A little round have run.

Hopes for thy cause, ennobling hopes I
How foolish all the fears!
Shamed were a faith that droops and gropes,

Since such accomplished years.

Our hearts are large with thankfulness;
We glory in the Lord;
His Spirit doth our spirits press
As we his grace record.

Short rest in camp, then forth for fight!
Welcome the long campaign!
Guided with meekness and with might,
Spread we Immanuel's reign.

Like the blue bending firmament,
That kingdom yet must span,
From shore to shore, a continent.
Redeemed to God for man.

CHARLES H. ROWE

Rev. Charles Henry Rowe was born in Guilford, Me., January 19, 1834, but his family and childhood home was in New Gloucester, Me. Here, when thirteen years of age, he was baptized by Rev. Joseph Ricker, d.d., then pastor of the Baptist church in that place. He was graduated at Colby University in 1858, and at Newton Theological Institution in 1861. August 29, 1861, he was ordained, and became pastor of the Baptist church in Holyoke, Mass. In the following year he accepted a call to the pastorate of the Baptist church in Augusta, Me. In 1864, he resigned in order to accept a chaplaincy in the army. In 1866, he returned to pastoral work at the Stoughton Street Baptist church, Boston. Here he remained until 1871, when he became pastor of the Baptist church at Weymouth. His subsequent pastorates have been, Wollaston Heights, 1874-8; Cambridgeport, 1878-81; Mystic River, Conn., 1881-4; and Whitman, Mass.,

1885-8.

From his mother, a woman of superior mind and deep devotional spirit, he inherited a fine literary taste and a special love for hymns sweet with the perfume of gospel grace and truth. Beside many contributions to the religious press, he has written several hymns and poems that have been widely circulated. One of these, "At Rest," is found in a volume of "Poems on the Death of President Garfield," published by Moses King, Cambridge, 1881. In 1886, the following hymn appeared in the Watchman, and has since been included in Rev. W. E. Penn's "Harvest Bells, No. 1," published by the John Church Company, Cincinnati, Ohio,

Nearer, Christ, to thee,
Nearer to thee;
In love and by thy cross
Thou drawest me;
While all my prayer shall be,
Nearer, O Christ, to thee.
Nearer to thee.

In the wide wilderness
Of sin astray,
A wanderer far from God,
Lost in the way;
But by thy grace I'll be
Nearer, O Christ, to thee.
Nearer to thee.

By thee the way appears
That leads to heaven,
And in the gospel word
Is mercy given;
Thy love it calleth me
Nearer, O Christ, to thee.

Nearer to thee.

Redeemed by precious blood
From sin and death,
The Spirit's quickening power
A living breath,
By faith I live to be
Nearer, O Christ, to thee.
Nearer to thee.

And when from earthly care
Thou bidst me come,
And in thy presence find
My heavenly home,
There shall I ever be
Nearer, O Christ, to thee.
Nearer to thee.

HENRY L. MOREHOUSE

Rev. Henry Lyman Morehouse, d.d., was born October 2, 1834, in Stanford, Dutchess County, N. Y. His father and grandfather were natives of Fairfield County, Conn., and were members and deacons of Baptist churches. At the age of twelve he removed with his parents and an only brother to Avon, Livingston County, N. Y., where he was reared in the habits of industry incident to a thrifty farmer's life. His academic course was taken at Genesee Wesleyan Seminary, a few miles from his home, and his collegiate course at the University of Rochester, Rochester, N. Y., from which he was graduated in 1858. He was converted early in 1857, and united soon after with the Baptist church in Avon. After the death of his father in 1859, he remained on the farm about two years, when, believing that he was called to the work of the Christian ministry, he entered, in 1861, the Rochester Theological Seminary, from which he was graduated in 1864.

After a few weeks spent in Virginia, in the service of the Christian Commission, he accepted a call to the pastorate of the Baptist church at East Saginaw, Mich., then a typical frontier city, full of speculation in lumber and salt. Here he remained over eight years, the first two of which he was a missionary of the American Baptist Home Mission Society, preaching frequently in the adjacent settlements. He was a trustee of Kalamazoo College, and of the Baptist Union Theological Seminary at Chicago, and president of the Michigan Baptist State Convention. Early in 1873, he accepted a call to the pastorate of the East Avenue Baptist church in Rochester, N. Y., a new interest, of which he was the first settled pastor. He was soon elected a member of the board of trustees of Rochester Theological Seminary, and from 1877, to 1879, in addition to his pastoral duties, he was corresponding secretary of the institution. In May, 1879, he was elected corresponding secretary of the American Baptist Home Mission Society, and entered upon the duties of this office in July following. The "Seven Years' Survey," presented to the society in 1886, shows what unprecedented strides the society had made during this period. Dr. Morehouse continues to fill this arduous and most responsible position. The honorary degree of doctor of divinity was conferred upon him by the University of Rochester in 1879.

The poetical element in Dr. Morehouse's nature found occasional expression during his college course, and led to his election as alumni poet for 1874. The poem which he delivered on that occasion, entitled "Problems of Being," is his most elaborate production. Several hymns written by him have found their way into the papers, and have been widely reproduced. Among them is the following:

Friend of sinners, hear my plea,
God be merciful to me;
Sinful though my heart be found,
Let thy grace much more abound;
In the riches of thy grace
Finds my soul its resting-place.

Thou, my Advocate with God,

Grant forgiveness through thy blood;

With my heart I now believe,

Thy atonement I receive;

Freely with my mouth confess

Thee, my Lord, my Righteousness.

Now I glory in thy cross.

What was gain I count my loss.

Count but shame my former pride,

Self with thee is crucified;

Cleanse me, clothe me in the dress

Of thy spotless righteousness.

Trusting thee, O Christ, my King,

Shall my soul thy praises sing;

Saved by thee, thou Holy One,

Not by works which I have done;

Heart and tongue confess again,

Thine the glory, Lord. Amen.

This hymn was first published in the Examiner, from which it was transferred to "Good as Gold," and in 1883, with the omission of the third stanza, to the "Baptist Hymnal." It has been exceedingly helpful to many souls.

MRS. ANNIE S. HAWKS

Who is not familiar with the hymn

I need thee every hour?

It was written by Mrs. Hawks, and with fitting music, composed by Rev. Robert Lowry, D.D., it was first sun oat the National Baptist Sunday School Convention in Cincinnati, Ohio, November 20, 1872. Since that time it has found its way into many church hymnals, and it has been translated and sung in many foreign languages. Rev. W. J. Batt, chaplain of the state prison at Concord, Mass., tells how an ex-prisoner, who had never had a home of his own, prepared a home, humble but tasteful, and then asked the chaplain to come and help him dedicate it. Together they entered the home—the man's wife had not yet come — and the service began. "Mr. B.," says the chaplain, "with evident brokenness of spirit, for he was naturally a proud man and not unacquainted with larger surroundings, could not refrain from some criticism upon his poor things; but his heart was so full that his embarrassment was only temporary, and he immediately went on with a firm purpose.

Mrs. Hawks was born in Hoosick, N. Y., May 28, 1835. For many years she has been a resident of Brooklyn, N. Y. Here about the year 1868, her pastor, Rev. Robert Lowry, d.d., discovered her gift as a hymn-writer, and induced her to exercise it for the advancement of the cause of Christ. One of the first of her hymns was the following:

Why weepest thou?

Whom seekest thou?

O wouldst thou see our Jesus?

Behold him near,

He marks each tear,

Our blessed, loving Jesus.

Why weepest thou,

Why seekest thou,

With doubting and repining?

O lift thine eye!

Thou shalt descry

His raiment near thee shining.

Believe him now;

Receive him now;

Look up, with faith and meekness,

To Jesus' blood

Which freely flowed

For all thy sin and weakness.

Believest thou?

Cease weeping now—

Thy soul he will deliver;

The cross he bore,

Our sins he wore,

And nailed them there forever.

D. HAYDEN LLOYDE

Mr. D. Hayden Lloyde was born in Springfield, Mass., June 11, 1835. Three years later his parents removed to the west, and settled in Bureau County, Illinois. As a child he evinced decided musical talent, and he early received musical instruction from his father, who was a music teacher, as well as a schoolmaster. When eleven years of age he sang alto in a church choir, and later he became a leader of singing in church and Sunday-school. At length he made the acquaintance of P. P. Bliss, from whom he received inspiration and encouragement, and for several years he devoted himself to the study and teaching of vocal music. Afterward he conducted musical institutes and conventions, and for many years he gave special attention to music for Sunday-schools. Since 1874, he has been a resident of Champaign, 111.

Mr. Lloyde has written many Sunday-school hymns, which, with music of his own composition, have been published in "Songs of Faith," "Shining Light," "Fount of Blessing," "Royal Songs," "Glorious Tidings," "River of Life," "Shining River," "Songs of Love," and other works.

The following hymn, written by Mr. Lloyde, is entitled "Mighty to Save," and was first published in the Sunday School Times:

Lead me, O thou precious Savior,
Safely lead by thine own hand,
Speak, I come to thee for guidance,
Traveling to the heavenly land.
Safe Supporter, sure Deliverer,
Cleanse me by thy power divine.

Brought by grace to see the fountain
From which cleansing waters flow,
I would trust thee now and ever;
Guide and bless me while below.
"Rock of ages, cleft for me,
Let me hide myself in thee."

While I live and through death's valley,
Lead me to the other side;
Bid my cares and fears to vanish,
Though the storms of life abide;
Safely to the haven guide me,
"O receive my soul at last."

JAMES W. WILLMARTH.

Rev. James W. Willmarth was born in Paris, France, December 23, 1835. His father, Rev. Isaac M. Willmarth, was the first American Baptist missionary in France. His early education was greatly impeded by a supposed affection of the eyes, but his thirst for knowledge led him to surmount formidable obstacles. Having been baptized at Grafton, Vt., in 1848, he studied theology with his father by help of a reader. His first service was in Chicago, as a missionary colporteur of the American Baptist Publication Society. July 26, 18G0, he was ordained at

Aurora, Ill. His pastorates have been at Metamora, Ill., Amenia, N. Y., Wakefield, Mass., Pemberton, N. J., and Roxborough, Philadelphia, where he still remains.

Mr. Willmarth is the author of several articles in the Baptist Quarterly. He has published also a sermon on "Election," preached as the doctrinal sermon before the Philadelphia Association in 1880; also "In the Name of Jesus," a small pamphlet, published by the American Baptist Publication Society. In the "Baptist Praise Book" (1872) is a hymn (740) by Mr. Willmarth, commencing

O Father, Lord of earth and heaven.

Its four stanzas are from a hymn of six stanzas, written in 1867, and first sung June 30, 1867, at a baptism of five candidates at Wakefield, Mass., then South Reading. It was published in some paper, probably the National Baptist, from which, with the second and sixth stanzas omitted, it was transferred to the "Baptist Praise Book." Subsequently the hymn was re-written for the "Baptist Hymn and Tune Book," in which its five stanzas were arranged as a baptismal chant (selection 33). The hymn as it there appears is as follows:

O Father, Lord of earth and heaven!
O Son Incarnate, Christ our King!
O Spirit, for our guidance given!
Hear and accept the vow we bring.

We own thee. Savior, crucified,
We own thee, Savior, raised to heaven;
With thee our souls to sin have died,
But now would rise as thou art risen.

Thy gospel, Lord, we would obey.
We follow, and thy hand shall guide;
We seek through Jordan's wave the way
That leads thy loved ones to thy side.

287

Now in immersion, wondrous sign.

We dedicate ourselves to thee;

Now seal the covenant divine.

And own us thine eternally.

We trust the pledge which thou hast given,

Of grace to keep us still thine own,

And dying, we shall rise to heaven,

To share thy glory and thy throne.

FRANKLIN JOHNSON.

In the Baptist Quarterly Review for July, 1882, appeared an article by Rev. Franklin Johnson, d.d., containing translations of some hymns and songs of certain German Anabaptists of the period of the Reformation. One of these translations is found on pages twenty-two and twenty-three of this volume, and a part of two others on page twenty-four. In 1883, Dr. Johnson published a small, tasteful volume entitled "Dies Irse, an English Version in Double Rhymes, with an Essay and Notes." As early as 1865, he had published in a religious journal a translation of the "Dies Irse ," and during the intervening years, at frequent intervals, he had returned to the task of giving a more perfect expression to his translations of this Latin mediaeval hymn. The thoroughness of his work appeared in this later publication, and the Atlantic Monthly, in a notice of his translation of this magnificent production, says, "As a whole it is worthy to take rank with the three best versions in the English language, and in selected stanzas is quite incomparable."

In 1886, D. Lothrop, & Co., Boston, published a translation by Dr. Johnson of two other

Latin hymns, "The Stabat Mater Speciosa," and "The Stabat Mater Dolorosa," with illustrations from the old masters. The same careful work appeared in these English renderings of these two well known hymns of the mediaeval church. In both Dr. Johnson has faithfully reproduced the meaning and emotion of the Latin originals. Both of these hymns, too, he gives in a translation adapted to the devotional use of Protestants.

> Hark! the angel hosts are singing
> Him who came to break our chains,
> And the skies with songs are ringing
> Over the dark Judean plains,
> For all Heaven, with countless voices,
> At the birth of Christ rejoices.

> Hail, thou happy babe and holy,
> Lying on thy mother's breast,
> Offspring of the Virgin lowly,
> Offspring of the Spirit blest.
> Child, and yet the world's salvation,
> Author of God's new creation.

> Long have prophets, saints and sages,
> This fair day of grace foretold,
> Chanting to the future ages
> What our favored eyes behold;
> Not a promise they have spoken
> To the weary world is broken.

> Wood and plain and lake and mountain,
> River falling from the height.
> Rain and snow and springing fountain,
> Storm and calm and day and night.

As your mighty Maker own him.
As your mighty Lord enthrone him.

Praise him, ye who are o'er laden
With the frosts of many days;
Praise him, youth, or man, or maiden;
Praise him, babes and sucklings, praise;
Worship him and bow before him.
And with sweetest songs adore him.

Dr. Johnson was born at Frankfort, Ohio, November 2, 1836. He was educated at Madison University, graduating from the Theological Department in 1861. In the same year he was ordained at Portsmouth, now Bay City, Mich., and became pastor of the Baptist church at that place. His subsequent pastorates have been at Lambertville, Passaic City, Newark, N. J., and Cambridge, Mass., the latter beginning in 1874, and closing in 1888. He has been in Europe four times, and studied at some of the German universities, among them Leipzig, Jena and Heidelberg, studying theology under Kahnis, and Old Testament interpretation under the elder Delitzsch.

Beside the hymns already noticed. Dr. Johnson has published "The Gospel According to Mark with Notes" (1873); "Moses and Israel" (1874); "Heroes and Judges from the Lawgiver to the King" (1875); "True Womanhood. Hints on the Formation of Womanly Character" (1882); "A Romance in Song. Heine's Lyrical Interlude" (1884); "The New Psychic Studies in their Relation to Christian Thought" (1887). He has also published several sermons and review articles, has been a frequent contributor to the religious press, and in 1876, with Dr. Lorimer, he edited the Watchman.

PHILIP P. BLISS 1838-1876

A useful life, early closed, was that of the well known song-evangelist, Philip P. Bliss. He was born in Clearfield County, Penn., July 9, 1838. His parents were Methodists, and at family worship, where daily there was the offering of praise as well as prayer, he received his first musical impressions. Such, too, were the sacred influences that surrounded him in his home from his earliest years that he could not remember the time when he was not a believer in Jesus Christ, and when twelve years of age he united with the Baptist church of Cherry Flats, Tioga County, Penn.

In 1864, Mr. Bliss took up his residence in Chicago, where, with George F. Root, he was engaged in conducting musical institutes, conventions, etc. He owed much by way of instruction and inspiration to William B. Bradbury, and one of his first published songs was a tribute to the memory of Mr. Bradbury. In 1874, Mr. Bliss accepted an invitation to engage in evangelistic work with Major Whittle, and his sacred songs became not only effective gospel utterances, moving hearts, but they soon made the name of the singer known in all parts of the land.

Mr. Bliss published his first musical work, "The Charm," in 1871. This was followed by the "Song Tree" in 1872, "Joy," and "Sunshine for Sunday Schools" in 1873, "Gospel Songs for Gospel Meetings" in 1874, and "Gospel Hymns and Sacred Songs" in 1875. In the preparation of this last book he was associated with Ira D. Sankey.

The following hymn has this added interest, that it was Mr. Bliss's last hymn:

I know not what awaits me,
God kindly veils mine eyes;
And o'er each step of my onward way
He makes new scenes to rise;
And every joy he sends me comes
A sweet and glad surprise.

One step I see before me.
'Tis all I need to see,
The light of heaven more brightly shines,

When earth's illusions flee;
And sweetly thro' the silence comes
His loving "Follow me."

O blissful lack of wisdom,
'Tis blessed not to know,
He holds me with his own right hand,
And will not let me go,
And lulls my troubled soul to rest
In him who loves me so.

So on I go, not knowing,
I would not if I might;
I'd rather walk in the dark with God
Than go alone in the light;
I'd rather walk by faith with him
Than go alone by sight.

In his later years Mr. Bliss became a member of the First Consecrational church in Chicago.

HENRY M. KING

Henry Melville King, d.d., was born in Oxford, Maine, September 3, 1838. When he was six years of age his parents removed to Portland, in the same state, where in the public schools he pursued his college preparatory course, graduating at the high school in 1855. In the autumn of that year, he entered Bowdoin College, and was graduated in 1859, with the highest honors of his class, his commencement part being a poem. With the Christian ministry in view he entered Newton Theological Institution, and was graduated in 1862. October 28, 1862, he was ordained in Portland, but returned to Newton as instructor in Hebrew, and assisted Dr. Hackett during the following seminary year. He then accepted a call to the pastorate of the Dudley Street Baptist church, Roxbury, Mass., succeeding Rev. Thomas D. Anderson, D.D., who had been called to the pastorate of the First Baptist church in New York city. Here his ministry was crowned with the divine favor, and though he received frequent calls to other churches and to professorships in theological institutions, he remained with the church from 1863, until 1882, when, greatly to the regret of his people he accepted a call from the Emmanuel Baptist church in Albany, N. Y., the church of which he is still pastor. He received the honorary degree of doctor of divinity from Colby University in 1877.

For many years, while pastor of the Dudley Street Baptist church. Dr. King was a member of the executive committee of the American Baptist Missionary Union, and also a trustee of Newton Theological Institution. After his removal to Albany he was made a trustee of Yassar College, and also of Rochester and Madison Theological Seminaries. From 1884, to 1887, he was president of the board of managers of the American Baptist Missionary Union.

To our denominational journals and reviews, Dr. King has been a frequent contributor. Beside numerous pamphlets, sermons, and two semi-centennial discourses— one for each of the churches he has served as pastor—he has published "Early Baptists Defended" (1880), being a review of Dr. H. M. Dexter's "As to Roger Williams," and "Mary's Alabaster Box" (1883), a volume of sermons. For the "Memorial History of Boston" (1881) he contributed an admirable sketch of the history of the Baptist churches in that city.

The following Christmas hymn by Dr. King, with music by Mr. Marsh, has also been published by Pond &Co.:

Angels sang the natal day
Of Christ, the Savior King;
And o'er the hills of Palestine
The Christmas sun did brightly shine,
And glory in the valley lay.
The morning of that sacred day—
Let us with angels sing.

Glory be to God most High,
And peace, good will to men;
For Christ the Lord was born today,
And in his manger-cradle lay.
The angels sang, and we reply,
And raise our voices to the sky,
And sing and sing again.

Prince of Peace, Almighty Lord,
He laid his glory by;
A loving Babe to earth he came
And Jesus, Savior, was his name.
He came to speak the living word,
Join earth and heaven in sweet accord,
And guide our souls on high.

Hail we now the new-born King,
Whose throne is in the sky;
Again he comes, a welcome guest,
To every lowly manger breast.
And "Glory be to God" we sing.
While heaven and earth with anthems ring,
And we with angels vie.

HEZEKTAH BUTTERWORTH.

Mr. Butterworth's childhood home was in Warren, R, I., where he was born December 22, 1839. His mother loved the old Methodist and Baptist hymns, and was accustomed to sing these while engaged in her daily tasks. In this way, from his earliest years, Mr. Butterworth was made familiar with very many of the songs of Zion. These hymn experiences of his youth led him in later years to write "The Story of the Hymns," an exceedingly interesting account of the origin of hymns of personal religious experience, published by the American Tract Society in 1875, and for which Mr. Butterworth received the George Wood gold medal. It was out of this experience, also, that he wrote the hymn, which has found a place in an English collection, commencing

> The church of Christ, our blest abode,
>
> Celestial grace is thine,
>
> Thou art the dwelling-place of God,
>
> The home of joys divine.
>
> Wherever for me the sun may set,
>
> Wherever I roam or dwell,
>
> My heart shall nevermore forget
>
> Thy courts, Immanuel.

This hymn appears in full in the cantata "Under the Palms." Many thousand copies of this cantata have been sold in this country and in England, and several of its hymns have been sung at Mr. Spurgeon's regular Sunday-service. It also has a place in "Heart and Voice," published by John Church & Co., with about twenty hymns written by Mr. Butterworth, many of them originally for the Ruggles Street Baptist church or Sunday-school, in Boston.

HENRY F. COLBY

Henry F. Colby, d.d., a son of Gardner and Mary L. R. Colby, was born in Roxbury, Mass., November 25, 1842. He received a thorough preparatory classical training, and entered Brown University in 1858, where he was graduated in 1862, delivering the Latin salutatory. He then commenced the study of law, but at length went abroad for travel. On account of a change of purpose in life, he abandoned his legal studies on his return, and entered Newton Theological Institution in the autumn of 1864. From this institution he was graduated in 1867, and in the latter part of that year he accepted a call to the pastorate of the First Baptist church in Dayton, Ohio, where he was ordained in January, 1868. Identifying himself with the religious and educational work of the Baptists of Ohio, he has served the denomination in that state as president of the Ohio Baptist Convention, and as a trustee of Denison University. He received the honorary degree of doctor of divinity from his alma mater in 1882.

The following hymn, written by Dr. Colby, was sung at the graduation of his class at Newton Theological Institution, June 26, 1867:

Waiting on the eve of labor,
Knowing not the coming day,
Bowing at thy throne, O Savior,
For a blessing, now, we pray.
Thou hast called us by thy Spirit;
Thou hast brought us to this hour;
Vain will be our best endeavors,
If we lack that Spirit's power.

Grant us then thy benediction,
Make us wise in word and deed,
Give us faith and love and patience,
Give us all the grace we need.
May we sow beside all waters,
Trusting thee the seed to keep;
May we, entering on the harvest.
Thrust the sickle in and reap.

Stand beside us, gracious Savior;
All thy promised aid impart;
Place thine arm of strength around us;
Let us feel thy beating heart.
Then, when days of toil are over,

When our latest sheaves are bound.

We will cast them all before thee.

Joying most to see thee crowned.

GEORGE C. NEEDHAM

Mr. Needham has become very widely known through his evangelistic labors. He was born about the year 1844, on the shore of Kenmare Bay, not far from the famous Lakes of Killarney, in the south of Ireland. His parents were Irish Protestants, and he received a religious training. His mother died when he was ten years of age, and her dying prayers were for the spiritual welfare of her children, who were gathered around her bedside. That solemn scene made an abiding impression on George. In his eighteenth year the great revival wave swept over Ireland, and the motherless boy was one of those who were reached by it. A year later he became connected with a business house in Dublin, and soon won the confidence and esteem of his employers. At the end of the year, however, against the protest of his employers, who made him flattering offers, and also against the advice of some of his friends, he relinquished his position, and gave himself to the work of an evangelist. His labors were so successful that he was at length invited to visit England, where his work in the vicinity of Mr. Spurgeon's birth-place brought him into intimate relations with the great London preacher. It is said that at that time he prepared to enter Mr. Spurgeon's college, then in its infancy; but Mr. Spurgeon, on account of Mr. Needham's usefulness in his calling, advised him to continue in it. In 1866, Mr. Needham, with Mr. H. Grattan Guinness, made an evangelistic tour of Ireland with marked results. In 1867, with the late Henry Moorhouse, he decided to visit the United States. He was detained, however, by the sickness of a sister, but for a short time only. Three months later, with her, he followed his friend. Mr. Needham landed in Boston, and on the next day he made a brief address at the noon meeting of the Boston Y. M. C. A. Invitations to preach soon poured in upon him, and with his well thumbed Bagster Bible he began to give "Bible Readings."

The following hymn, by Mr. Needham, first appeared anonymously in Dr. A. J. Gordon's

"Vestry Hymn and Tune Book" (1872), and has been transferred to other collections:

I stand, but not where once I stood

Beneath a load of guilt;

My Savior, Jesus, bore it all,

For me his blood was spilt;

bless the Lord exalt his name;

He gave himself for me;

He died upon the shameful cross

To set the captive free.

I stand, but not on Calvary's mount.

Before the blood-stained cross;

Though still on it my faith doth rest,

And count all else but dross;

bless the Lord! I do believe

That Jesus died for sin.

And on that cross he shed his blood

To make the guilty clean.

I stand, but not beside the grave

Where once my Lord did lie;

The cross and grave he left behind,

And took his seat on high;

bless the Lord! the work is done.

With God I'm reconciled;

And risen with the risen Christ;

He owns me as his child.

I stand even now within the vail,

In union with my Lord,

Beyond the power of death and hell;

I know it from his word;

O bless the Lord! assured thereby,

In him we are complete;

We walk by faith, but soon, in sight,

Our gracious King well' greet.

ELIZABETH A. NEEDHAM.

Mrs. Elizabeth Axnable Needham, wife of Geo. C. Needham, the evangelist, was born of Puritan stock, in Manchester, Mass. As a child, she was religiously thoughtful, and leaving her young companions, she loved to study her Bible amid the wild solitudes of her grandfather's estate. Her life thus very naturally took on that coloring of quiet seriousness and earnest gravity which since have been characteristic of her. She did not, however, neglect the different branches of secular study. She had careful instructors, who delighted to guide her thoughtful mind. But as a girl, with steadfast purpose she devoted her best powers to the interpretation and presentation of Bible truth. Her studies in this direction have borne rich fruit. Since her marriage to Mr. Needham, she has often accompanied him in his evangelistic tours, and her Bible readings, marked by womanly grace and refinement, have also been marked by the richer graces of the Spirit. She is a woman of strong faith. The Christian Herald, referring to her, says: "When her husband explained to her before marriage the plan of his life, never to contract a debt, and that he had gone without food in his evangelistic work rather than borrow a dollar, she heartily commended the plan, and rejoiced in his purpose."

The following hymn, written by Mrs. Needham, is from a collection of hymns compiled by Rev. H. L. Hastings, entitled "Songs of Pilgrimage" (1886):

"All night in prayer" —while others slept,

Or, heedless, their wild revels kept,

In lonely spots, oppressed with care,

The Savior spent his nights in prayer.

"All night in prayer" — 't is joy to know
I have such comfort in my woe;
And whilst I watch, his pity share.
Who often spent like hours in prayer.

"All night in prayer" — I love to think
His hand doth mix each cup I drink;
And for my blessing doth prepare
Each night of weariness and prayer.

"All night in prayer"—O Savior, Christ,
My sins deprived thy life of rest;
And love for me didst make thee bear
The sorrows of those nights of prayer.

"All night in prayer" —ah! morn shall come,
A morn whose light shall guide the home;
Its dawn will scatter gloom and care,
And joy shall crown our nights or prayer.

C. C. LUTHER

Among Baptists there have been, and there are still, a large number of successful evangelists. Mr. Luther has devoted himself to this department of Christian service. He was born May 17, 1847, in Worcester, Mass., where his parents are members of the First Baptist church. After completing his college preparatory course, he was employed for two years as a journalist. He then entered Brown University, where he was graduated in 1871. During his senior year he was converted, and united with the church to which his parents belong. On leaving college it was his purpose to make journalism his lifework, and until 1876, he was connected with papers in Springfield, Mass. He was then gradually led to see that the Lord had other purposes concerning him. For nearly a year he accompanied Rev. S. H. Pratt in his evangelistic work, singing the gospel which Mr. Pratt preached. Then he, too, began to preach, and from that time he has been earnestly engaged as an evangelist. For several years he labored as a lay evangelist, but June 25, 1880, he was ordained by the church at Worcester, of which he is a member. His work, which has been limited almost wholly to Baptist churches in eastern Massachusetts and Rhode Island, though he has visited places in New Hampshire, Connecticut, New York, New Jersey and Pennsylvania, has been greatly blessed, and large accessions have been made to the churches which he has served.

The use of sacred song in gospel meetings Mr. Luther well understands, and he has written about twenty-five hymns, to which he has added music of his own composition.

A few days later he handed them to George C. Stebbins, who composed for them the beautiful music which accompanies them in "Gospel Hymns." Music of his own composition Mr. Luther added to these words subsequently. The hymn, as written by Mr. Luther, is as follows:

"Must I go, and empty-handed?"
Thus my dear Redeemer meet?
Not one day of service give him,
Lay no trophy at his feet?

"Must I go, and empty-handed?"
Not one lost one homeward guide?
Ne'er proclaim the love of Jesus,
How for sinners lost he died?

Not at death I shrink nor tremble,
For my Savior saves me now;
But to meet him empty-handed,

Thought of that now clouds my brow.

Oh, the years of sinning wasted!
Could I but recall them now,
I would give them to my Savior,
In his service gladly go.

O, ye saints, arouse, be earnest,
Up and work while yet 'tis day;
Ere the night of death overtakes thee,
Strive for souls while still you may.

WILLIAM A. SMITH.

Rev. William A. Smith was born in Cincinnati, Ohio, December 29, 1847. He received his collegiate education at Brown University, Providence, R. I., where he was graduated in 1870. With the profession of law in view he studied at the Law School in Albany, N. Y., graduating in 1872. He was admitted to practice in the courts of the State of New York, but in 1877, he decided to enter the Christian ministry, and commenced the study of theology. In October, 1878, he received ordination as a Baptist minister, and the same year he was called to the pastorate of the First Baptist church in Hamilton, Ohio. In 1879, he became pastor of the Third Baptist church in Cleveland, Ohio. In 1881, he was called to the pulpit of the Perkins Street Baptist church in East Somerville, Mass., the parish lying partly in Boston and partly in Somerville.

Mr. Smith has written and published the following books: "The Student's Hand-book of Commercial Law," "Who is Responsible?" and "The Spinning Wheel of Tamworth." He is also the author of many hymns, published for special occasions, in addition to those which have found their way into collections; among them the following, entitled "The Sweeter Thought";

'Tis sweet when morning wakens,
And leaves the couch of night,
To cast athwart the darkness,
Her golden radiance bright;
'Tis sweet to look to heaven,
And breathe upon the air.
With grateful hearts overflowing,
The voice of thankful prayer.

'T is sweet when twilight shadows
Are gathering thickly round,
When evening bells are ringing
In low, melodious sound;
'T is sweet to leave the labor
And cares of anxious days.
To worship in his presence.
And raise the song of praise.

'Tis sweet in youth's bright morning,
When hope inspires the breast.
And every zeal and effort
Are into service pressed;
'T is sweet to trust our Father,
And on his help rely,
To feel that on us ever
Is fixed his watchful eye.

But sweeter far it will be,
If in the hour of death
I can but sing his praises
With life's last lingering breath;

Yes, sweeter far than ever,
I feel —I know 't will be,
If I can hear him whisper
The message, "Come to me."

ALBERT A. BENNETT.

In 1886, there was published anonymously "A Collection of Hymns," arranged with especial reference to the wants of the First Baptist church in Yokohama, Japan. The compilation was the work of Rev. Albert Arnold Bennett, one of the missionaries of the American Baptist Missionary Union stationed at Yokohama. Of the two hundred and thirty hymns in this collection twelve were written by Mr. Bennett. The following is number 220:

Oh, for a stainless record!
Oh, for a spotless name!
Oh, for that praise of heaven,
Without which fame is shame.

Oh, to be good and noble;
To help to make men good!
Oh, to deserve that plaudit
Where "hath done" equals "could"

Oh, for the course well ended!
Oh, for the race well run!
Oh, for the crown God giveth
To all who crown his Son!

For this I pant and labor,
And powerless cry to thee;

Great Help, thou God Almighty,

Say thou, "The thing shall be."

Mr. Bennett was born in Philadelphia, Penn., April 16, 1849. His father, Edward A. Bennett, was a deacon of the Fifth Baptist church in that city. With this church Mr. Bennett united at an early age, during the pastorate of Rev. J. B. Simmons, d.d., by whom he was baptized. From the time of his conversion he was active in church and Sunday-school work, and early consecrated himself to service in the foreign mission field, with a special interest in Japan. Having graduated with honor at Brown University in 1872, he entered the Baptist Theological Seminary in Chicago, where he was graduated in 1875. From 1875, to 1879, he was pastor of the Baptist church in Holliston, Mass. He resigned his pastorate in order to engage in mission work, and having been appointed a missionary to Japan, he sailed with his wife (a daughter of Rev. B. W. Barrows) from San Francisco, in November, 1879, and on his arrival in Japan entered upon the work to which he had so long looked forward with deep interest and many prayers. The "Japanese Hymn Book," commenced by Dr. N. Brown, was completed by Mr. Bennett.

JOHN B. MULFORD.

Rev. John Brantly Mulford was born in Philadelphia, Penn., September 2, 1851. His grandfather. Rev. Joseph H. Kennard, d.d., was the founder, and for nearly thirty years the pastor, of the Tenth Baptist church; and he was baptized by his grandfather when twelve years of age. He took his theological coarse at Crozer Theological Seminary, and was a member of the class of 1876. His first settlement was in Sewickley, Penn., where he became pastor of the Baptist church, August 1, 1876. January 1, 1878, he became pastor of the Baptist church at Somerville, N. J., where he remained until July, 1881. His next pastorate was at Wheeling, West Virginia, whither he was sent by the Home Mission Board in New York to aid in saving an old church from extinction and to protect the society from a loss of money loaned. Having accomplished this, he accepted a call from the First Baptist church in Atchison, Kansas, and entered upon his labors in December, 1883. There he still remains. He is a member of the board of directors of Ottawa University, also of the State Home Mission Board, and is one of its executive committee.

Mr. Mulford is the author of several hymns written for the most part at the request of Rev. Robert Lowry, d.d. One of these was written in Wheeling, West Virginia, November 4, 1881, as the conclusion of a sermon on the text, "And everything shall live whither the river cometh."

The following hymn by Mr. Mulford, is in "Joyful Lays":

O glorious God! eternal and wise,
Thou Maker of worlds, and Lord of the skies;
To thee would we lift glad carols of praise,
For all thy rich gifts and wonderful ways.
When earth without form lay mantled in night,
Thy lips spoke the word, and there was light;
When man in his strength come forth from thy hand,
He found his first dwelling a Paradise land.

O bountiful God! attentive and kind,
Thou fullness of light to souls that are blind,
To thee would we yield the tribute of love,
Tor blessings on earth and mansions above.
The mercies of life are held in thy hand.
The angels of help around thee now stand;
For every earth-want and every soul-need.
As beams of the morning with succor they speed.

O all-loving God! benignant, and pure,
Thou Savior of souls, whose promise is sure,
To thee would we give the love of our hearts,
And take of thy grace with all it imparts;
The cross of thy Son, all crimson with blood,

Assures us of life beyond the dark flood;

For Jesus has died our ransom to pay,

To lead us in triumph to glory's bright day.

ARTHUR S. PHELPS.

Arthur Stevens Phelps, third son of the well known hymn-writer, Rev. S. Dryden Phelps, d.d., and grandson of Rev. James H. Linsley (one of the compilers of "Select Hymns," 1836), was born in New Haven, Conn., January 23, 1863. He was baptized at the age of thirteen; began to preach at nineteen; spent a year in Brown University; in 1886, was graduated B.A. at Yale University, and entered the Yale Divinity School. The following hymn, first printed in the Christian Secretary, April 8, 1885, a few months after it was written, is number 1218 in "Songs of Pilgrimage" (1886), compiled by Rev. H. L. Hastings:

Help me, my Lord, to grow

More like to thee,

Thy wondrous love to know,

Thy face to see.

Lord fill my soul with light,

Dispel the gloom of night,

And make me through thy might

More like to thee.

Though rough the road may be.

Jagged and steep,

Lord, though I may not run,

Upward I'll creep.

When nightly shadows fall,

When doubts and fears appall,

Then may I rise from all,

More like to thee.

Or if my footsteps sink
la doubt's dark wave,
May I like Peter cry,
Lord Jesus, save I
So by my faith to prove
Thine all redeeming love;
Oh, make me, heavenly Dove,
More like to thee.

And when from Pisgah's height
Canaan I view;
When faith shall change to sight,
Old things to new;
Then in a nobler song,
Through all the ages long,
I'll stand amid the throng,
Made like to thee.

GERMAN BAPTIST HYMN WRITERS AND THEIR HYMNS

GOTTFRIED W. LEHMANN 1790-1882

Gottfried Wilhelm Lehmann was born in Hambarg, Germany, October 23, 1799. Soon after his birth his parents removed to Berlin, the capital of Prussia. While a youth he went to Leer, in East Friesland, to learn the saddler's trade of his uncle. But not long after, he came to feel that this was not to be his occupation for life, and near the close of 1817, he returned to Berlin, where he became an engraver and lithographer. While in East Friesland, he was attracted to the Christian faith, and soon after his return to Berlin he joined a circle of believers who were interested in the furtherance of the work of Christian missions, the circulation of Bibles, and the cause of temperance. In order to procure Bibles at a low cost Mr. Lehmann applied to J. G. Oncken, of Himburg, who was at that time an agent of the Edinburgh Bible Society, now the National Bible Society of Scotland. In this way, between these two men an acquaintance was formed which was to be of great importance to the cause of Christ in the Fatherland.

This was in 1830. Oncken was baptized by Dr. Sears at Hamburg, April 22, 1834. Lehmann, who by independent study of God's Word had quite early been convinced of the necessity of believer's baptism, was baptized with six others, May 14, 1837, by Oncken, in a lake near Berlin. On the following day this little flock of disciples was organized as a Baptist church, and Lehmann was appointed pastor, although he still continued his business tasks. At first, almost unsurmountable difficulties and severe persecutions were encountered by these Berlin Baptists. In 1838, Mr. Lehmann entered the service of the American Baptist Missionary Union, and devoted one-half of his time to missionary work. In 1840, he went to England, where in Salter's Hall Chapel, Cannon Street, London, he was ordained June 29. The revolution of 1848, brought to the German Baptists in Prussia entire liberty. Many and extensive missionary tours were made by Lehmann into eastern Prussia, where great success attended his labors. He also again visited England, and collected funds for a chapel in Berlin. At length the Baptists in Berlin, through his labors, secured a comfortable home, which became the headquarters of wide-spread activities.

Mr. Lehmann was one of the founders of the Berlin branch of the Evangelical Alliance. Although he was stricken down by disease several times, he lived to see the Baptist church in Berlin receive the rights of incorporation, and died February 21, 1882. Mr. Lehmann possessed the gift of leadership, and with Oncken and Robner guided the Baptist movement in Germany many years. It would be difficult to overestimate the value of his services, and his labors were blessed to the awakening and conversion of a large number of devoted Christian men and women.

SIGISMUND KUPFER 1803-1882

Sigismund Kupper was born in 1803, in Berne, Switzerland, where he studied theology, and later was connected with the Free Evangelical Society, a company of pious members of the state church banded together for the evangelization of the canton of Berne. In 1848, having previously married Miss Julia Haller, a most estimable lady, he emigrated to this country. Meeting with Baptists on his arrival in New York, he became convinced of the scripturalness of their views, and united with the First German Baptist church in that city. Soon after he was ordained, and accepted the pastorate of the First Baptist church in Newark, N. J. In 1850, he went to St. Louis, and became pastor of the German Baptist church in that city. While there, he baptized Prof. Rauschenbusch. After withdrawing from his work in St. Louis, he spent the most of his remaining life in retirement, in Highland, Ill., but supplied for a time the First German Baptist church in Buffalo, N. Y. These later years of his life he devoted to the study of the Scriptures, to a very fruitful and spiritual correspondence, and to the preparation of contributions in prose and verse for Der Sendbote, the German Baptist paper published in Cleveland, Ohio. Mr. Kupper was a man of earnest piety, sound theological training, and his sermons were full of thought, and excellent food for the soul, though they failed to attract the masses on account of defects in his delivery. He died full of years, and highly esteemed for his own and for his work's sake, about the year 1882.

The following hymn by Mr. Kupper is 455 in "Die Pilgerharfe":

In anthems of praise, O church of the Lord,
Now join your glad voices in blessed accord,
United to Christ in a covenant sure.
Which rests on God's promise and ever must endure.

We're witnesses, rescued from sin and the grave,
By Jesus, who came both to seek and to save;
With him we are buried to the world and its strife,
And with him are risen to newness of life.

We joy as we look upon this sacred bath,
As together we journey o'er life's thorny path;
The mind of the Spirit our guide day by day.
While faith joyful looks to the prize far away.

Descend now upon us thou Spirit divine.
And to the dear Savior our hearts all incline;
The light of thy presence upon us let fall,
The witness of grace bestow on us all.

Redeemed of the Lord, let anthems of praise,

As you press toward the light, your glad voices raise;

The bright land of promise provides blissful rest.

And Jesus invites you to come and be blest.

JULIUS KOBNER 1807-1884

Julius Kobner was born June 11, 1807, at Odensee, capital of the island Fuhnen, and next to Copenhagen the most important place in Denmark. As the son of the head rabbi he was brought up in all the traditions of Jewish lore, receiving careful instruction in a good school. Later he became an engraver, and having entered into a marriage engagement with a young lady of noble birth, the young couple, on account of the difficulties in the way of such a union in their native land, left Denmark, and took up their residence in Wandersbeck, Germany. Here they renounced Judaism, entered the state church, and were married by a special act of grace from the Danish king.

It is not known that at this time Mr. Kobner was especially interested in religious things. Somewhat later, while residing in Lubeck, he was on friendly terms with Dr. Geibel, pastor of the Reformed Church. Afterward he earned a livelihood as a play-writer in Hamburg. But while in Hamburg he made the acquaintance of John G. Oncken, who made known to him the way of life so clearly that soon he could say of the Messiah, "Rabbi, thou art the Son of God, thou art the King of Israel."

May 7, 1836, Mr. Kobner was baptized by Oncken. Until 1852, he assisted Oncken as pastor of the Baptist church in Hamburg and also as a missionary. An earnest student, he was interested in the wide field of knowledge, and made himself familiar with the Greek, Latin and English languages, in addition to the Hebrew, Danish and German languages with which he was already familiar. From 1852, to 1866, he was pastor of the Baptist church in Bar, Rhenish Prussia, a church of which he was the founder. In 1866, he went to Copenhagen, where he labored until 1879. He then returned to Barmen, and in 1883, became pastor of the Baptist church in Berlin. Here he closed his work, dying February 2, 1884, one month after Oncken's death, and nearly two years after the death of Lehmann.

The following translation of this hymn, by David Chandler Gilmore, of Rochester, N. Y., appeared in the Examiner, July 29, 1886:

All perfect, holy majesty
Enthroned above the skies,
The Lord through all eternity!
To thee we lift our eyes.
That we are nothing well we know,
Yet every heart rejoices so,
That thou art great and glorious,
And holdst thy scepter forth to us.
Before thy face
Refuse us not a place.

A company of sinners we,
We all have made thee grieve;
But in thy changeless love we see
Our safety. We receive
From Jesus Christ our righteousness;
We stand before thee in this dress;
And Abba, Father, can we say;
And all our hearts rejoice always—
Rejoice in thee,
Here is it good to be.

In God how great our blessedness;
A man is on the throne
Who all the weight of weariness

313

And human scorn has known.

His day of triumph is begun,

What shall withstand Jehovah's Son?

Send us thy mighty word today,

Victorious bear the spoil away,

With heart and hand

Be present in our band.

CONRAD A. FLETSCHMANN 1812-1867

Conrad A. Fleischmann was the pioneer German Baptist missionary in the United States. He was born in Nuremberg, Bavaria, April 18, 1812. Here he was brought up in the Lutheran faith. Having learned a trade, he set out in his nineteenth year to complete his apprenticeship in other cities. In Geneva he made the acquaintance of some earnest Christians, by whom he was led into a fuller light of the gospel of Christ. This was in 1831. Soon after, he was baptized at Basel, and in obedience to his convictions of duty he now entered upon a course of theological study at Berne. Three years later he commenced Christian work in the Emmenthal. In 1837, he returned to Nuremberg, and in the following year, at the invitation of George Muller, he visited Bristol, England, and in 1839, he came to the United States for the purpose of doing missionary work among his countrymen.

He began his work in Newark, N. J., and in October, he baptized three converts, the first fruits of his labors. Others followed. Later he went to Reading, Penn., where great success attended his way among the Germans there. In 1842, he removed to Philadelphia, where he organized a German Baptist church. During his pastorate there he did missionary service in other parts of the country. In 1852, the first Conference of German Baptists was held, and Mr. Fleischmann, by appointment of the Confederate, commenced in the following year the publication of Der Sendbote, then a monthly paper. The first meeting of the General German Baptist Conference was held in 1865. Der Sendbote was now made a weekly paper, and Mr. Fleischmann became associate editor. October 15, 1867, after preaching an impressive sermon from the text, "Thus said the Lord: set thy house in order, for thou shalt die, and not live," his long and eminently useful career was suddenly terminated by death. Mr. Fleischmann was a devout, earnest, affectionate disciple of the Master, and loved the work of winning souls to Christ. His services as founder of the German Baptist churches in the United States wall long be remembered.

AUGUSTUS RAUSCHENBUSCH

Prof. Augustus Rauschenbusch, d.d., was born in Altena, Westphalia, Germany, February 13, 1816. His father, from whom he received careful early instruction, was pastor of the Lutheran church in that city. When fourteen years of age he entered the gymnasium at Elberfeld, and four years later he entered the theological department of the University of Berlin. Here, under the influence of Neander and other pious friends, he was led to a saving knowledge of the truth. Later he studied natural science and theology at the University of Bonn. When his father died in 1841, he was made his father's successor; and his earnest evangelical efforts at Altena were greatly blessed. But he was not at ease under the restrictions of his position, and in 1846, he crossed the Atlantic to labor among his countrymen in the United States. He preached a short time in Missouri. In 1847, he was placed in charge of the German tract department of the American Tract Society in New York. While in this position he was led to examine the question of baptism, and as a result of his investigations he accepted Baptist views, and was baptized in May, 1850. In 1851, he labored awhile in Canada, and organized the first German Baptist churches there, though he did not sever his connection with the American Tract Society until

1853. He then visited his native land. Returning to the United States with a party of emigrants in 1854, he settled with them in Missouri. In 1855, he organized a German Baptist church in Gasconade, Mo. In 1855, at the request of the New York Baptist Union, he organized the German Department of the Theological Seminary in Rochester, N. Y., and received an appointment as professor. This he filled with great acceptance, performing a most valuable service for the German Baptist churches in the United States, until the summer of 1888, when he resigned on account of ill health, and returned to his native land, bearing with him the love and honor, not only of his fellow-countrymen in the United States, for whom he had so long and faithfully labored, but also the love and honor of all who, during his work in this country, had in any way been associated with him, or had known his work. May his last days, amid the scenes of his youth, be crowned with abundant blessings.

Once where flows the sacred Jordan,
Christ was buried beneath the wave.
See the waters swelling round him,
In this emblematic gravel
See how glowed his tender love
For the sinful, when he strove
With the mightiest powers infernal,
Snatching souls from death eternal.

Yes, for us on Calvary dying,
He from sin has made us free,
Life and fullest pardon winning,
Blessedness for you and me.
His we are from this glad day,
Follow him in his own way,
Uncomplaining, his cross bearing,
He for us our nature wearing.

Therefore on, ye well-loved children;

Are you from the curse made free?

Glows your heart with love for Jesus,

Crucified upon the tree?

Ye who bear his sacred name.

Follow him through floods and flame.

Where our Head has gone before us,

We may tread, his banner o'er us.

PHILIPP BICKEL

Rev. Philipp Bickel D.D., was born September 7, 1821, in Weinheim, Grand Duchy of Baden, Germany. His education he received at Bender's Collegiate Institute in Weinheim. In 1847, he was apprenticed to a notary public, preparatory to state service. On account of his participation in the revolution in Baden in 1848, however, he was compelled to leave his native land and, in the summer of 1848, he made his way to the United States. Here for a time he found employment as a printer and as a teacher. In the winter of 1851, he was converted under the preaching of Rev. J. Coggeshall, and was baptized in Lake Michigan, near Waukegan, Ill. Not long afterward the conviction ripened that it was his duty to preach among his own countrymen the gospel he had received. To fit himself for this work, he .availed himself of the theological course at the Rochester Theological Seminary. After his graduation in 1855, he entered upon missionary work among the Germans, in Cincinnati, Ohio, where he succeeded in organizing a German Baptist church. As the pastor of this church he was ordained in September, 1857. Here he built a chapel, and published the first German Sunday-school paper. In 1865, the German General Baptist Conference appointed Mr. Bickel president of the newly organized German Baptist Publication Society, and withdrawing from the pastorate he removed to Cleveland, Ohio, which became the Society's headquarters. Here he built the German Baptist Publishing House in 1871, and superintended the Society's publication work, which included the editorship of Der Sendbote. As a recognition of his scholarly worth, Denison University conferred upon him the degree of doctor of divinity. In 1878, by appointment of the American Baptist Publication

Society, and at the request of prominent Baptists in Germany, Dr. Bickel returned to his native land to re-organize the publication work of the German Baptists in Hamburg, which has since that time been his residence. In this work Dr. Bickel has been successful. Beside superintending the publication work, he edits Der Walirheitszeuge, and in various ways he is performing a service for the Baptists of Germany, which is gratefully recognized.

Six of Dr. Bickel's hymns are in "Die Glaubensharfe." One of them (611) is the following:

Take my heart, O Father, make it.
Wholly and for aye thine own;
Holy Spirit, melt it, break it,
Soften into flesh this stone.
Liker thine may it be growing.
Savior, thou its sovereign art;
While my soul unfolds, up going,
Meek and lowly keep my heart.
Father, shelter it from evil;
Bid it find in thee its home;
Help it world, and flesh and devil,
By thy strength to overcome.
God, in Jesus' blood and anguish
Cleanse my heart, and give it rest;
When in darkest hours I languish,
Comfort thou my troubled breast.

GREGOR SPECK

Gregor Speck was born in Ettlingen, near Carlsruhe, Baden, Germany, November 17, 1826. He was brought up in the Roman Catholic faith, and was educated in the seminary for teachers in his native place. Afterward, until July, 1849, he was engaged in teaching in the district of Gengenbach. In 1850, he came to the United States, and shortly after his arrival in New York he took up his residence in New Brunswick, N. J. Here he played the organ in the Roman Catholic church. But coming under Protestant influences, and having been led by the grace of God to accept Jesus Christ as his Savior, he was baptized in January, 1853, and united with the First German Baptist church in New York. About this time Mr. S. S. Constant opened a mission Sunday-school in 38th Street, among the German people there, and Mr. Speck was invited by the First German church to take charge of a German day school in connection with this Sunday-school. He accepted the position, and for fifteen years he devoted himself to the interests of this day and Sunday-school. It was a blessed work, and a blessing followed his earnest labors.

Among the German Baptist churches, when he entered upon this work, the Sunday-school was little known. There were no German Sunday-school papers nor hymn books. Mr. Speck opened a correspondence with Rev. P. Bickel, then a German Baptist missionary in Cincinnati, Ohio, deeply interested in Sunday-school work, who commenced the publication of a Sunday school paper, Der Muntere Saeman, which is now in all German Baptist Sunday-schools. He also encouraged Mr. Bickel to publish a Sunday-school hymn book. The first edition of "Das Singvogelein" contained only fifty-two hymns. This collection has been enlarged from time to time, and the seventh edition, now in use, has two hundred and twenty-two hymns.

JOHANN D. FEDDERSEN.

Johann Feddersen was born at Deetzbiill, "Kreis" Jondeni, Duchy of Schleswig, November 3, 1836. His father, who was a merchant in that place, died early, and when Johann completed his school-life he went to Husnm to learn the bookbinder's trade. It was here that the greatest of all changes in his life took place, for here he gained a living faith in the Son of God. In the spring of 1853, Husnm was devastated by a fire. After this fire a quantity of old books were stored in the garret where Johann slept, and he spent his Sundays and leisure hours in looking over these old books. Among them he found a copy of David Hollagen's "Evangelische Gnadenordnung," which impressed him because of the stress the author laid upon the necessity of a new birth, together with the fact that through a recognition of one's misery in sin, and through the forgiveness of sin in Jesus' blood, is there obtained a consciousness of peace with God. He resolved to make an effort to obtain this boon, and the Lord blessed the reading of that old book to his heart in such a manner that one evening in June, 1853, he could exclaim with unspeakable joy, "God's spirit bears witness with my spirit that I am his child and heir." He now had peace with God, and henceforth he has lived in the blessed sunshine of his grace.

In his twenty-first year he began to express in verse the feelings that stirred his young heart, and a series of religious poems was the result. These were brought together, and published in 1864, at Hamburg, with the title "Zions Heder." From this collection °I take the following, entitled "Nur Ihu" — "Him Only":

> O sweet and precious Lamb of God,
> On whom once fell the chastening rod,
> Who bore ray sins upon the tree,
> I ever have enough in thee.

> In thee, in thee, and thee alone!
> If thou didst not for me atone,
> If I dared not to go to thee,
> All hope had long since fled from me.

> Since Christ my sins has now forgiven,
> And made of me an heir of heaven,
> From this glad hour my heart shall be
> At peace with him to whom I flee.

> Without him how could I each day
> Tread joyfully the narrow way?
> Apart from him who gave me breath,

That were to me destruction, death.

But he remains my lasting choice,
And in his blood I still rejoice.
The cleansing blood that makes me free,
Which flowed on Calvary for me.

A sweet and precious Lamb of God,
On whom once fell the chastening rod,
Who bore my sins upon the tree,
I ever have enough in thee.

Mr. Feddersen's home is at Elmshorn, in the Duchy of Holstein, and he is a member of the Baptist church there.

HERMANN WINDOLF.

Hermann Windolf was born at Gmnenplan, Duchy of Brunswick, Germany, April 28, 1846. He was converted when sixteen years of age, and united with the Baptist church at Einbeck, in Hanover. Through the mission paper published at Hamburg, and Der Sendbote, he became interested in missions, and love for his Master awakened in him a desire to be employed in the work of giving the gospel to the heathen. But it pleased the Lord, he says, to keep him in the school of patience, and teach him lessons which would be useful to him in the work upon which he was to enter. His father was a mason, and he served an apprenticeship with him. He received instruction also in an institute of technology. In 1865, he attended the theological school at Hamburg, with which at that time Oncken and Reibner were connected. He studied the Gospel of John under Oncken. Not less stimulating and faithful, he says, was the instruction of Reibner. Returning to his trade, he devoted a part of his time to evangelistic work. For two years (1867—1869) he labored as a missionary at Herford, in Westphalia. From 1873, to 1877, he performed a like service in Brunswick. At the close of 1877, he sailed with his family for Queensland, Australia, where he landed February 20, 1878. During the remainder of that year he served the German Baptist church at Fassifern and Mount Walker as pastor. From 1879, to 1884, he was pastor of the German Baptist church at Marburg and Upper Brisbane River. On account of impaired health he was laid aside for a year and a half. Since 1886, he has been pastor of the German Baptist church at Engelsburg. His ministry has been greatly blessed in the conversion of souls, and four new chapels have been erected in connection with his labors.

WALTHER RAUSCHENBUSCH

Walther Rauschenbusch, son of Dr. A. Rauschenbusch, was born in Rochester, N. Y., October 4, 1861. In 1865, his mother, with her three children, went to Germany for a year's sojourn. At the end of the year, Professor Rauschenbusch expected to join his family for a brief rest in the Fatherland. But he was delayed until 1868. These three years, Mrs. Rauschenbusch, with her children, spent in Neuwied on the Rhine, and at Barmen. A part of the year 1868-9, was devoted to travel. After the return of the family to Rochester in 1869, Walther, who at the time was familiar with the German language only, attended English and German schools alternately until 1877. Then he entered the Rochester Free Academy, and began the study of the classics, graduating in 1879. After his graduation, instead of entering college he went to Germany, where he was admitted to Unter Secunda, in the gymnasium at Gutersloh, Westphalia, a Christian institution of high rank. Here he remained three years and a half, completing the course in the usual time. During the last two years he led his class, and was graduated in March, 1883. For six months he traveled in Germany and England. Returning then to Rochester, he entered Rochester Theological Seminary in September. He also took a partial course in Rochester University, and received the degree of B.A. in 1885. From the Seminary he was graduated in 1886. Before graduating, he had accepted a call to the pastorate of the Second German Baptist church in New York. Here he remains, abundant in labors, and fulfilling his ministry with large success and growing influence.

While in Germany Mr. Rauschenbusch became intensely interested in literary studies. In poetry, especially, he took delight, and read the best authors in different languages. He gave expression also to his own thoughts in verse, and some of his productions were printed.

SWEDISH BAPTIST HYMN WRITERS AND THEIR HYMNS

The quickening of spiritual life during the last half century in Sweden, with which Baptists have been so prominently identified, has manifested itself in the praise-songs of God's people. New psalms, to tunes not heard before, have borne to God the worship of his saints.

Fully as often, however, the divine Spirit has infused itself into the old hymns, sublime in poetry and grand in music, contained in the hymn book of the Established Church. From the ditties of the day the pious Swede will evermore return to the inspiring anthems of Spegel, Franzen and Wallin.

The new hymns have come from various sources. In the beginning of the Baptist movement, about 1850, hymns written by Lutheran clergymen in Finland, showing a marked Moravian tendency, were very generally sung by the "Pietists" of Sweden. A free, evangelical spirit was evinced in the religious songs of the Countess von Posse and Mrs. C. O. Bergh, two highly gifted Lutheran ladies. Their hymns were incorporated by Mr. P. Palmquist, a Baptist publisher, in a collection entitled "Hymns for the Sunday-school," and also in "The Songs of the Pilgrims." The first edition of this latter book was published in 1859, and a second and considerably enlarged edition in 1862. About four hundred thousand copies of this hymn book have been sold, and new editions are continually appearing. Some of the hymns in this collection were written by Baptists.

The first Baptist hymn-writer in Sweden was Rev. Gustavus Palmquist. The mother of this pioneer in Baptist work was led to Christ by the admonition of her youngest boy crying to her on his death-bed, "Read, mother! Sing, mother!" Born in Pilabo, Sweden, May 26, 1812, and converted at the age of thirty-two, Mr. Palmquist, while on a visit to the United States, was baptized at Galesburgh, Ill., and there he was ordained, July 27, following. Both in the United States, and in Sweden after his return, he proved himself a powerful preacher. When he established the first Baptist theological school in Sweden, in 1857, he was found to be a very acceptable teacher. His contributions to the "Songs of the Pilgrims" were mostly translations from familiar English hymns, but not a few were originals. Many a soul has been led heavenward in aspiration, and has had spiritual affections rekindled by words like these:

Had I the wings of a clove I would fly

Far, far away, far away,

Where sin and death cannot reach me on high,

Far, far away, far away;

Up to that land where the sun nevermore

Hides in the clouds on eternity's shore.

But all its brightness forever doth pour,

Far, far away, far away.

Mr. Palmquist died in Sweden, September 18, 1867. His last words, repeated in English, were, "The precious blood of Christ."

In the midst of the most exacting duties, at the head of a large business firm, Mr. Peter Palmquist, a younger brother of Rev. G. Palmquist (born in 1815, died 1887) found time to write some hymns characterized by his firm faith and great intellectual strength.

Rev. T. Truve, pastor of the Gottenburg Tabernacle, has translated a collection of Sunday-school songs that has been published by the Oerebro Sunday School Union. This collection has had a wide circulation.

In 1881, Rev. J. Stadling submitted to the Triennial Conference a collection of five hundred and fifty hymns, entitled "The Psalmist." It was compiled for the most part from existing collections, viz., the "Lutheran Hymn Book," the "Songs of the Pilgrims," etc. But it contained quite a number of new versions of hymns previously translated, some new translations, and a few originals. It is a valuable work, and contains excellent music.

The Swedish Baptist churches in the United States use for the most part "The Psalmist," or "The Songs of the Pilgrims." In Minneapolis and St. Paul they use hymns newly translated, printed on slips, and distributed every month. A collection of hymns has been published by Rev. E. P. Eckman, of Stromsburg, Nebraska. Another collection has been published by Rev. Frank Peterson, of Minneapolis, Minn. Neither of these collections, however, has been widely circulated.

DANISH AND NORWEGIAN BAPTIST HYMN WRITERS AND THEIR HYMNS

Rev. J. Kobiffer, who has been mentioned in connection with German Baptist hymn writers and their hymns, was a Dane by birth, and though he labored chiefly in Germany, yet he did a most enduring work in his native land, being the founder of the Danish Baptist mission in 1839, and serving twelve years as pastor of the Baptist church in Copenhagen. To the Danish Baptist churches he gave a hymn book ("Troesstemmen") similar to the one which he prepared for the German Baptist churches. In it are many of his own hymns, among them not a few of a superior order. By the Baptists of Denmark his hymns are preferred above all others.

Another Danish hymn-writer. Rev. Niels Nielson, was born in Denmark in 1809. He became a Baptist in 1840, was soon after ordained as a Baptist minister by Oncken and Kobner, and was for many years a leader of the Baptist cause in Denmark. For some time he was compelled to endure much persecution, but through his efforts at length liberty of conscience was secured in Denmark. He compiled the first hymn book prepared for Danish Baptists by one of their number. It was published in 1854, and contained one hundred and eighty-two hymns. Considering the circumstances under which it was published, this was an excellent book, and a great blessing to the Danish Baptist churches. Most of the hymns were taken from earlier Danish hymn books, but the collection included some translations by Nielson from the German; also a few originals, the two (8 and 185) best of which are included in the Baptist Danish hymn book published in this country in 1887, entitled "Salme-og Sangbog." In 1859, Nielson's hymn book was re-published in an enlarged form, and included many Swedish hymns translated by himself. About twenty years ago he came to the United States, and was pastor of the Danish Baptist church in Chicago. Subsequently he removed to Kansas, where he continued his pastoral labors. Here he closed a useful and honored life in 1887.

Rev. S. Hansen, one of the oldest Baptist pastors in Denmark has composed nearly one hundred hymns and spiritual songs, some of which are of considerable merit, and are found in Kobner's "Troesstemmen," and also in the Danish hymn book, "Salme-og Sangbog," published in Chicago in 1887. As he has taken a very active part in inculcating Baptist principles in Denmark, he has incurred the bitter hatred of the clergy of the Lutheran state church. In 1868, he published a poem, in which he set forth with some severity the evils of that church and its priesthood. For this he suffered persecution, and finally was imprisoned three months. Of its kind this poem was a master-piece. He has now in manuscript a complete "History of the Baptists of

Denmark," which will be published in 1889, when occurs the fiftieth anniversary of the establishment of Baptist mission work in Denmark.

Rev. Peter Sorensen, a native of Denmark, and now nearly eighty years of age, residing in Wisconsin, has published a hymn book containing about three hundred hymns, all of his own composition. For a while this book was used by some of the Baptist churches in Denmark, but as the author is of a somewhat mystical turn of mind, and as most of the hymns are nothing but religious the book has not come into general use. On account of the deep spiritual character of these hymns, however, some of them have been included in later Danish collections. In his earlier ministerial life Mr. Sorensen did much in spreading Baptist principles in Norway.

Rev. N. Larsex is a leading preacher among the Baptists of Denmark. He has been the editor of the Baptist paper in Denmark since its establishment, in 1856. In this paper, the Evangelisten, many excellent hymns from Mr. Larsen's pen have appeared, and, prominent among them, hymns for the different seasons of the year. Some of these hymns have found their way into the "Troesstemmen," "Salme-og Sangbog," and other collections.

Rev. M. Larsen, pastor of the Baptist church in Copenhagen, has written some excellent hymns, and translated a few from the German, Assisted by Rev. S. Hansen, he has compiled a most excellent singing book for the use of the Baptist Sunday-schools in Denmark.

Rev. J. S. Lux, pastor of the Baptist church in Bath, Minn., came from Denmark to the United States when a boy. He is now one of the foremost preachers in the Danish-Norwegian churches in this country. A few excellent hymns are from his pen, and he was one of the committee that prepared the new Danish Baptist hymn book, "Salme-og Sangbog."

Rev. H. a. Reicheistbach, pastor of the Baptist church in Council Bluffs, Iowa, also came to this country in early life. With excellent gifts as a preacher and an organizer, he has labored among the Scandinavian Baptist churches in the west for nearly a quarter of a century. He has assisted in compiling two hymn books for general use in this country. The first was the " Missions-Harpen," published in Chicago in 1873, and the second the "Sahe-og Sangbog." He has also compiled and published a small Sunday-school hymn book, "Den syngende Evangelist," consisting for the most part of translations of "Gospel Hymns," found here and there in Scandinavian papers. He is also the author of a few original hymns.

As it is not more than twenty years since the establishment of Baptist mission work in Norway, there is not as yet much that can be said concerning Norwegian Baptist hymn writers. Mrs. Sjodahl, the wife of a Baptist minister, has written a few hymns, which the Baptists in Norway love to sing, and some of them have found their way into a book compiled by a committee of the Norwegian Conference. Rev. P. Helbrostad, also, has written a few excellent hymns, one of which (number 366) is found in the "Salme-og Sangbog." Mr. Helbrostad assisted in compiling the Norwegian Baptist hymn book. He has also published a most excellent Sunday-school hymn book, which is used in Baptist Sunday-schools in Norway, and also by some Norwegian Baptist Sunday-schools in this country. He is the editor of the Norwegian Baptist paper, and is most highly esteemed for his excellent Christian spirit, and his great ability as a preacher and leader of the Baptist churches in Norway.

FRENCH BAPTIST HYMN WRITERS AND THEIR HYMNS

The Baptists in France have as yet no hymn book of their own. Nearly all of them use the "Chants Chretiens" in common with other independent churches of that country, the hymns of the McAll Mission, together with half a dozen hymns on baptism, adapted from English baptismal hymns. In fact, in all of the Protestant churches in France, but little attention until recently has been paid to the service of song in the house of the Lord. The selection in use in the National Reformed churches is composed of Psalms in verse and of some "Cantiques" taken from "Chants Chretiens," and contains about two hundred hymns in all. In most of the Independent churches in the south of France, the hymn book in use is the "Recueil de Cantiques de Geneve et Lyon," which contains about two hundred hymns, most of which were borrowed from the "Chants Chretiens."

In recent years the McAll Mission in Paris has made much use of Christian song in its evangelistic services, and its "Cantiques Populaires " is now extensively used in all of the Protestant churches throughout France. This collection contains two hundred and forty-three hymns, some of which are from the "Chants Chretiens," "Cantiques du Reveil," "Psaumes et Cantiques," but a large number, about seventy, many of them translations of familiar English and American hymns, were written by Ruben Saillens, who since 1873, has been the assistant of Rev. R. W. McAll in his mission work in Paris. At the present time (1888), Mr. Saillens is in charge of the Baptist church in Paris, though still connected with the McAll Mission.

Mr. Saillens was born June 24, 1855, at St. Jean-du-Gard, in the Cevennes, the mountain district made famous by resistance of the Huguenots to Louis XIV. Even now the Cevennes abound in Huguenots. Of the four thousand inhabitants in St. Jean-du-Gard, three thousand nine hundred are Protestants. In this place about forty years ago a free church was organized, the members of which held Baptist views. Mr. Saillens' father, who was one of these, removed to Marseilles, then to Lyons, where he labored as an evangelist. In 1871, at Lyons, the son was converted, and in May of the following year he was baptized by his father. He then went to

London, and entered Mr. H. Grattan Guinness' Training Institute for Home and Foreign Missions. There he remained one year, and at Christmas, 1873, he crossed over to Paris to engage in evangelistic work with Mr. McAll, who was then laying the foundations of his now well known mission. In entering upon this work they could avail themselves of only a few gospel hymns, and these were not very well adapted to the work. Mr. Saillens accordingly undertook to meet this deficiency, and since that time he has written a large number of hymns, many of which are now very familiar in Protestant churches in France, Switzerland and other French-speaking communities. He has also written and published a large number of poems and tracts. It is his purpose, in connection with our Baptist work in Paris, to prepare a hymn book for use in the Baptist churches of France. Mr. Saillens, in 1877, married the fourth daughter of Rev. J. B. Cretin, the oldest Baptist pastor in France, and the author of a series of tracts and books which have done much to advance Baptist interests in France.

The French Baptists on this side of the Atlantic, like the Baptists in France, have no hymn book of their own. The oldest hymn book used in the French Baptist churches in Canada, which I have seen, is the "Recueil de Cantiques Chretiens a L'Usage des Eglises du Canada," which was compiled by " un Pasteur de la Mission de la Grande Ligne," and published in 1851. Rev. A. L. Therrien informs me that this pastor of the Grand Ligne Mission is "our much loved and venerable brother Normandeau, an expriest, converted at Grande Ligne forty-five years ago, and who still (1886) preaches the gospel at the age of seventy-four." In the preface the compiler says that he has endeavored to make a selection which will meet the demands of each Christian denomination. He includes, accordingly, hymns suitable for the baptism of adults, seven in number, and also two hymns to be used at the consecration of infants.

The hymn book now in ease in all the French Protestant churches in Canada and the United States, including the French Baptist churches, is entitled "Chants Evangeliques pour le Culte Public et l'Edification Particuliere avec Musique a Quatre Parties." It contains hymns by Felix Nelt, B. Pictet, C. Malan, A. Vinet, A. Monod, Merle D' Aubigne, and other writers of less note. In the supplement are seventeen added "Chants Evangeliques."

There would be a gain to our French Baptist brethren on both sides of the Atlantic if, with like wants, they could unite in the preparation of a hymn book adapted to these wants. A tie would thus be formed, which could not but be helpful to them in their widely separated fields of labor.

WELSH BAPTIST HYMN WRITERS AND THEIR HYMNS

Among the earlier Welsh Baptist hymn writers was Rev. Benjamin Francis, pastor of the Baptist church at Horsley-down, England, and well known as a writer of English hymns. He was born in Wales in 1734, and, retaining the use of his native tongue, he often returned to the scenes of his childhood, and preached to his countrymen, and composed hymns for their use in their religious meetings.

Rev. David Saunders, of Merthyr Tyfdil, South Wales, was also a prolific hymn writer. His hymns, like those of Mr. Francis, were mostly doctrinal, although by no means destitute of tenderness.

Rev. Joseph Harris (Gomer), of Swansea, South Wales, published a collection of hymns in 1821. For many years this was a favorite book with the Welsh Baptists. In it were a large number of hymns by the celebrated Christmas Evans, the apostle of Wales; also by Rev. Morgan John Rees, who emigrated to this country from Wales about the year 1800, the father of Morgan John Rees, who died not long ago in Brooklyn, N. Y. Mr. Harris was the author of many hymns, and his book is still in use in Baptist churches in Wales.

Rev. John R. Jones, of Ramoth, North Wales, published a valuable collection of hymns, including many of his own compositions, also hymns by Robert Gwilym Du and Dewi Wyn Eiffon.

Rev. Daniel Jones, for many years pastor of the Welsh Baptist church in Liverpool, England, published a collection of hymns for use in his own church, and in the Baptist churches of Wales. He was a hymn writer of considerable note.

Rev. Robert Jones, of Llanllyfui, North Wales, also published a collection of hymns in the Welsh language.

In 1838, Rev. William H. Thomas published in Utica, N. Y., an American edition of Rev. Joseph Harris' collection of hymns, for use in the Welsh Baptist churches in the United States. Later the three Welsh Baptist Associations appointed Rev. John P. Harris, then of Minersville, Penn., now of Nanticoke, Penn., to bring out a new and revised edition of this book. This edition was published at Pottsville, Penn., in 1857, by Richard Edwards, and was adopted by the Welsh Baptist churches. It contained one thousand and fifty-two hymns. Many of the hymns in Mr. Thomas' book were omitted. Others were added, among them the best old hymns in the language; and there was added an appendix containing about fifty hymns, composed by Mr. Harris for use on Independence Day, at anti-slavery gatherings, temperance meetings, etc. Mr. Harris was born in Pembrokeshire, South Wales, January 27, 1820. He was converted in his sixteenth year, and soon after was invited by the church to exercise his gifts in preaching. In 1842, he was graduated at the Baptist college in Haverfordwest. Soon after he came to the United States, and was ordained to the work of the gospel ministry in 1843, at the Second (Welsh) Baptist church in Remsen, N. Y. He labored among his countrymen in the anthracite coal regions, in farming districts, and in some city churches, preaching in the Welsh language until 1882. Since that time he has preached in English, and has built up a very promising church in Nanticoke. During his ministry he has baptized about seven hundred converts. He has given, since his arrival in this country, considerable attention to literary work, and has published several works for Welsh Baptists; also a monthly magazine called the Western Star, of which he was editor seven years.

The book compiled by Mr. Harris has been out of print for some time, and a hymn book prepared by Rev. Lewis Jones, entitled "Llawlyfr Moliant," Hand Book of Praise, imported from Wales, has taken its place. This book is the one now generally used by the Welsh Baptist churches in the United States.

The most recent Welsh Baptist hymn book published in this country is "The Baptist Musical Measure." It contains Welsh and English hymns, and is designed for use at the English and Welsh services so commonly held in the Welsh Baptist churches in the United States. It was compiled by several Baptist ministers of the Welsh Baptist Association of eastern Pennsylvania, and was published in 1887, in Utica, N. Y., by Thomas J. Griffith.

BAPTIST HYMN WRTIERS AND THEIR HYMNS IN SPAIN

Baptist Mission work in Spain was commenced in 1869, by Prof. W. I. Knapp, Ph.D., who, discovering a field for Protestant evangelical labor, entered it as an independent missionary. Success attended his efforts, and August 10, 1870, Prof. Knapp organized a Baptist church in Madrid, with thirty-three members. The promise of the mission at the close of the year was such that Prof. Knapp was appointed a missionary of the American Baptist Missionary Union, and under his direction the work of the mission was carried forward with energy and success at Madrid, Alicante, Valencia, and other places. Having seen the work well established. Prof. Knapp resigned his connection with the Missionary Union in the summer of 1876, leaving the various mission stations under the charge of native evangelists.

Prof. Knapp was born at Greenpoint, Long Island, N. Y., March 10, 1835. His collegiate education he received at Madison and New York Universities. After his graduation at Madison University in 1860, he became professor of modern languages in that institution. Subsequently he was professor of ancient and modern languages in Vassar College. He went to Europe in 1867. After leaving the service of the Missionary Union, Prof. Knapp became secretary to the American Legation in Spain, and Spanish correspondent of the London Times. In 1879, he was appointed professor of modern languages in Yale College, a position which he has most creditably filled, and which he still holds.

Prof. Knapp's collection of hymns is now on of print, and the book in use by our Baptist missionaries in Spain at the present time is an undenominational collection of two hundred and fifty-nine hymns, entitled "Himnario Evangelico." It was compiled by Mr. A. R. Fenn, an English missionary, who for many years has represented the Plymouth Brethren in their mission work in Madrid. He is more of a musician than poet, and with the exception of some translations and adaptations of his own, the book comprises hymns taken from hymn books already in use among Spanish-speaking peoples on both sides of the Atlantic.

335

BAPTIST HYMN WRITERS AND THEIR HYMNS IN MEXICO

The first Protestant evangelical work in Mexico, so far as I can ascertain, was done by Baptists. In the spring of 1862, a young Englishman, John W. Butler, came to Monterey. There he made the acquaintance of Mr. Thomas M. Westrup, who, born April 10, 1837, in London, in the humble sphere of artisan life, and with scanty opportunities for obtaining an education, made his way to Mexico in 1852, to assist his father in the erection of a flour mill there. He had been brought up in the faith of the Church of England, and it was far from his thoughts that he should ever become a pioneer Baptist preacher. He had been seriously inclined, however, from his early years. The influence of his parents, especially of his mother, who loved and tried to follow the Savior, was good. But the world, above all the world in Mexico, is not a friend to grace; and so his attachment to Christ was only a weak, wavering, halting sentiment until 1862, when the efforts of Mr. Butler, the death of his mother, and acquaintanceship with Rev. James Hickey, in the order here named, were blessed to his awakening and consecration to Christ.

Rev. James Hickey was a Baptist minister, who on account of his aversion to slavery and the civil war left Texas in 1861, and took up his residence in Matamoras. He was originally from the west of Ireland, where he was born in 1800. At the request of Mr. Butler and Mr. Westrup, he came to Monterey in November, 1862. Mr. Westrup gives the following account of the results of this visit:

"I was charmed with brother Hickey's teaching and books, though bred an Episcopalian, and really ignorant of theological and denominational questions. I joined him, and gave him such assistance as I could. Other foreigners, including my father, were willing to assist, but desired to keep the work undenominational. This they could not do. The real worker was a Baptist, and the consequences were unavoidable. We were soon left severely alone. Two Mexicans and I were baptized January 30, 1864, and the same day the First Baptist church w\as organized with five members."

Mr. Westrup was ordained and chosen pastor of the little flock, as Mr. Hickey was agent of the American Bible Society in Mexico. At the close of 1864, the church had twenty members. Mr. Hickey died in December, 1866, and Mr. Westrup was made his successor as agent of the Bible Society. In 1869, Mr. Westrup resigned this position, and early in 1870, he accepted an appointment of the American Baptist Home Missionary Society, as missionary to Mexico. A printing-press was purchased for his use, and distinctive missionary work was commenced. Since that time the work has gone forward, and is now well established, with suitable head-quarters in the city of Mexico.

Before his baptism Mr. Westrup had translated a few English hymns and psalms into the Spanish language. Later, on account of the demand for song in the service of the sanctuary, he renewed his efforts in this direction, and since that time he has composed about one hundred and fifty hymns, most of which are sung by the various evangelical congregations in Mexico, being included in the hymn books of other denominations.

BAPTISTS HYMN WRITERS AND THEIR HYMNS IN GREECE

In 1873, a hymn book, for the use of the Baptist mission in Greece, was published at Athens by Rev. D. Z. Sakellarios, a missionary of the American Baptist Missionary Union. It was entitled "Sacred Hymns." These hymns, one hundred and forty in number, were selected from such evangelical hymns in the Greek language as were at hand; and one of them, number 109, was altered to make it suitable for use on baptismal occasions. There were in the collection no hymns by Baptist writers.

To these "Sacred Hymns" were added thirty-six hymns for Sunday-school use. In later editions Mrs. Sakellarios added seven hymns to the first part, making one hundred and forty-seven in all. These were partly translations and partly originals.

Adaline (Edmands) Sakellakios, a daughter of Benjamin and Laura Sprague Edmands, was born in Charlestown, Mass., February 19, 1830. The gift of song she cultivated in childhood, and as she advanced in life she became proficient in instrumental music, receiving instruction both upon the piano and the organ from the best masters in the city. Birthday anniversaries and social family meetings she remembered with contributions in verse, while some of her poems were printed in several of the journals of the day. Under the pastorate of Rev. T. F. Caldicott she gave her heart to the Savior and her life to his service. She was baptized April 28, 1850, and became an active member of the Charlestown Baptist church, teaching in the Sunday-school, singing in the choir, and ready to aid in every good work. Although other inviting fields of labor opened to her, no call came until the Macedonian cry was heard "Come over and help us." This cry she could not fail to recognize, and after mature deliberation and much prayer, she accepted it as a divine call, and gave her life to mission work in Greece. March 30, 1866, she was married to Rev. D. Z. Sakellarios of Athens, Greece; and in April following she sailed from New York for her new home. She reached Athens early in May, and there she spent twenty-one years in her Master's service. She died at Athens, July 24, 1887, and was buried in the Protestant cemetery, where rest so many others who have given their lives for Greece.

BAPTIST HYMN WRITERS AND THEIR HYMNS IN INDIA

In a letter from Moypauldiggy, Bengal, under date of January 6, 1797, Rev. J. Fountain writes:

"Brother Thomas has translated Dr. Watts' 88th hymn, second book, 'Salvation! the Joyful Sound,' &c., and I have taught the congregation at Moypauldiggy to sing it to Sydenham tune. They sing it every Lord's day in time of worship. We are also learning it at Mudnabatty. The people of this country know nothing of music as a science. They never saw a musical character in their lives, but it is astonishing to hear how tune ably they sing together. We sing Boshoo's Bengal hymn every Sabbath. Brother Carey's pundit has an excellent voice and fine ear; he will learn any tune by my singing it over with him a few times. Brothers Carey, Thomas and myself, when together, can sing in three parts. The first evening we were together (after I had briefly related what the Lord was doing in England, when I left it) we joined in singing the 421st hymn in your [Dr. Rippon's] Selection entitled ' Longing for the Latterday Glory,' an event which none have greater reason eagerly to desire, than we in this wretched country."

Dr. Carey wrote other hymns, one of which is still in use. Smith, in his Life of Carey, says: "He had thus early (1798) brought into the service of Christ the Hindoo love of musical recitation, which was recently re-discovered, and now forms a most important mode of evangelistic work when accompanied by native musical instruments."

Krishnu Pal, the first heathen convert baptized by Dr. Carey, was also the author of a number of hymns in Bengali. One of his hymns was translated by Dr. Marshman, Dr. Carey's associate, and has found a place in most English hymn books in all branches of the Christian church down to our own time. It is as follows:

O thou, my soul, forget no more
The Friend who all thy misery bore;
Let every idol be forgot,
But, O my soul, forget him not.

Jesus for thee a body takes,
Thy guilt assumes, thy fetters breaks.
Discharging all thy dreadful debt;
And canst thou ever such love forget?

Renounce thy works and ways with grief,
And fly to this most sure relief;
Nor him forget who left his throne
And for thy life gave up his own.

Infinite truth and mercy shine
In him, and he himself is thine;
And canst thou then, with sin beset.
Such charms, such matchless charms, forget?

Ah no; when all things else expire,
And perish in the general fire,
This name all others shall survive.
And through eternity shall live.

A translation of another hymn by Krishnu Pal, on "Salvation by the Death of Christ," is in Miss M. E. Leslie's "Eastern Blossoms, a Story for Native Christian Women" (1875).

Krishna's acquaintance with the missionaries commenced in this way: At his work as a carpenter he had broken his arm, and Mr. Thomas, Dr. Carey's associate, was called to set the broken limb. Having done this, the missionary embraced the opportunity to speak a few words for his Master to those present. The words found a lodging-place in the carpenter's heart, and he called on the missionary later for further instruction. His wife and daughter also became interested. December 22, 1800, Krishnu, and Gokol, his brother, renounced their caste by sitting down to eat with the missionaries. That evening Krishnu, his wife and daughter, offered themselves for baptism, and were received. When it was known that Krishnu had renounced his caste, and become a Christian, there was intense excitement in Serampore, and a mob of two thousand persons appeared before his house, and dragged him and his brother before a magistrate, but they were soon released. The wife and daughter now hesitated to declare their allegiance to Christ. Gokol, also, drew back. But Krishnu was steadfast; and December 28, 1800, with Dr. Carey's son Felix, then a lad of sixteen years, he was baptized in the Ganges in the presence of the English governor. Dr. Carey, in a letter to Dr. Rippon, dated April 8, 1801, says:

"The ordinance was administered in the river just opposite to our house. The river here is a full half mile wide. We had a good number of people, Europeans, Portuguese (natives), and Hindoos. I addressed them in the Bengal tongue. We sung a Bengal translation of the 451st hymn of your 'Selection.'"

Jesus, and shall it ever be,

after which I prayed, and descended into the water. Afterward Brother Marshman addressed the by-standers in Bengallee. I felt joy at this triumph of the cross over superstition, and I believe we all felt much joy in the Lord."

In a letter dated Serampore, March 18, 1801, Dr. Carey announces the baptism of the wife of Krishnu, February 22. Of Krishnu's daughter, Andrew Fuller, writing at Kettering, March 26, 1802, having received letters from Serampore up to September, 1801, says: "Krishnu's eldest daughter, who was not baptized, but of whom hopes were entertained, has been seized and carried away by force by the man to whom she was betrothed. But when beaten, and in the utmost peril of her life, she bore a noble testimony for Christ, and expressed her determination, whether she lived or died, to live or die a Christian." Mr. Fuller also announced the baptism of Gokol, Krishnu's brother.

Krishnu soon began to preach the gospel, and he had the privilege of baptizing hundreds of his countrymen. He died of cholera, in 1822.

A Bengali hymn book was early published at Serampore, but the hymn book in this dialect, which has been in use by the English Baptist missionaries during the post fifty years, was published in Calcutta. It was edited, and to a great extent it was prepared, by Rev. J. H. Pearce, who also composed many of its hymns. Mr. Pearce's Bengali hymns were for the most part in English meters. The natives, however, greatly prefer their own meters, regarding English meters as harsh. The collection also contains a large number of native hymns. "Any Bengali," says a missionary, "will write verse to order."

The Urdu hymn book contains three hundred hymns, including the first two classes of hymns in the Hindi hymn book, together with a large number of original Urdu and Hindi hymns. This Urdu hymn book was compiled by Rev. R. F. Guyton, and published at Delhi about the year 1880.

At the Orissa Baptist Mission hymns were composed and circulated before the first hymn book was printed in 1844. Rev. A. Sutton, d.d., was the compiler of this collection, and of its three hundred and ten hymns he was the author of one hundred and seventy-nine. In the preface Dr. Sutton says: "The compiler of this volume of hymns apprehends that there are very few of them respecting whose paternity any jealousy will long be felt, but as inquiries are constantly arising in relation to our India Christian literature, recent as is its origin, which can rarely be answered, he has thought it desirable to give a general clue to the parties who have furnished these hymns. Of his own contributions he may remark that most of them are simply transferred from the Bengali, with such alterations as the Orissa required. Others are translations of English hymns, or suggested by English hymns; and a few are originals. He supposes similar remarks may be made in reference to the other contributions. Some of the translations from the Bengali were made at the commencement of his literary course, when he was unable to translate all the verses, or thought it unnecessary to do so; but having once obtained currency, he found it difficult to alter them for the present edition."

In this collection thirty-four hymns are by Rev. C. Lacey, and sixty-five by Gunga Dhar, the first Orissa convert There are fifteen other contributors, of whom one supplies six hymns. Of the whole number of hymns in the collection, twenty-four are in English meters. The remainder are in the native measure, adapted to the old ballad tunes of the country. The subjects include all those most commonly found in English hymn books, such as the attributes and works of God, the love and grace of Christ, the death and resurrection of Christ, Christ as a Savior, the Holy Spirit, regeneration, faith, the scriptures, the Lord's day, baptism and the Lord's supper, etc.

With the exception of about forty hymns retained in the new selections, the hymns in Dr. Sutton's collection are no longer in use. In the present collection, made up of selections printed from time to time, there are three hundred and two hymns from twenty three contributors, of whom thirteen are living. In this collection twenty-two hymns by Gunga Dhar are retained. These contain much genuine Christian teaching and true poetry, and some of them seem destined to remain in permanent use. Makunda Das heads the list of contributors with one hundred and forty-five hymns, nearly half of the whole number. He has been called the Dr. Watts of Orissa, and his hymns have undoubtedly rendered much useful service in expressing the best Christian sentiment, and in deepening the spiritual life of the churches. He has also prepared poetical versions of the four gospels, and the books of Psalms and Proverbs.

In 1879, Mrs. Annie H. Downie, of Nellore, wife of Rev. David Downie, d.d., published a collection of "Christian Hymns, Selected and Reduced to Music from the Native Airs." This was the first collection of Telugu hymns with music ever published. It was a work of great labor, as Mrs. Downie in its preparation was obliged to catch the notes of these hymns from singers as best she could. But it was a much needed work, as hitherto no two congregations connected with the mission sang the same hymn in the same way.

A new Baptist Telugu hymn book was published in 1887. It is entitled "Telugu Hymns in Native and English Meters. For Public and Private Worship." Mrs. Downie was chairman of the committee that had this work in charge. In the preface she says:

"This collection of Christian hymns is the work of a committee appointed at the Jubilee of the American Baptist Telugu Mission held in Nellore, February, 1886. It contains many of the best hymns used in nil previous collections published by our mission. It also has a number of choice hymns from the Delta Mission Collection, for which we are indebted to our brethren at Nursapur. It also contains a number of hymns from the excellent Dawson Collection, for which we thank Dr. Murdock of the Madras Tract Society."

"Beside these selected hymns, the collection will be found to contain a large number of new and original hymns. Some of the choicest of them are by Chondari Purushottam, of Cuttack, in the Orissa mission. Quite a number of original hymns by members of our own native churches are included in the collection, not so much for their special excellence, though they are by no means wanting in some degree of merit, but chiefly because of the special interest attaching to them in being our own, and also to encourage whatever native talent we have in this direction. The English meters are usually translations by our own and other missionaries."

The number of hymns in this collection is one hundred and eighty-seven, of these forty-four were written by Chondari Purushottam. He is a convert from some Sudra caste of Hindus, and of Telugu birth. For a long time he was employed as a catechist in connection with the London Missionary Society, and is the author of many tracts commending Christianity to his countrymen. His "History of Salvation" is said to be a work of undying fame, admired even by pundits of classical learning. The diction is at once musical and elevated, and the work breathes a spirit of earnest devotion throughout. In recent years he has been connected with the Baptist mission at Cuttack, where, full of years, he is still (1887) serving his Lord as far as his strength permits. Dr. Lyman Jewett says of Purushottam: "I have heard him spoken of by our intelligent Telugu Christians, who knew him well, as a 'learned man.' I think he is now over seventy years of age and blind. Among those who are always found at the Sabbath services and weekday prayer meetings, he is one. He is full of Christian love. One of his hymns of which we never tire is on 'The Raising; of Lazarus.'"

T. Yohan, connected with the American Baptist Telugu mission, is the author of thirty-four hymns in this new collection. Others connected with this mission, who have hymns in the collection, are as follows: B. Ambrose, five hymns; M. Ragavallo, five hymns; A. P.

Veeraswamy, three hymns; Mrs. Jewett and Mrs. Clough, three hymns; J. Burder, two hymns; V. Appiah, two hymns; Mrs. Jewett. Mrs. W. W. Campbell, R. Sashiah, R. Lutchmi-Nursu, B. Kotiah and T. Benjamin, each one hymn.

BAPTIST HYMN WRITERS AND THEIR HYMNS IN BURMA

During the earliest years of the Barman mission, singing was not a part of native Christian worship. Dr. Judson cannot sing, there were no hymns, and the native prejudice against the introduction of singing was strong. According; to the native mind, singing was not only foreign to all proper ideas of worship, but was one of the things interdicted by religious law and custom. It was intimately associated with theatrical performances. However, after much opposition, as tradition runs, the missionaries determined to introduce singing into worship. Dr. Judson composed the first hymn, "Shway pyee koung-gin," and Dr. Wade became responsible for the music. Notwithstanding the efforts put forth by the missionaries, singing did not become popular, and after a considerable time, according to one report, was abandoned. At any rate, it did not come into general favor until the arrival of the Cutters and Hancocks. Mrs. Cutter and Mr. and Mrs. Hancock were fine singers, and under their direction and skill all prejudice disappeared, and music was established as a part of sacred worship.

In speaking of Burman and Karen hymnody, it must be borne in mind that the hymns in those languages, with a few exceptions, which will be noted in their place, are written according to western ideas of versification, and have nothing in common with the style of the indigenous poetry of the country. Indeed, the natives of Burma, uninfluenced by missionary ideas, would not regard the hymns as poetical. It would not be possible to sing native poetry to western music.

Rev. E. a. Stevens, d.d., contributed eighty-nine hymns to the Burman hymn book. These are chiefly translations or adaptations of English hymns, but there are some which are original. Dr. Stevens was born at Sunbury, Liberty County, Georgia, January 23, 1814. Educated at Brown University and Newton Theological Institution, he sailed for Burma, October 28, 1837. He was a man of rare purity of spirit and unassuming piety, and was greatly beloved by his brethren. Dr. Judson committed to him the editing and publication of his Burman and English Dictionary. Much of his life was spent in literary work as editor of the Burman monthly religious newspaper, a translator of histories, a writer of commutaries, and the compiler of a concordance. At one time, his wife says, he spent every Sunday evening, after preaching, in the preparation of a hymn. His hymns have clearness of thought, ease of expression, and correctness of style. Dr. Stevens died in Rangoon, June 19, 1886.

Rev. E. O. Stevens, son of Dr. Stevens, has twenty-seven hymns in the Burman hymn book, and has published others since its compilation. He was born in Burma, December 17, 1838, and was educated at Brown University and Newton Theological Institution. He returned to Burma as a missionary in the autumn of 1864, and settled at Rome, where he has since remained. Speaking the Burmese as a vernacular, he uses it with facility in the translation of hymns.

Mrs. Caroline J. (Harrington) Simons has twenty two hymns. She was born at Brookfield, Mass., October 28, 1811, and died at Maulmain, May 1, 1843, after eleven years of mission service. Her hymns are among the best in the Burman language.

Rev. James R. Haswell, son of Rev. J. M. Haswell, D.D., has nineteen hymns. He was born at Amherst, Burmall September 4, 1836. He graduated at Madison University, and sailed for Burma as a missionary in 1859. He died of cholera, May 20, 1877. Burman was a mother tongue to him, and he used it with great eloquence in preaching. His hymns have much of the sonorous, stately movement which characterizes the religious language of the people.

Sarah Boardman Judson wrote fifteen hymns. Her Burman hymns have the easy grace and happy expression which characterize her English verse. Mrs. E. C. Judson, in her Life of Sarah B. Judson, in a note at the close, says:

"The following translation of one of Mrs. Judson's hymns may be admitted as a tolerable specimen of her labors in this department, though it has been found difficult to preserve the simplicity of the original, and the sentiments lose much of their force by being transformed to another language and a different scene. The first two stanzas, especially, convey a distinct and positive meaning to Burmese converts, which can never be appreciated by those who worship God beneath genial skies, with none to molest or make them afraid."

Fourteen hymns were written by Rev. Lovell Ingalls, all of which are probably original. He was born at Worcester, N. Y., August 21, 1808. After completing his education at Hamilton Literary and Theological Institution, he sailed from Boston, September 20, 1835. His mission life was spent at Mergui, Akyab and Rangoon. He died at sea, between Calcutta and Rangoon, March 14, 1856. His hymns are simple and didactic.

Rev. J. M. Haswell, d.d., prepared thirteen hymns. He was born at Bennington, Vt., February 4, 1810. After he graduated from the Hamilton Literary and Theological Institution, he sailed for Burma, September 22, 1835, and spent the most of his life at Amherst and Maulmain. He became thoroughly acquainted with Peguan and Burman, translated the New Testament into Peguan and prepared many Peguan and Burman tracts. He died at Maulmain, September 13, 1876. The style of his hymns resembles that of his son.

Rev. Lymais Stilsox is .credited with ten hymns. He was born at Meredith, N. Y., in 1805; sailed for Burma, October 28,1837; retired from the mission December 23, 1851, on account of ill health; and died March 23, 1886. The mathematical works which he published in Burman have been valuable in the education of native youth, and are in use at the present time. His useful missionary life was brought to an end by the permanent weakness and ill health which resulted from a brutal attack made upon him by Burman robbers who sought to obtain the funds in his hands as mission treasurer. His hymns are smooth in style.

Rev. N. Brown, d.d., one of the most scholarly and versatile missionaries ever connected with the American Baptist Missionary Union, was the writer of nine hymns. He sailed for Burma, December 22, 1832. He passed several years at Maulmain, and it was at this time that his Burman hymns were written. One of them, a translation of "There is a happy land," has always been exceedingly popular.

Rev. John Wade, d.d., has seven hymns. He was born at Otsego, N. Y., December 10, 1798; educated at Hamilton Literary and Theological Institution; and sailed for Burma, June 22, 1825. On the opening of the first Burman war he and Rev. Mr. Hough were seized, imprisoned, and twice made ready for execution. They were saved by the British after their victorious assault on Rangoon. Dr. Wade spoke both Burman and Karen fluently-. He rendered the Karens the invaluable service of reducing their language to writing. He also prepared a Karen dictionary, a scholarly Karen thesaurus, and other works in the Karen language. In Burman he is known by his dictionary of Buddhism and his excellent tracts. His life was a quiet one, and whatever came from his pen exhibits great painstaking, but his hymns are somewhat faulty in meter. He died in Rangoon in 1873.

SGAU KAREN HYMN WEITERS.

Mes. Calista Vinton is the largest contributor to the Sgau Karen hymn book. Of the four hundred and forty-two hymns which it contains, two hundred and sixteen are attributed to her. Although only thirty-four of these hymns are marked as translations, most of the remaining one hundred and eighty-two are adaptations of English hymns. Her father's name was Holman. She was born at Union, Conn., in 1809. After her marriage with Rev. Justus H. Vinton, she sailed with her husband from Boston, for Burma, July 3, 1834. Her death occurred in 1865. She was a woman of great energy of character, and indefatigable in her labors for the Karens. After her husband's death in 1858, she guided the large Rangoon Sgau Karen mission with great success.

Her numerous hymns are smooth and flowing in style, and she has the honor of bearing much the same relation to Karen hymnody as Watts does to English hymnody. She could not sing and her son says, that in the preparation of her hymns, she sometimes failed to appreciate and employ the proper quantity demanded by the meter of the verse in which she was writing. Her husband, however, had a delicately sensitive musical ear, which led him to detect immediately any error in rhythm. Defects of this kind were corrected by her with great facility. She used to attribute much of her ease in versification to an exercise enforced upon her in her school days, by which she was made to turn a sentence into as many ways of expression as were possible and yet allow the retention of the idea, but she unquestionably had a large natural talent for hymn writing. Beside her hymns which appear in the hymn book, she was the author of many published ones, which still exist in manuscript.

Her son, Rev. J. B. Vinton, d.d., contributed sixty hymns to the Sgau Karen hymn book, of which forty-eight are marked as translations. He was born in 1840, and after completing his education at Madison University, N. Y., joined the Rangoon Sgau Karen mission, which had received so much labor from his parents. The Sgau Karen was a vernacular to him, and he used it with perfect fluency and great skill. Dr. Vinton died at Rangoon, June 23, 1887.

Fifty-four hymns, of which forty-five are marked as translations, are from the pen of Rev. B. C. Thomas, who was a native of Massachusetts and educated at Brown University and Newton Theological Institution. He arrived at Tavoy, Burma, May, 1851, but the principal part of his devoted life was spent at Henzada whether he removed after the annexation of Pegu province. He was the founder of the prosperous Sgau Karen mission in that district. He died in New York City, June 10, 1868, four days after his arrival in his native land, and was buried at Newton Centre, Mass. He was a man of rare piety, and his pure, sweet and zealously consecrated life was a benediction to all who knew him. His style is easy and the rhythm generally pleasing to the ear.

Rev. D. A. W. Smith, d.d., son of Rev. S. F. Smith, D.D., of Newton Centre, Mass., inherits some of his father's poetic ability. He has furnished forty-one hymns, of which thirty-four are marked as translated. He is the author of the original hymn sung at the dedication of the Ko Thah Bu Memorial Hall at Bassein. His birth took place at Waterville, Me., June 18, 1840. He was educated at Harvard University, and Newton Theological Institution. At one time he had charge of the Henzada Sgau Karen mission, but is now president of the Rangoon Karen Theological Seminary. Much valuable Christian Karen literature has come from his pen. He shares with Mr. Thomas and Dr. Vinton the honor of translating some of the most beautiful and precious hymns of the English language into Karen.

Nine hymns, of which three are marked as translations, are the work of Rev. E. B. Cross, d.d. He was born at Georgetown, N. Y., June 11, 1814, was educated at Hamilton Literary and Theological Institution, and sailed for Burma, October 30, 1844. His first station was at Tavoy, but in 1861, he removed to Toungoo, where he has made his home to the present time. He has been a voluminous writer in Karen on religious and mathematical subjects, and has published a Karen translation of a Bible dictionary, and some commentaries in that language. He has also given much time to the revision of the Karen New Testament.

Rev. Francis Mason, d.d., was the author of many hymns, only nine of which have been preserved in the Sgau Karen hymn book. He also compiled a volume of hymns in the Bghai Karen dialect which was used until recently in the Bghai churches. Several Burman hymns composed by him are found in the Burman hymn book. This versatile man was born in Yorkshire, but emigrating to America in his youth, he was educated at Newton Theological Institution. He sailed from Boston, May 24, 1830. His life was spent in Tavoy, until 1853, when he went to Toungoo, to open a mission for the Karens, upon the mountains of that district. He was the translator of the Karen Bible. He was an able linguist, and published works in Burman and Pali as well as Karen.

His "Burniah," lately edited and enlarged by Theobald, is still the standard work on the ethnology, geology, fanna, and flora of the country whose name it bears. He died at Rangoon March 3, 1874. His hymns are written in the style of native Karen poetry, whose characteristics he was very successful in reproducing. Each line consists of seven syllables. The thought is expressed in couplets, resembling the parallelism of Hebrew poetry. In many cases the second line of the couplet differs from the first line only in a slight change of the closing words. It is impossible to sing these hymns to western tunes. They can be fitly used only with the plaintive, weird, strangely sweet, native Karen music. Hence at the last revision of the hymn book with Dr.

Mason's consent, many of his hymns were replaced by those which could be sung to western tunes.

Four hymns are the work of Mrs. Miranda Vinton Harris, of which one is marked as a translation. She was the sister of Rev. J. H. Vinton, and the second wife of Rev. Norman Harris. Her birth took place at Wellington, Conn., April 10, 1819. After fifteen years service in Burma, she died at Shwaygyeen, September 9, 1856. Her life was heartily devoted to Christ, and her missionary service very effective. Her memory is still warmly cherished by the Karens. The poetic style of her hymns is beautiful. One hymn, based on the English translation of Psalm cxxxix "Lord, thou hast searched," etc., is used with great frequency in divine worship.

Mrs. H. M. (Norris) Armstrong- has furnished two hymns. After spending several years in the Karen mission, she married Rev. W. F. Armstrong of the Maritime Provinces, and entered the Telugu mission sustained by the Baptists of those provinces. She is now engaged with her husband in English and Telugu work at Maulmain, Burma.

Rev. W. F. Thomas, son of Rev. B. C. Thomas, Rev. A. Banker, d.d., and Mrs. J. E. Harris have each furnished the translation of one English hymn. Rev. Mr. Thomas was educated at Brown University and Newton Theological Institution. He arrived in Burma in 1880, and took charge of the Henzada Sgau Karen mission which was founded by his father. He speaks Karen and Burman as vernaculars, and resembles his father in character, energy and consecrated service. Dr. Bunker was born in 1836, educated at Waterville College and Newton Theological Institution, and sailed for Burma in 1865. He has spent his time in arduous and successful service in the northern half of the Toungoo Karen mountains. Mrs. Harris' home now is in Hamilton, N. Y.

There are six native Karen hymn writers. Moung Loonee, who is about thirty-eight years old, was carefully educated under the care of the Yintons and speaks English fluently. He is a medal scholar in law, and is an advocate in Rano-oon. No other Karen has ever undertaken the translation of English hymns with success. Twelve of his sixteen hymns are marked as translations. The meter and general character of these hymns are reproduced in Karen in an excellent manner.

Sau Quala is the author of nine hymns. His history is exceedingly interesting. He has been called the second Karen apostle. His conversion was due to the first sermon of Ko Thah Byu, the first Karen apostle. He was ordained in 1846, and in December, 1853, he went to Toungoo, where he ranged the mountains and preached the gospel. Eighteen hundred and sixty were baptized in one year and nine months, and twenty-eight churches were organized. After more than ten years' labor on the Karen mountains, he returned to Tavoy, where he spent the remainder of his life, which was at one time clouded by a fall into sin. He died in 1880, at a goodly age. His hymns are original and are written in the pure, native Karen style which was adopted by Dr. Mason for his hymns.

Sau Eh Hpau wrote two hymns. According to Rev. Dr. Vinton, he was a Maulmain Karen preacher. A Karen of a similar name lived at Mergui at one time, and was the author of a number of hymns which the native Christians refused to sing after his apostasy.

SHAI HYMNS

Of the eighty-seven hymns in the Shan hymn book, seventy-nine have been prepared by Rev. J. N. Gushing, D.D. Of these four are original hymns. The others are translations or adaptations of English hymns. Dr. Gushing was born in Attleborough, Mass., May 4, 1840. He was graduated in 1862, at Brown University, and at Newton Theological Institution in 1865. Two years, 1866, and 1867, he spent a Newton as instructor in Hebrew. He then entered the service of the American Baptist Missionary Union, and was assigned to Burma. His principal work has been in connection with the Shan mission. He has translated the Scriptures into the Shan language, and in many ways done much to advance the work of the Missionary Union in Burma. In recognition of his scholarly worth Brown University, in 1881, conferred upon him the degree of doctor of divinity.

One hymn was translated by Rev. F. H. Eveleth. He was born in Durham, Me., March 21, 1843, was graduated at Golby University in 1870, and at Newton Theological Institution in 1873. He arrived in Burma, in the spring of 1874, and has performed a valuable service as a missionary of the Union.

Three hymns were prepared by Shway Wa, who is a native of the principality of Mone. For a number of years he was the chief scribe of the Saubwa of Theinnee. He is a man about thirty-five years old and is a good Shan scholar. He has been the principal native assistant of Dr. Gushing in the preparation of his translation of the Scriptures into Shan. Shway Wa was baptized in 1882, and has thus far led a consistent Christian life. During Dr. Gushing's absence in America, Shway Wa acted as chief Shan interpreter in connection with the English occupation of Upper Burma. Recently, much against the wishes of English officials he has voluntarily resigned his position as interpreter, and a salary of one hundred rupees a month, to assist in the revision of the Shan Scriptures at a salary of thirty rupees a month.

Two hymns by Toonla are translations of Burman hymns. He was born at Toungoo after his parents had immigrated thither from Shanland. He was educated in the Shan mission school, and was baptized in 1871. He is about thirty years old, and has been a preacher, although not always a consistent Christian. He is now in the employ of the English government as an interpreter.

Saug Myat, who prepared a translation of two Burman hymns, was a native of Mone. He was a man of some natural ability, but before the close of his life fell into grievous sin. Professing penitence he died in 1835, at about the age of thirty-five years.

BAPTIST HYMN WRITERS AND THEIR HYMNS IN ASSAM

The Assamese are not a musical people, but our missionaries from the beginning of their labors among them have sought to cultivate in the converts a love for Christian song. The first Assamese hymn book, compiled by Dr. N. Brown, was printed in 1845. A revised and enlarged edition, containing one hundred and eighty-two hymns, was published in 1850. A third edition, containing two hundred and seventy nine hymns, followed in 1860. The last edition, enlarged to three hundred and fifty-two hymns, and thirty-two Sunday-school hymns in a supplement, was published in 1873. Rev. Nathan Brown, d.d., whose early missionary life was spent in Assam, he reached Assam in March, 1836, and remained there until 1855 —contributed to the Assamese hymn book eighty hymns, viz., thirty-two originals and forty-eight translations.

Rev. Miles Bronson, d.d., who reached Assam a little more than a year later than Dr. Brown, and settled at Gowahati, contributed to the Assamese hymn book two or three original hymns, and about eighteen translations, among them some of the more recent English hymns, as "Hold the fort," and " He leadeth me."

Of the native hymn writers Nidhi Levi Farwell ranks first. He was the first Assamese convert, and was baptized by Dr. Bronson, June 13, 1841. He was for many years the chief assistant in the mission press work. He wrote one hundred and thirteen hymns, of which only six or seven were translations. His wife, Abby, wrote one hymn, and Mrs. Bronson's school girl, Sophia, also one hymn. Batiram Dass one of the early converts, and afterward a preacher, wrote twenty hymns.

Eight hymns in the collection were taken from the Bengali hymns of Carey and Marshman. Thirty-three were contributed by the preachers pundits, native Christians of Sibsagor, Nowgong and Gowahati.

A revision of the Assamese hymn book is already called for, and Rev. P. H. Moore of Nowgong has undertaken the work. It will contain about fifty new hymns in Assamese. These are mostly translations from English hymns contributed by Assamese Christians, Sardoka, Kandura, and others j also by some of the missionaries.

BAPTIST HYMN WRITERS AND THEIR HYMNS IN CHINA

Under date of February 8, 1888, Rev. S. B. Partridge, of Swatow, where he has been stationed since 1873, as a missionary of the American Baptist Missionary Union, sent me a package of hymn books in Chinese. The books were numbered one, two, three, four. In a letter which accompanied the package, Mr. Partridge wrote: "Fifteen years ago we were using No. 1, which had been in use some years. It was printed from wooden blocks. I cannot tell by whom the hymns were written, nor by whom the book was compiled. Dr. Ashmore collected a number of hymns from various sources, which in 1875, I arranged, and to which I added a few and had No. 2 printed. No. 3 is practically the same as No. 2, but was changed by Rev. W. K. McKibben to adapt it to the Hakka dialect. Miss Fielde had a part of the same book put in a simple style, to be used as a primer in teaching women. About three years ago, feeling the need of a larger collection of hymns, we concluded to adopt the hymn book which R. H. Graves, d.d., had prepared. In order that we might have a few hymns that our church members were familiar with, I compiled a supplement. Two or three hymns in the supplement were written by the teacher who is our assistant in the theological school. Many of the hymns in this supplement are translations, or adaptations, but I cannot tell you by whom the work was done. I think, however, that very little of such work has been done by Baptists, except what has been done by Dr. Graves, whose hymn book I consider a most valuable addition to Chinese church literature."

Dr. Graves, who is a missionary of the Southern Baptist board stationed in Canton, published in 1876, a hymn book in Chinese, entitled "Songs of Praise to the Lord." It contained about two hundred and eighty-six hymns, of which about twenty were original hymns by Dr. Graves, and between sixty and seventy were translations, by Dr. Graves, of familiar English hymns. The remaining hymns in the collection were selections from other Chinese hymn books, being mostly translations of hymns in the English and German languages, with some hymns composed by missionaries and Chinese converts. In its arrangement Dr. Graves' book followed the arrangement of the "Baptist Hymn and Tune Book," issued by the American Baptist Publication Society.

Dr. Graves was born May 29, 1833, in Baltimore, Md., was graduated at St. Mary's College, in his native city in 1851, and was baptized by Dr. Richard Fuller, of whose church he became a member, and under whom he studied for the ministry. He was ordained as a missionary to China in April, 1856, and reached Canton, in August of the same year. Here, and in the vicinity of the city, he has labored. For a number of years past, he has been pastor of the Chinese Baptist church in Canton. On account of the ill health of his wife. Dr. Graves is at present in the United States.

In a note written since his return to this country, Dr. Graves says: "Dr. Hartwell informs me that a small collection of hymns, was published in the Shanghai colloquial dialect by Rev. A. B. Cabaniss of the Southern Baptist mission, also a larger one by Rev. T. P. Crawford of the same mission, and this, I am informed, has been enlarged by Rev. Dr. M. T. Yates. Our English Baptist brethren have a collection, I believe, in Mandarin colloquial."

357

Rev. J. R. Goddard, who has been a missionary of the American Baptist Missionary Union at Ningpo since 1867, writes under date of January 23, 1888: "Here at Ningpo, and in the stations connected with the eastern China mission, we use a hymn book prepared about twenty-five years ago, and revised three or four times since, principally by members of the American Presbyterian mission. It contains translations and original hymns by members of all the missions here. The contributions from Baptist sources, however, are very few. Dr. Knowlton prepared three translations, one of the hymn beginning, 'Lord, thy perfect word,' another, 'The morning light is breaking,' and the third, 'Today, the Savior calls.' S. P. Barchet, m.d., at present in connection with our mission, made a translation of the hymn, 'Jesus is our Shepherd.' These are all the Baptist contributions." A small Chinese hymn book was published in Bangkok in 1838. The first hymn in the collection was composed, it is believed, by Siang, a Chinese preacher at Bangkok. Several editions of this small book have been printed, the last in 1881, containing one hundred and thirty-five hymns and six forms of prayer, the first of which is the Lord's prayer.

Rev. Fung Chek, who is now pastor of the Chinese Baptist church in Portland, Oregon, has published a collection of hymns consisting of translations by himself of some of the hymns in "Gospel Hymns" and some familiar Sunday-school hymns, together with five or six hymns of his own. Fung Chek is a native of a village near Canton, where he was baptized in 1871. He spent several years in California, and was ordained in 1880, in Portland, Oregon.

The following is a translation of an original hymn by Rev. Fung Chek. It is entitled "The Uncertainty of Earthly Things:"

Earthly things are uncertain as the waves;

Now comes gladness, then comes sadness.

Do not say that joy is true joy;

And true grief is not unending grief.

Grief usually proceeds from joy.

In the midst of joy there is always a sting of grief.

All comes from our first parents breaking God's law;

After generations became the slaves of sin.

Thanks to God's helpful grace,

Who sent his Son to bear our crimes,

To deliver us from sin and to save us,

That our souls may dwell in bliss.

When our souls are in heaven at God's side,

Contrition and sighs will all be over;

Our joyful songs will never cease

Of praise to the Savior's bleeding love.

BAPTIST HYMN WRITERS AND THEIR HYMNS IN JAPAN

Properly speaking Baptists in Japan have had three hymn books. The first, in Roman characters and kata kana, or square letters in parallel lines, was published about the year 1874. The second, in Roman characters and hira gana, the script or running hand (in separate books), was published in 1876. The third in hira gana (only the page captions, names of tunes, etc., being in the Roman characters) was published in part in 1884, or 1885, but was not completed until after the death of Dr. Nathan Brown in 1886. It makes a volume of three hundred and eighteen pages. In the preface Rev. Albert A. Bennett says:

"Should any honor be attached to the preparation of the present hymn book, it belongs to the late Dr. Nathan Brown. Years ago, when it was commonly said that 'the Japanese cannot sing,' he commenced work on hymns for them, and his rendering of the Lord's Prayer was probably the first Christian hymn in their language. The first hymn book that he published, was a very modest little volume, but it from time to time gave place to larger ones, and the present edition is supposed to be the largest collection of Japanese hymns yet published. On this, Dr. Brown labored till his palsied hand could no longer hold a pen." One day, while at work on his Japanese hymn book. Dr. Brown remarked, " I have got as far as the hymns on heaven." It was a fitting time for the aged saint to bring his labors to an end, and closing a long and useful life he passed over into the celestial country.

"In some cases," says Mr. Bennett in his reference to this hymn book, "an initial letter has been affixed to indicate the author's name, or the book from which the hymn was taken. Dr. Brown exerted himself to ascertain the names of composers and translators, but the information he obtained was comparatively meagre, and it is feared that some of that meagre information has been lost."

The collection contains, also, quite a number of the familiar "Gospel Hymns."

Beside Dr. Brown, who is credited with fifteen hymns, the Baptist writers represented in this collection are Rev. W. J. White, English Baptist missionary, Miss Clara A. Sands, of the American Baptist Missionary Union, and the following natives : K. Nakagawa, K. Ikeda, Rev. T. Suzuki, Rev. S. Torigama, and Rev. T. Kawakatsu.

Mk. White, who has three hymns in the collection, was born April 19, 1848, at Brockhurst, a suburb of the ancient town of Gosport, in the south of England. In 1870, he went to Japan, and was engaged six years in educational work. In order to prepare himself for missionary work, he then returned to England and entered the Pastor's College connected with the Metropolitan Tabernacle in London. After a short course of preparatory study, Mr. White offered himself to the committee of the Baptist Missionary Society, and Was cordially accepted as a missionary October 8, 1877. September 6, 1878, he was designated for the work in Japan at a meeting held at Brockhurst, and on the 18th, of the same month he sailed for his field of labor. On his arrival in Japan, he entered upon his missionary career in Tokyo, where he has since labored with many evidences of the divine blessings.

Miss Sards, represented in the collection by five hymns, was born in Southport, N. Y., July 27, 1844, and was educated in the Female College at Oxford, Ohio. In October, 1873, she was baptized at Salamanca. N. Y., and September 2, 1875, she was appointed a missionary of the American Baptist Missionary Union to Japan. She reached Yokohama the same year, and there she has since labored with great diligence and success.

K. Nakagawa, who has six hymns in the collection, was for a long time one of the teachers in the school connected with the mission at Yokohama, but was at length excluded from the church on account of his inconsistent walk. He has recently expressed a desire to return, and it is hoped that he may yet sing again the hymns of faith and hope which he wrote while a member of the mission.

K. Ikeda has three hymns in the collection. He is engaged in missionary work as a native preacher at Odawara, and is an earnest Christian worker.

Rev. T. Suzuki, who has nine hymns in the collection, is pastor of the native church at Kobe, and assists Mr. Rees in his mission work. He is an earnest, prayerful man, and, humanly speaking, was converted through hearing a sermon by the lamented Rev. J. Hope Arthur. Mr. Arthur could poorly speak the language and Mr. Suzuki could poorly understand what was said; but the Spirit was present to aid and to enlighten, and caused the listening Japanese to know the Word that became flesh.

Rev. S. Torigama, the author of two hymns in the collection, is the pastor of the church at Tokyo, and assists Mr. Fisher in his work. He is a devoted Bible student, and a consecrated worker.

Rev. T. Kawakatsu, was the earliest of the Japanese ordained Baptist preachers, although the youngest of the three. He was Dr. Brown's assistant in the translation of the New Testament, and is now pastor of several of the native churches. He is an exceedingly useful member of the mission, and is greatly beloved by all the brethren. He has eight hymns in the collection.

BAPTIST HYMN WRITERS AND THEIR HYMNS IN AFRICA

The missionaries connected with the English Baptist Mission in Congo-land have a hymn book, containing about twenty hymns, printed at the Edwin Wade Printing Press, Underbill Station, Congo River. Other hymns have been prepared, and are in use, but only these have been printed. Rev. J. H. Weeks, of San Salvador, writes: "We have nearly forty hymns, but we have printed only those which we have repeatedly tested and found correct. When a hymn is first translated, we use it at our stations for some time, alter it if it is needful until it is as near perfect as we can get it, and then we print it." Some of the hymns in this collection are originals, and some are translations of well-known English hymns. All have been prepared since 1880. The translations in the collection were made by Rev. T. J. Comber, Rev. W. H. Bentley, Rev. J. H.

Weeks, Rev. H. Dixon, and two natives, Kavungu and Mantu. The original hymns were composed by Rev. T. J. Comber, Rev. W. H. Bentley, and Rev. J. H. Weeks.

Rev. T. J. Comber was one of the pioneers of the Congo mission, entering upon his work in 1878. Other members of his family have been engaged in mission service in Africa. His sister died at Cameroons. His brother, Dr. Comber, at Ngombe, Congo. Another brother is still connected with the Congo mission. Rev. T. J. Comber died on the steamship Lulu Bohlen, June 27, 1887, off Loango, a French settlement several miles north of Banana, and was buried at Mayumba, two hundred miles north of the mouth of the Congo. Among his last words were these:

"Oh Christ, thou art the fountain,

The deep spring-well of love;

The springs of earth I've tasted"

His companion failed to catch what followed. Dangerously ill with remittent fever, Mr. Comber was placed on board the Lulu Bohlen, in hope that a sea voyage would restore him to health. But his work was done, and submissively he yielded to the Father's will. With gifts and graces that fitted him in a marked degree for successful missionary work, he performed a service, in laying the foundation of the Congo Mission, that will long be remembered in Africa as well as in his native land.

The hymn book in use in the mission on the Congo conducted by the American Baptist Missionary Union was printed in London in the early part of 1885, by some English friends of Rev. C. E. Ingham, one of the oldest Congo missionaries. It contains eighteen hymns. Of these, eight were by Henry Craven, six by C. H. Harvey, two by H. J. Petterson, one by N. Westlind and one by C. B. Banks.

C. H. Harvey joined the mission in 1880, and has proved a most valuable member of this heroic company. He has labored at Matadi, Palabala, Banza Manteke and Lukungu, where he is now stationed. He possesses a superior knowledge of the Ki-Kongo language, into which in 1886, he translated the Gospel of Mark.

H. J. Petterson is a Swedish Baptist missionary, who has done valuable pioneer service on the Congo. He established the Equator Station. At present he is connected with the Swedish Baptist mission at Mukimbungu.

Nils Westlind, also a Swedish Baptist Missionary, has translated the Gospel of John into the Ki-Kongo language, and is the author of valuable notes on the Ki-Kongo. He, too, is now connected with the Swedish Baptist mission at Mukimbungu.

C. B. Banks accompanied Petterson to Equator Station from Stanley Pool, and is now at this important inland station.

Other hymns have been prepared since the hymn book now in use was published in London. Rev. Henry Richards, whose work at Banza Manteke is without a parallel in the history of African missions, has translated several hymns. Mr. Richards went to the Congo in 1878. After traveling considerably, and aiding in building Lukungu, he finally established a station at Banza Manteke, where he has remained, and where he has witnessed almost Pentecostal blessings. Here he buried his first wife, Mary Richards, November 13, 1881. He has translated the Gospel of Luke into Ki-Kongo. His hymns, with added hymns by Mr. Harvey, were printed at Palabala by Mr. Clark, Herbert Probert and the late Mr. White.

J. McKittrick has made one or two excellent translations. He has written one or two hymns, also, in the Kilolo language at the equator.

In 1886, J. B. Eddie composed several hymns in Kilolo at the Equator Station. Like Dr. Sims he has great linguistic powers. He has a good knowledge of Kiyousi, and speaks with facility the Ki-Kongo. At present he is preparing a dictionary of the Kilolo.

Made in United States
North Haven, CT
16 November 2023

44113139R00200